PEAKS AND LAMAS

ༀ་ཨཱ་ཧཱུཾ་གུ་རུ

TO

THE FOUR LAMAS

The Hermit Abbot of Lachhen
The Lama Dawa, Bursar of Spituk
The Lama-painter, Konchhog Gyaltsan of P'hiyan
The Lama Wangyal, of Drepung, Lhasa

*who for my benefit and for the good of all creatures
set in motion the Wheel of the Doctrine*

THIS BOOK
IS REVERENTLY DEDICATED

Marco Pallis

PEAKS
AND LAMAS

READERS UNION
by arrangement with Cassell & Co. Ltd.
LONDON 1948

This volume was produced in 1948 in Great Britain, in complete conformity with the authorized economy standards. First published in the
unabridged version in England in 1939 by Cassell & Co. Ltd., it has
been newly set in Garamond 11 point, and printed at Frome by Butler
& Tanner Ltd. It is one of the books produced for sale to its members
only by Readers Union Ltd., of 38 William IV Street, Charing
Cross, London, and of Letchworth Garden City, Hertfordshire.
Membership of RU may be made at all bookshops and particulars are
obtainable from either address

Contents

Illustrations

Maps and Diagrams

Publishers' Note

THIS edition of *Peaks and Lamas* has been specially prepared for Readers Union members by Marco Pallis. While it omits certain passages of the first edition which are unnecessary for popular reading, together with a section on Tibetan art, the publishers feel that these omissions in no way do violence to the author's narrative and argument

INTRODUCTORY NOTES

A FORMAL preface would serve no useful purpose in this book. All that had to be said has found a better place in the actual narrative: there is no object in preparing the reader's mind for things that he will discover soon enough for himself. I shall therefore confine myself to giving a few explanations of a purely practical nature, concerning the spelling of place-names and the use of special terms. At the same time I shall be discharging the pleasant duty of thanking the many friends without whose help the book could neither have been written, nor the work done, which furnished the excuse for writing it.

Spelling of Indian and Tibetan Names. I have all along tried to reproduce the correct sounds, as spoken, and have disregarded the original spellings. Therefore the name of a celebrated monastery in Ladak, though spelt Himis on maps, is here written Himi, since in conversation I have always found the *s* to be muted. Similarly in referring to a Tibetan valley that lies near the north frontier of Bhutan, I write Hlobrak, instead of the orthographically correct Lho-brag. The name of a certain divinity called Chenrezig is so written here, though by its spelling it would be Spyan-ras-gzigs. The book is intended in the first place for the general reader, not for scholars; the latter will in any case know what the spelling should have been. The only exceptions to this rule of writing phonetically are names such as Lhasa and Darjeeling, which are now practically English words. To have turned Lhasa into Hlasa, because it is so sounded in Tibetan, would have been pedantic and confusing.

In the Tibetan language, generic terms derived from places are made by the addition of the suffixes -pa, -wa, or -ba. Thus a man of Ladak is Ladakpa, a Londoner is Londonwa. By this method many circumlocutions like "a man of Kham" can be avoided. I have therefore permitted myself its free use: in the example given I should simply say Khamba.

Phonetics. Vowel sounds may be taken as being roughly like the continental ones, say in Italian. The diphthong *au* in Indian words and the modified vowels *ö* and *ü* in Tibetan should be pronounced as in German.

In a few Indian words stress accents have been added, wherever the tendencies of English were likely to predispose people towards wrong accentuation. Nine Englishmen out of ten, who have not had some connection with India, will call the capital of Kashmir, Srinagár, instead of the correct Srinágar, unless the stress is marked as I have shown it.

Aspirated consonants need special attention. Both in the Indian and Tibetan languages the *h* sound must be distinctly pronounced, even after *p* or *t*. To make sure that no one falls into the error of reading *ph* with an *f* sound, or *th* as in "then," I have marked an apostrophe thus: *p'h, t'h*. In the word *t'hanka*, meaning a painted scroll, the *t'h* should therefore be spoken as in "tha*t* *h*ouse."

For the sake of accuracy I have followed scholars in indicating a particular sort of *t* and *d* sound that is found in Tibetan thus: *ṭ* and *ḍ*. They occur in words where the main consonant is followed by a muted *r*, which lends to the preceding letter a slightly explosive character. To produce it, the tongue must be pressed hard against the palate. The words *Ṭulku*, an Incarnation, and *Ṭashilhunpo*, the great monastery near Shigatze where the Panchhen Lama resides, are a case in point: so also is *Ḍikhung*, the name of another monastery.

My thanks are due to a large number of people who have assisted me in a variety of ways. I have indeed been surprised at the trouble taken on behalf of both expeditions by all sorts of busy people, from Maharajas and officials downwards. Not the least of the rewards that have fallen to me and my companions have been the many friendships that have arisen in this manner, both at home and in the East, both among our own people and with Indians and Tibetans. I can assure all who have contributed information, advice, gifts or any other form of help to us, that their kindness is neither forgotten nor forgettable.

To Pamela Freston my debt is beyond all thanks. The whole book passed through her hands three times, and received from her a most rigorous, though sympathetic, criticism, which got rid of countless clumsy passages and other faults of style. I have reckoned that she pointed out over two thousand major and minor blemishes. Her contribution has been such that I look on her now not so much as an adviser, but rather as a collaborator.

MARCO PALLIS.

GANGES AND SATLEJ

(1933)

Part One

GANGES AND SATLEJ]

(1953)

THE BIRTH OF AN EXPEDITION

THE story of two Himalayan journeys which fills this book presented a peculiar difficulty in the telling, because of the many and sometimes bewilderingly sudden alternations of mood required of the reader. At one moment, in our company, he would be living on the purely physical plane while pitting every ounce of strength against a giant of the mountains; or else in the midst of flower-filled meadows or in a secluded glade of the primeval forest, he would be recovering from the fatigues of defeat or success. Yet directly afterwards, having moved on but a few short miles, he would be found sipping tea from silver-mounted bowls and exchanging formal courtesies with representatives of one of the earth's most civilized peoples; or again, with intellect whetted to its keenest edge, he would be trying to keep pace with the descant of some contemplative recluse upon a theme of pure metaphysic.

To have suppressed some of the contrasting elements, leaving the others in a position of unchallenged preponderance, would have been simple; advisers were not wanting who urged this course. But somehow, when it came to be tried, the journey so described seemed to be no longer the same that I remembered: a stranger had gone on it, a man more single-eyed than the author. I resolved, therefore, to risk a long story and to relate the adventures of our party in all their diversity, allowing the pendulum to swing where and when it willed, leaving out nothing that really mattered, and only praying that my would-be companions might have the patience to adapt themselves. Whoever is willing to bear with these apparent caprices, will find, I hope, as I have done, that the bodily exertion of climbing, by forcing the mind to lie fallow for a time and concentrate on purely animal needs, will have prepared it in just the right way for subsequent excursions into more subtle realms. There is some advantage in first reducing mental, no less than physical, weight, before calling on the spirit, thus lightened of its ballast, to take flight towards the stars.

Indeed, there is everything to be said for letting unaccustomed impressions soak in slowly, without system, to find their own level in their own time. A vague idea, born of some chance event, presently ripens into sharper definition as fresh incidents bearing on it occur at intervals and are pieced together with other impressions already stored in the consciousness. The first allusion may have been superficial and soon forgotten, while one turned from the path to attempt some peak which caught one's passing fancy. Later, the same question comes up again. Possibly an increasing fluency in the language, fruit of daily practice, has enabled one to debate it seriously with some person qualified to throw light on it. So one is led on by small, discontinuous steps, till at length one is swept into very deep waters.

And now at last the hour has come to pack up our baggage and set out on this our first visit to the mountain ranges of the East. It is All Fools' Day, 1933, and the group of five well-seasoned climbing friends is waving farewells to parents and relatives, and drawing the fire of cameras on the dockside at Liverpool, where the good ship *Custodian*, which is to be their home for the next four weeks, is taking on its last belated bits of cargo.

The members of the party must now be introduced by name:—RICHARD NICHOLSON, a son of the famous builder of yachts, and a fellow-musician of mine, for many years my companion on almost every climb, both in the Alps and at home; F. E. HICKS, a schoolmaster and notable rock-climber and ski-runner, one of the strongest and gentlest of men, owner of physical and mental gifts blended in such a nice proportion as to make him, to my mind, the very ideal of an all-round mountaineer; C. F. KIRKUS, who works in Insurance, one of the two or three best rock-climbers in this country, pioneer of many new routes, especially in Wales [1]; DR. CHARLES WARREN, a man of considerable Alpine experience, who afterwards acted as Medical Officer on several Everest expeditions; lastly, myself, rather older than the others, with a number of Alpine seasons behind me and an affinity for Oriental, especially Indian, History and Art, dating back to early childhood: a reasonably

[1] He eventually lost his life in a raid over Germany while serving with the R.A.F.

4

strong party, and even-tempered, a thing which counts for much in the wilds.

When the last cable that joined us to England had been cast loose and the ship began to move out into the river, there was a brief moment of excitement; then a pleasant feeling of relaxation began to steal over us, to which we had long been strangers; for the preliminaries of such an expedition, new to every one of us, which had occupied our leisure for twelve months or more, had been strenuous: drawing up lists of equipment and estimating rations, unpacking parcels, sorting, checking, repacking, weighing, working out a foolproof method of cataloguing simple enough not to break down under field conditions, consulting every accessible authority living or printed and sifting their often contradictory information, cadging contributions in kind from sympathetic firms, poring over maps, or, ensconced in armchairs before the fire, calling up those alluring phantoms which by and by materialized into feasible plans—these were but a few of our occupations.

In addition, certain items of equipment had to be put to practical trial so as to preclude the danger of unpleasant surprises on the mountain. The most plausible design often hides lurking weaknesses which are only detected through actual use. Clumsiness in handling tackle too, due to ignorance of the appropriate drill, may entail exhausting struggles in the rarefied air of high altitudes. We held sleeping-bag parades, tentless, on the windy summits of Ben Nevis and Snowdon in midwinter, following them up with a grand dress-rehearsal, tents and all, played under mock-Himalayan rules, as realistic as we could devise them, in the Valais Alps. Nothing was taken on trust: there were no serious mishaps when the hour came for real testing.

Fair weather attended us from the outset of the voyage; but some days elapsed before we began to feel inclined for anything except sleep. After we had rounded Gibraltar, however, and entered warmer seas, and turtles with orange shells had swum past, and we had looked on the ineffable transparency of the Algerian mountains still clothed in winter snow, our torpid energies began to reassert themselves. As we were the only passengers on board, the jovial Irish captain gave us the run of his ship and a number of "rock-climbs" were soon discovered. The most important activity, however, was connected

5

with the study of languages. The *Custodian* was promptly converted into a floating university; in every corner you could have found grammars and dictionaries left by students who had been diligently compiling useful vocabularies under headings such as "On the March," "Pitching Camp," "Buying Food in a Village," "Visiting a Shrine," when they were summoned to the saloon by the clang of the dinner-gong.

In the tropics, while lying on the deck sunbathing and watching the shoals of flying-fish skimming the crests of waves like volleys of silver arrows, we concocted strange dialogues, now Hindustani, now Tibetan. The classic "Have you taken the pen of my uncle? No, you will find it in your grandmother's garden" was replaced with "Is there a camping-ground in the woods behind the village? No, it is on the glacier to the east of the mountain pass." Presently, as the combining of phrases began to come more easily, they were tried on the dog, that is to say, on members of the Lascar crew, who at first affected not to know the language at all for Hindustani, till one day it dawned on them, when they broke out into such volubility that they left us all guessing.

Many people intending to travel in the Himalaya are, in the matter of languages, ready to accept a rather low standard, ignoring the rules of grammar, and contenting themselves with a hundred words or so. No doubt this can be made to do for elementary needs, and even for forging the links of a genuine, if inarticulate, comradeship with the native porters. But it seems a pity to put up with such a narrowing of possibilities; for most English people are not nearly so incompetent at languages as they imagine, and good teachers are to be found to help them over the more awkward stiles. The reward for trying lies in the possibility of a real exchange of thoughts with the inhabitants of a foreign country, which is surely one of the greatest joys of travel.

For us, so occupied, four weeks slipped by all too quickly, and it was with mixed feelings that we saw the mangrove-fringed coast near the mouth of the Hoogli slowly loom into sight and knew that it was the last time we should hear the cheery voice of Captain O'Connor summoning us to his cabin, at the end of the day's work, to join him in a "sundowner." But there was a thrill in the thought that this turbid waterway, with its jute factories and barges, its feathery palms and slimy mud-flats, suited to the siestas of crocodiles, was a mouth of

6

the selfsame Ganges which we were about to follow all the way to its source, goal of many pilgrims, where it issued from the parent glacier.

Calcutta saw us for the inside of a day; at night we made our way to Howra terminus and entrained for Dehra Dun, the railhead for the hill station of Mussoori. As we walked down the thronged platform we noticed a white cotton thread apparently endless, extending away from us into the distance; it might have been taken for the clue bestowed on Theseus by Ariadne, to guide him through the labyrinth. Moved by curiosity we traced it out; but our Minotaur proved to be an obese, elderly Bengali, white-robed and clutching the inevitable, untidily-furled umbrella, who was waddling along through the tittering crowd, all unconscious of the mirth he was causing by reason of the reel of cotton in his pocket ever unwinding, the free end having caught itself somewhere on the way. As no one seemed to be making a move, one of us picked up the strand and, nudging the old *babu* on the elbow, handed back his straggling property. The old fellow gathered it up with a startled movement, and then broke out into such effusive thanks, that our simple action might have been an unprecedented act of chivalry. Could it really have appeared out of the ordinary? Or did his pompous gratitude mask some age-long reproach?

We spent the railway journey, or at least its waking hours, gazing out of the window. Charming rural scenes, familiar through the miniatures of the Rajput school in London museums, passed before us, villages of reddish mud and thatch surrounded by mango trees, hump-backed cattle watched by half-naked urchins, grazing upon what seemed bare earth (for it was near the end of the hot weather), women in gay saris—it must have been a festival day—waiting their turn at the well or walking home with the gait of princesses, their polished brass pots balanced on their heads. By a queer reversal, it felt as if all this was meant to illustrate the miniatures, instead of the contrary being the case. With what deep understanding those old artists had caught hold of the spirit of village life, where beats the real heart of India.

A number of sites of historical interest flashed by. Here was Benares, sacred city of the Hindus; over its many-stepped bathing places and conical-roofed temples towered the twin minarets of the Mughal Aurangzib, who, unlike his ancestors, was no builder, and erected them there principally in order to impress his non-Moslem subjects. We also caught sight of Jaunpur, glorious in the stately Saracenic gateways of its numerous mosques, the former capital of a dynasty bearing the proud title of Kings of the East, now reduced to a quiet country town.

Later came temple-girt Ayodhya, scene of the childhood of India's epic hero, Rama, mighty bender of the bow. In the station a family of brown monkeys was waiting, father, mother and frolicking babies, apparently hoping to catch the next stopping train.

But what astonished us most of all on the journey across India was the abundance of animal life: we saw foxes, jackals and monkeys; and a great variety of birds. Remembering the songless countryside of so much of Europe, one was tempted to ask how it was that this Indian plain, densely inhabited and cultivated since remote times, was still able to support so large an animal population. Surely the interests of some, at least, of the creatures which we saw, must be competing to a certain extent with those of man. Does the explanation lie in the fact that Hindus, in their abhorrence of killing, for which people sometimes presume to ridicule them, are ready to overlook a moderate toll levied by animals on their crops, and do not make this into an excuse for wholesale extermination, though these Indian peasants have little enough to spare, as compared with many of their fellows in other countries?

One of the minor peculiarities of an Indian tour is the sheer hopelessness which attends any search for a drinkable cup of tea, although this is the land which contains Darjeeling and Ceylon. Neither prayers nor threats will make the Indian servant on the railways or in hotels believe that every Englishman does not like his tea *ystrang*, that is to say of such a consistency that I could easily have written this book by filling my fountain-pen from the teapot. As to serving a jug of hot water with the tea-tray, that is simply not done, not even in good hotels. If pressed, the waiter, after a prolonged show of incomprehension, will first take away the pot and dilute the ink, or if one goes on insisting, he will go and fetch a second teapot full of boiling water: but the convention, as we know it at home, is simply not recognized. It is strange that the British, who have succeeded in imposing so many of their institutions on their imperial possessions, should have failed over this. It is

8

as if the Indians said: "You have conquered us in other ways; in this one thing, a thing moreover very close to your hearts, we defy you!"

Early on the second morning we woke up in a climate markedly cooler: we were passing through a belt of jungle; when we emerged, we saw hills at last. Then the train drew up alongside Dehra Dun platform, and we stepped out to shake hands with Dr. R. Maclagan Gorrie, a distinguished member of that admirable service the Department of Forests, who bade us welcome to the Himalaya. His help and advice at this stage were invaluable, for we suddenly felt tongue-tied by shyness and in no mood for making decisions. He piloted us through our first awkwardness, interviewed candidates for the post of head-porter and selected one who had been overseer to a gang of road-menders, a Hindu of the name of Jai Datt. Dr. Gorrie also took two of us for a whole day in his car across the lovely forested Dun to call on H.H. the Maharaja of Tehri-Garhwal, in whose principality our mountains lay. To the prince also and to his prime minister our thanks are due, for the kindness of their reception and for their readiness in arranging all facilities.

Clouds hung low on the ridge, and we walked up the short distance into Mussoori, from where the motor road ends, through a fine drizzle. A regimental band was giving selections from light opera on the parade and the doubtful cheerfulness of the tunes seemed to add a touch of melancholy to the rawness of the evening. Knots of Garhwalis huddled in shop doorways, their brown blankets drawn over their heads. We passed a lighted shop-window which displayed a fashionable frock draped superciliously on its lay figure. A young man in evening dress rolled by in a rickshaw. As we turned down off the parade towards our hotel there was a sudden crash overhead as a band of monkeys hurtled out from among some scarlet rhododendrons, chasing one another across the road, and disappeared down the hillside.

That first evening we assembled for dinner only four out of five: one member of our party was confined to his room indisposed, truly a matter for agitation. We were on the threshold of our adventure and a man gone sick already! What precaution could possibly have been neglected? Had we not let our insides be turned into a bacteriological laboratory and our skins into sieves with I know not how many innoculations? It was in vain that other visitors in the hotel explained that

it was the commonest thing to be slightly upset by the sudden
rise from the plains to eight thousand feet. He who has come
with ambitions to climb to a height of twenty thousand or
more, is loath to believe himself of the same clay as ordinary
hotel guests. His mind is prone to wildest alarms about nameless exotic diseases. Little was said, but a jumpy uneasiness
lurked behind the desultory conversation as we drifted in and
out of one another's rooms or up and down the veranda,
listening to the whirring of cicadas or stopping to examine the
unfamiliar moths round the electric lamps. In the light of later
experience how easy and how unfair it is to laugh at those
exaggerated fears!

The sun rose in a clear sky next morning and for a brief
hour or two the matchless panorama of the Gangotri peaks was
uncovered. Our goal stood outspread before us; catching that
first glimpse of the land of our dreams, what a passionate
eagerness welled up in us to set out, leaving all tedious last-
minute organization to run itself. We longed to start, not the
day after the day after to-morrow, but in that very instant,
along the winding tracks that cross the seventy miles of forested
foothills to the base of the snowy ranges. Whoever has had
experience of a get-away into the Himalaya must be familiar
with this impatience. One remembers several evenings standing
knee-deep in the debris of packing, to watch the twilight in
the valleys snuffed out by the over-hasty fingers of sub-tropical
nightfall, and sighing because yet another day's work stands
between oneself and departure. The vow is fiercely registered
each time to travel lighter and yet more light: and in fact, if
it is to be purely a question of travelling, that is easy enough,
as we have since found out; but when the programme includes
mountaineering, with its siege tactics, a certain minimum of
climbing gear and provisions for spending several weeks on
glaciers is unavoidable, and that minimum when stacked
together in one place can look disconcertingly elaborate.

Before 1933 few expeditions had gone up from Mussoori.
There was no precedent behind the formation of a *bandobast*
such as exists, for instance, in Kashmir. This was not without
its compensations, for we escaped the regiment of touts which
falls upon the greenhorn in those other places, with its nicely-
graded tariffs based on the degree of "roughing it" required
or apprehended: so much for tents, chairs, tables, camp-beds,
commodes, and tin baths, with slight reductions on omitting

10

any one or other of these almost indispensable articles. How we laughed on a certain morning three years later in Kashmir when we rode up behind a young servant trotting along with the meat-safe strapped to his shoulders and Sunday's joint visible through the wire on its white china dish! But if we enjoyed the advantage of being early in the field in Mussoori, there was correspondingly more for a stranger to find out and more work to be done.

The hotel manager kindly made over to us one of his sheds in which to complete the packing and interview porters and candidates for the all-important office of cook. Several mornings were spent down there weighing up loads on a spring balance, squeezing out any object regarded at the last minute as superfluous, and all the while fending off the inquisitive, the hasty, the officious would-be helpers, who buzzed like a cloud of blue-bottles round the door, threatening at any moment to reduce everything to a state of chaos. The bazaar knew, of course, all about the expedition, and besides those whose names had been entered officially on the head-porter's list, countless hopefuls hung round from morning till night. It was during these operations that a little Puck-like fellow called Urbi Datt first caught my eye. We used to pick two or three assistants from the crowd and one day the lot fell to him, a happy chance, since he was to turn out the most able of any of our servants during this early part of our travels. We soon saw that here was a first-class man, from his unhurried manner, his quickness to catch on to an idea, and his ability not to meddle in matters that did not concern him. Also he had a way with the crowd which was an invaluable protection when one's back was turned.

At home we had read a good deal about the sufferings of mountaineers at the hands of their cooks, though the grumblers rather betrayed themselves by having made no serious effort to change cooks. It seems so unnecessary to put up with un-wholesome food. The Englishman's readiness to allow a low standard to be imposed on him and his almost criminal timidity about experimenting with outlandish cookery, partly accounts for these tales. A man may be an expert in cooking the food he usually eats, and at the same time may make a hopeless failure when invited to reproduce the foreign recipes which his sahib demands. How else can one account for the fact that though skilful cooks abound in India, so much of the food served up to Europeans there is uneatable? In the long run it is better for the digestion, as well as pleasanter, to experiment a little in the native dishes which one's cook already knows how to prepare, than to expect him to try his hand at the English style at short notice. If he is a professional he will at first assume that English dishes are expected of him; but he will probably be overjoyed and begin to turn out food of a very different quality when firmly told that one prefers to feed like an Indian.

We inquired of Urbi Datt if he would take on the job, but he very properly replied that being a strict vegetarian he was afraid of being asked to handle what was ritually impure. Though disappointed we still hesitated, because a few interviews with professional applicants for the post did not tend to predispose us in their favour. We had heard that the sub-division of functions had gone far in India, but the question was how far? Did custom entitle the cook to demand one menial to fetch water for him, a second to scour his dirty pans, a third to blow up his fire and a fourth to carry the food to the sahib's table? Or was this simply jobbery? We saw our caravan growing into an army. When it came to a request for a cook-house tent to shade the meats from the sinister influence of hooded crows or even of a passing cloud, suspicion turned to conviction. Here was nothing more or less than a ramp to provide a couple of months' employment for brothers and cousins and in-laws.

Eventually a porter named Maidar Singh was chosen. For a few extra annas he was prepared to do his share of carrying, as well as our own domestic work. He was a big, rough fellow whose shirt protruded from beneath a tight-fitting blue waist-coat even on the hottest of days and who professed, with what turned out to be false modesty, to know very little about cooking. Actually, I think, he was nearly first-class, and we soon learned our place and abandoned any amateurish attempts at interference with his art. He managed to gather three help-mates for the kitchen, including one of suitable caste to do the washing up, which he himself was not allowed to touch. But as they all carried ordinary loads and were counted the same as other porters, he was welcome to them.

Maidar Singh was a child in his habit of fishing for praises: "That was a very nice curried chicken you gave us this evening; I hope we shall have it often." "Ah! Ah!" he purred, drinking in our words. A few minutes later there would be a scratching

12

at my tent-flap. "What is it, Maidar Singh?" "Did the Sahib like the curried chicken? Was it good?" "But certainly, Maidar Singh, I told you so. You must do some again to-morrow." "Ah! Ah!" A quarter of an hour would pass and the identical ceremony had to be gone through again. "Ah! Ah!"

One other controversy led to prolonged heart-searchings. It is a convenience when trekking to carry personal belongings in one's own rucksack and to be independent of servants. It had been hinted, however, by some of the initiated that this practice would at once lower our prestige. We were by no means above taking hints; quite the reverse, for in our hearts we did feel some diffidence in setting out to control sixty or seventy men in this unfamiliar land. The climax came when it was realized that if we carried packs the head-porter must do likewise; naturally he could not be seen walking unburdened behind his loaded masters. Jai Datt was much dashed when his nice new rucksack was handed to him, for he was a man of rather feeble character, morbidly sensitive about losing face. His redeeming feature was that he never tried to abuse or bully his subordinates. There had been some difficulty in securing anyone better for the job, as the man engaged for us before we left England had gone off to Everest at short notice. Dr. Gorrie had done the very best possible in the time.

I forget if Jai Datt resorted to the persuasion of tears on the first or second day. "Please don't make me carry it," he whimpered. "Everyone on that route knows me for the friend of important people, of forest rangers and even deputy-collectors. What will they think when they see me with a load like a coolie? They will make a mock of me." "But, Jai Datt, they will see us carrying packs too: we will walk beside you whenever you have to go through a village." In the end he was forced to yield and his forebodings proved unjustified; but he never felt easy about it, and took every opportunity of handing over his rucksack on the quiet to one of the other porters.

It is to be hoped that we did not socially demean the rather pitiable Jai Datt. As to ourselves, what with one thing and another, our loads became of quite respectable weight; but this, far from losing us the respect of our porters, enhanced it notice-ably. In fact it produced a crop of topical jokes. A man would come up and feel my pack. "That's quite heavy. Why not get a fresh porter?" (That, doubtless, with an eye to providing an extra job for some cousin.) "I'm doing it for practice. If I lose

13

my money and all else fails, I shall take up the profession of coolie." This sally never failed to bring the house down.

At last the morning of May 10th came: all was in readiness, "venesta" cases and kitbags were stacked according to their several marks; ice-axes and an awkward parcel of skis—which, when carried upright, turned its owner into the likeness of a monster praying-mantis—were standing in a corner, ropes and line were neatly coiled and the pile was completed by a couple of empty kerosene tins grandiloquently called "canister" and used for fetching water, washing the sahibs' socks and shirts, or for the sahibs themselves to wash in. The march appointed for the first day was a short one, only seven miles, to a camping-ground called Magra, near which was a shop where the men could buy food to last several stages out of their first day's pay. No one could understand why I insisted on everyone reporting at the store-shed as early as six-thirty, with a view to an eight o'clock start. If truth must be told, I did not wish to air my still halting Hindustani or to make a display of incompetence in controlling men, under the critical eyes of those of the hotel residents who might have been tempted to look on. It was better to know that they were all safely ensconced in their beds.

It is extraordinary how, till one has tried, one fails to think of quite simple expedients such as ordering the porters to stand in a line so that they should pick up their loads one by one. The management of these matters was left to Jai Datt; for we had yet to plumb the depths of his incapacity. Almost all the men pressed forward simultaneously and settled on the pile of waiting loads like swarming bees, each man determined to weigh every one of the sixty-five packages with his own hands, in search of the lightest. In vain we shouted above the uproar that they were all equal, fifty pounds, neither more nor less. For a few moments confusion threatened, while poor Jai Datt stood turning the leaves of his notebook and sucking a pencil, his usual signal of distress. Then somehow, probably with the help of Urbi Datt, the hubbub was stilled and in small groups the men started off down the road.

There is a special excitement belonging to any first occasion. For pure delight what can equal a first day's trek out into a fresh landscape? On such an occasion the commonest object fascinates; every viewpoint, every plant, bird or beetle. The business of the day, reaching a destination, becomes quite secondary. I for one, am given to peering inside thistles and

14

turning over dockleaves for fear of missing something. It does not worry me if the local inhabitants stop and stare at the mad foreigner.

It was misty that morning and the air was softly caressing. Before turning north off the ridge towards Magra, we stopped to take a last look at the plains. The clouds had lifted, revealing the white stony bed of Lady Ganges, where she issued from the mountains, winding away endlessly. The sound of many cuckoos calling in the woods below came as an almost annoying surprise. In that exotic landscape the cuckoo which, like the nightingale, suggests a copse with primrose, dog-violet and anemone—the heralds of an English spring—had no place. Rounding a corner, we came upon a clump of tall rhododendron, trees rather than bushes, carrying their dark leathery foliage and clusters of blossoms upon smooth, russet-coloured branches. A pair of Himalayan pie floated off into the woods, trailing their graceful powder-blue tail feathers behind them. No homely associations could outlive that sudden vision of crimson blooms and brilliant plumage, and we walked on engrossed again in the examination of the new and the strange.

The path had veered sharp left over the crest now, and we found ourselves beginning to drop down the farther slope, following a small ravine. "I, no other, supervised the making of this bit of road," exclaimed Jai Datt proudly. At last, in a grove of fir we caught the glint of fires. Our men had already made themselves at home; some were engaged in carrying water from the stream, others were squatting over stew-pots, or merely enjoying that sweet art of doing nothing which we are, to our loss, on the way to forgetting in this hard-driven society of ours. This was Magra, our first camp in the wilds.

THE PILGRIM WAY TO GANGOTRI

CERTAIN anxieties attend the setting of a first camp. The whole carefully planned system of packing becomes open to suspicion if, on this occasion, a tent is discovered without its attendant pegs; nor is the suspicion allayed if out of another tent-bag there clatter enough pegs to anchor a marquee. The porters have not been drilled in the handling of your particular brand of tent; confusion and damage may result if you cannot keep their zealous hands off the gear while you yourself carry out a demonstration pitch. Indian porters seem constitutionally slow at learning the principles of guy-ropes. Even after repeated and patient coaching they keep reverting to their own idea of tightening, which is to stick a peg through the ring at the end of the line, pull hard and then force the peg into the ground, using a stone to hammer it home if it resists. If the adjustment of some other guy-rope causes their line to slacken, they up-root the peg and haul on it again ; but light fabrics or aluminium pegs will not stand such treatment for long; that is why tent-pitching and striking should never be left entirely to underlings.

At Magra, a fortnight's walking lay between us and Gaumukh, source of the Bhagirat'hi, one of the several head waters of the Ganges, itself the continuation of the great Gangotri glacier. Gaumukh means Cow's Mouth. It is the Hindu custom to attach symbolical names to the salient features in a landscape, the intention being to conjure up ideas rather than to refer to historical events or to evoke the memory of famous men. The Ganges, which plays so prominent a part in Hindu symbolism, is pictured as having its source in the mouth of that gentle, patient creature, the chosen type of the animal kingdom, whose protection is enjoined on all Hindus. To a stranger in his ignorance "Cow's Mouth" might seem an unromantic name for one of Nature's grandest display-places: yet, when the meaning is made known, one revises one's

16

opinion. Looking with the eye of a pilgrim at the flood of waters gushing forth from amethystine caverns concealed beneath the ice, a sculptor might have found inspiration in the name and felt moved to carve some great animal head, a sphinx-like Colossus, through whose jaws the waters of the infant Ganges might flow.

The second morning's march continued the descent into the valley of the Aglar. The unforgettable memory of that day was a magnolia bush at a curve of the road; its few flowers were of shell-like purity, their frilled petals shaded to a deep rose. The trunk and branches were gnarled and twisted into shapes so fantastic that one would have said it had been consciously trained to serve as a model for some divine old Chinese artist. Each man stopped as he caught sight of it in breathless amazement. At a later stage we found more magnolias, larger and covered with flowers; but that first one contained the quintessence of them all, an unfading picture imprinted on our minds.

Between us and the Bhagirat'hi valley there still lay two passes, each about 8,000 feet high. Twice we saw the Gangotri peaks from these points of vantage across the wooded foothills. For the second pass it was desirable to make an early start, since the descent on the farther side was said to be long and hot. With the dawn we broke up our camp on the hillside at Chapra, below the first pass, and plunged down into the cool shadow. At the bottom we paddled through a shallow torrent in which a Hindu devotee was performing his morning ablutions; we had noticed him the night before, sitting in deep thought in a villager's garden among opium poppies and tobacco plants. He had greeted us with a motion of the hand and a dreamy, far-off look; our passing scarcely distracted him for a second from the vision that held him.

For a couple of hours we climbed up the opposite hillside. Peasants here and there were tilling narrow strips of field, walking behind the small wooden harrows drawn by slow, plodding oxen; little boys, the colour of the soil, were sitting on the ploughs, using their scanty weight to drive the plough-shares deeper. About eight o'clock we arrived on the col. I remember how we all stood in silence before the glorious line of peaks glistening in the early morning sunlight. Close at hand on either side a soft breeze was brushing across the barley, while overhead eagles wheeled against the blue. The porters

17

came up close behind us, some of them bringing handfuls of yellow raspberries. As each man topped the pass he sang out boisterously in praise of the Holy Ones. "Hail to Jamnotri!" (source of the Jamna). "Hail to Gangotri!" "To the white lord of Kedar, homage!" (Its Weisshorn-like pyramid occupied the centre of the picture.) "To Badrinath," (sacred to Vishnu) "all Hail!" We would willingly have gazed all day, but the thought of the heat, awaiting us in the valley below, made us cut short this joyous moment and we set off on the descent to Dharasu.

Our way followed the Bhagirat'hi valley, now making height steadily, now rising suddenly, when rocky narrows forced the path to take a higher level. We had got into our stride now, arrangements were working smoothly, and we felt in a carefree frame of mind, able to let our attention wander among the countless new things which met us at every turn. To allude to them all separately would need a volume; so I will first describe a typical day, and afterwards mention one or two happenings that stood out with special prominence.

We usually woke about five and, while breakfast was cooking strapped up our holdalls and struck the tents; for the porters would be already hovering round impatient to get off in the cool. Then, after indicating a place some fifteen miles away for the next camp, we let them straggle off, each at his own pace; the faster ones, to whom things first needed on arrival had been entrusted, forged on ahead, while the older ones trudged behind slowly. We were then free to employ our own time on the march as we pleased, pausing to take photographs or to bathe in an inviting pool or to pass the time of day with some friendly pilgrims bound like ourselves for Gangotri.

This valley is sacred to Shiva, the Aspect of the Hindu Trinity who stands for the transformative and also, but only by extension, for the destructive function in the Godhead. We passed many small temples, like elongated beehives; almost all were dedicated to Shiva under one of His aspects, such as Conqueror of Demons or Lord of the Cosmic Dance: within, in lieu of an image, there is often placed a black conical stone, the phallic emblem of the God. The corresponding valley on the East of the Gangotri mountains in British Garhwal, that of the Alaknanda, is consecrated to the cult of Vishnu, the Aspect that is the complement of Shiva's, that of creation and preservation; His temple at Bradrinath draws a still larger yearly pilgrimage.

The pilgrims themselves belonged to every province of India and came from all ranks of society. First we met a sturdy peasant, half hidden under a huge bundle of bedding overflowing from his long wicker basket, like the ones used in Switzerland, which was slung over his back. On the top of it his wife was perched, her legs dangling: yet the Orient is called ungallant! Then we came across a wealthy dame, borne aloft in her palanquin on the shoulders of four stout attendants, looking, but for her clothes, like one of her eighteenth-century predecessors, the pious Austrian or French great ladies, Romeward bound.

I remember also a mysterious person whom we passed and repassed frequently, a very tall man in a flowing toga, with eyes that pierced like stilettos, his coal-black hair gathered up in a knot, in his hand an iron-shod staff like a spear. He strode along haughtily, and whenever he came upon a big stone that had rolled on to the path, he picked it up as if it were a feather and tossed it over the precipice with a gesture of disdain that was rather terrifying in its suggestion of power. We thought of him as the god Wotan, disguised as the Wanderer—for he really might have stepped straight out of *Siegfried*. When he brought his staff sharply down on the rock, I momentarily expected sparks to fly out.

Many *Swamis*, or devotees wearing saffron robes and turbans, each of them carrying a drinking pot of burnished metal, passed us by. Most of them eyed us coldly, as if suspicious of our presence: their demeanour came as somewhat of a shock after the unfailing smiles and salaams of the common pilgrims. There was also another class of devotees to be found in large numbers, so-called *Sadhus*, men naked save for a loincloth, besmeared with grey ash from head to foot, their faces often made to look repulsive by blotches of ochre. The conception of the true *Sadhu* is an exalted one: he is the type of the spiritually independent man, who asks guidance of no power but his inner light, and has passed beyond all that social life can give, whether rights or duties. For him, renunciation implies no idea of sacrifice of the "good things of the world"—that conception, peculiar to European monasticism, is unknown to India, Tibet and other Oriental traditions: this is an important point to grasp, lest one be drawn into a false analogy. On the contrary, the genuine *Sadhu* rejects the world "with pleasure, just as a man would find satisfaction in taking off a filthy and ragged

19

garment." He makes himself like an outlaw, abandoning the privileges of family and caste in the present, of past fame, of aspiration for the future life, and tramps the highways, begging for his meagre livelihood, driven on by the wind of the spirit, that bloweth where it listeth.

This way, however, is not for the many: by no means all the ascetics who frequent sacred places can approach it. There is also a host of hangers-on, charlatans usurping the title, who, to do them justice, adopt uncomfortable existence, but whose spiritual status would, in others respects, take some proving.

In the afternoon we used to go ahead of the porters to choose the best site for a camp in beautiful surroundings. Having read of the uncleanness which spoils many usual camping-grounds in Garhwal, we made a point of avoiding them and choosing ground of our own, not too close to villages. It is a better plan not to leave this important matter, affecting both comfort and pleasure, to head-porters, who will of course invariably do as everyone else does and pick for preference some fly-infested area in the middle of the village, near a stream which receives the sewage of all the houses. Indians are extremely clean as far as their persons, clothes and eating-vessels are concerned, but utterly insanitary in their use of ground in the vicinity of habitations. Within a radius of two miles round Gangotri temple, for instance, the soil is badly polluted. Near villages or cultivation one cannot be too careful about the water: in fact we never risked drinking it unboiled till we were past human settlements. Lest anyone should be tempted in the midday heat, we made it a rule that each European must carry in his rucksack a flask of boiled water. Should any man desire to undertake a worthy work of piety, he might try to instal a system of simple latrines along the pilgrim route: I should like to see it established not as an innovation in the name of foreign hygiene, but rather as an offering to Shiva, for a purification of His holy ground.

It is lucky that carcasses of cows and goats are dealt with by the vultures, which circle continuously overhead at a great height, and scan the country for dying animals. Outside the village of Uttarkashi we came upon a dozen of them which had just finished picking a skeleton clean. How magnificent they looked as they flapped their mighty wings, and how different from the listless captives of our zoos, which are made into a gazing-stock for the supposed education of children. It

20

is surely base ingratitude towards a fellow-creature, which, even from the narrow point of view of our own self-interest, should be saluted as the unpaid ally of the sanitary squad and the health inspector.

After pitching tents and making tea, the work of the day was by no means over, for some of us at least. News that we had a doctor in our midst spread quickly, and soon a long string of people demanding medicine appeared at the edge of the camp. First they had to be sorted out, and then the doctor examined each in turn. One of us acted as his interpreter and helped to dispense in small envelopes the pills or powders which he prescribed. We saw some sad, and many amusing, cases.

One man reported various symptoms, affecting almost every limb and organ in the body, which seemed hard to square with his appearance of robust health. Pain in the shoulder, in the hips, headache, shivering, what next? Fever?—the thermometer belied him. "There is nothing wrong with you, why do you come and waste our time?" cried the doctor. "Oh! no, Sahib," he answered. "It's not I who am ill, it's my wife. She lives at the village back yonder, two days' journey away. You can give me the medicine."

Another man demanded something for his horse, also not present. All this had to be carried on in full publicity, with the whole village enjoying the show. Some of the bystanders, bitten with a desire to share in the excitement, were seized with sudden ailments and looked quite crestfallen when the doctor refused to prescribe for them like the others.

At long last came the big meal of the day, supper, usually a curry of sorts; and then half an hour's yarning round the camp-fire, in which some of the porters joined, reduced everyone to somnolence. By eight-thirty or nine we were all asleep.

The commissariat proved an unqualified success, thanks to the fresh food we bought daily and to Maidar Singh's skill in cooking it. During the course of travel in the hills, one learns to know the essential requirements, what must be brought from home, and what can be purchased locally. Experience has shown that in most districts the village shop can be relied on for flour, rice, lentils, *ghi* (clarified butter), sugar, onions and pepper. Eggs, milk, and often a few vegetables such as potatoes, a kind of spinach and large sweet radishes can be bought direct from the peasants. We accustomed ourselves to a diet of these foods; our imports only amounted to a few luxuries.

The quality of the native foodstuffs is on the whole excellent; the fatal cult of whiteness and regularity of shape has not caused half their goodness to be "purified" away, nor has their flavour been dissipated in the crazy worship of size and number.

The highest-lying villages in Garhwal, along the Tibetan border, are inhabited in the summer months by a semi-nomadic tribe called Jadhs or, farther to the east, Bhotias. These people are a typical frontier product, mixed racially and in tradition, who make the best of two worlds in any border dispute. The Tibetan half predominates in the Jadhs, however; six days out of seven they are Buddhists and, when not wearing European cast-offs purchased while they are wintering on the edge of the Indian plain, they clothe themselves in Tibetan style. In summer they pasture their flocks and ponies in the uplands, or cross into Tibet to barter Indian produce for a consignment of salt or borax.

A party of Jadhs happened to be encamped near a place called Kot'h Bangla the afternoon we arrived there. Their gaily-coloured tents, unusual clothes, and flat faces at once attracted our attention. We stopped to stare and they, for their part, returned the compliment with interest. Then I took my courage in both hands and spoke a short sentence in Tibetan, my first remark in that tongue to a native of the land. There was stony silence till I spoke again; then everyone burst into roars of laughter, shouting, "Why, he's talking Tibetan, he's really talking Tibetan!" It was rather disconcerting to have one's linguistic efforts laughed at with such unconcealed frankness; but it was not long before I discovered that what tickled their sense of humour was not so much my halting speech, as the extraordinary fact that a white man should speak in Tibetan at all! There was among them one man in particular who caught my eye; we asked him to visit us so that we might continue the new talking-game. Sure enough, he turned up in an hour's time, bringing a young Jadh with him, and spent the rest of the afternoon in our company. Mutual sympathy developed from the start. We found out that he spoke, and even could write, Hindustani as well as Tibetan, and what was still more exciting, that he was no Jadh, but came from Poo on the Satlej, a place which stood on our itinerary for Part Two of the expedition's programme: for it was our intention to climb at Gangotri till the rains broke and then to cross the Ganges-Satlej watershed to a district beyond the monsoon's influence,

22

and passing through Poo, to attempt, as a grand finale, the ascent of the great peak of Riwo Pargyul. Our new-found friends seemed to have turned up providentially; before they left our camp that day we had invited them both to join us. The man of Poo asked for a brief delay in order to go back and consult his wife, but promised to bring an answer before the day was out.

In the evening he returned with the glad news that everything was settled and that he and Djun Singh, his friend, who looked as strong as a young bull, would most certainly come with us as far and as long as we liked. As if to seal the compact, he made me a present of a little wooden bowl with a silver base and received a knife in exchange. His name was Odsung in his own country; but he kept the alternative one of Ishwar Singh for use when associating with Indians. In time he was to become the head of our porters, and three years later both he and Djun Singh joined us again in Sikkim: far-reaching results from a chance meeting by the roadside. Ishwar Singh's rapid decision to throw in his lot with total strangers, for a journey of six hundred miles, was characteristic of Tibetan independence and love of roving.

PORTERS AND SAHIBS

FOR the man who loves trees and plants, even if he be no more than an amateur, the walk along the Bhagirat'hi is one long succession of delights; for each day's gain in height is faithfully reflected in corresponding changes of vegetation. Dharasu, the point where one enters the valley at the low level of 2,500 feet, lies in a warm zone in which even small palms are found—outposts of the flora of the plains. The blue-grey of the long-needled pine colours much of the landscape. White roses are massed along the path for miles on end; *Erythrina*, the coral tree, lends here and there a touch of fire; this part of the valley is the favoured home of the pink magnolia.

At about 7,000 feet, that king of forest trees, the Himalayan cedar or deodar, makes its appearance, its roots clinging to ledges on the cliff face, its trunk leaning precariously out over the swirling rapids. A few miles short of a place called Gangnani the road crosses temporarily to the left bank and penetrates a belt of mixed forest, maple, oak and chestnut, of almost tropical density. The shed petals of tree rhododendrons turn the path into a crimson carpet, as if in expectation of a royal progress. Jasmine and wild hops wreathe the boughs with festive garlands. The tender shoots of bamboo, so delicate yet so impenetrable, bar the way to the interior of the forest, guarding the glades where the wild peonies gleam like folds of white satin.

One more day, and the scene changes to typical Alpine country, a flat-bottomed valley through which the Bhagirat'hi winds along its shingly bed, hardly recognizable for the same stream as the raging torrent lower down. Mixed woods have disappeared and the hillsides are uniformly forested with stately deodars; violets look up from the grass; the light airs bring with them the fragrance of thyme. One is glad to pull on a sweater, for in mid-May the snow is still lying quite low and evenings soon turn chilly.

24

At the farther extremity of this valley there is a small hamlet called Harsil where, according to our programme, we had planned to make a three days' halt in order to pay off our Mussoori coolies and replace them by local men, better inured to the rigorous climate of the glaciers. We had been counting on the Jadhs to furnish the whole of our new personnel, but found that at that date only a few advanced bands had yet come up from the winter grazing-grounds; the remainder were still scattered down the valley. The only alternative was to make up the number from near-by villages, though we knew that the nomads, whose life is one long trek, would have answered our purpose far better than the peasants, whose hearts were in their fields and who elected to come for the pay, but came reluctantly. There was, however, no choice, so word was sent to the village headmen stating our requirements which they promised to supply.

Meanwhile at our end there were also jobs to be done. First, we had to decide who were the four best men to keep with us at our glacier camp for work on the mountains. As recently as 1933 it was still generally believed that Europeans were only just capable of becoming sufficiently acclimatized to climb their peaks, and that in the absence of native porters to do their fetching and carrying for them they had hardly a hope of success. For one European climber to go high, several natives had to accompany him. It is not difficult to calculate what a multiplication of personnel and baggage resulted from this hypothesis: for the attendant natives themselves needed food and shelter, which entailed again more porters and so on for ever. In fact, it could be proved mathematically that by this process one European party would eventually involve the whole human race, and still the problem would be no nearer solution.

Our complement of only four porters was probably rather short commons, since it meant less than one coolie per European: we found in practice that we wasted more of our own energy than we could afford in long-distance carries over the glaciers. I have said four; but in reality they were but three and a half, for one of the men selected, our new-found friend from Poo, Ishwar Singh, was not very strong and did not undertake serious carrying. He more than made up for it, however, by being the perfect caretaker of a camp, ready to turn his hand to anything, and a suitable man for sending down to the villages to order fresh supplies or to engage porters to clear our stuff when the climbing was all over. His friend, Djun Singh, the Jadh, was a powerful fellow. The other vacancies were filled by two young men from British Garhwal, one of whom was an old soldier, in more senses than one, who had served with the Garhwal Rifles. He was perpetually saluting and clicking heels; but he was active as a cat on rocks. He also performed prodigies of weight-lifting and speed on steep slopes. Had we asked for his life he would have given it; but that did not preclude his trying to score off us in petty ways from time to time. Apart from that, as a mountain porter he could not have been bettered.

A further job at Harsil was the dumping of half our baggage which, not being immediately required, was intended for use during the second or Satlej part of the journey. Everything was handed into the charge of the district forest ranger, a very obliging Hindu who stored it in a safe place against our return from the glacier.

The third job was a melancholy one for all concerned, the paying off of the old set of porters who had served us so faithfully. Nine days of acquaintance may not seem long, but the Indians, when treated considerately, attach themselves easily; the men seemed genuinely sad to be leaving us as they walked up in turn to the box that served as a table to receive their wages.

This opportunity must be taken of testifying to the uniform level of honesty that we have found among the mountain peoples. In 1933 we changed porters five times and employed Indians, Jadhs, Tibetans and Kunáwaris from the Satlej. During the whole time we did not miss so much as a lump of sugar; not that we took precautions, we soon learned that it was a waste of trouble. Everything was strewn about the camp. In how many countries of Europe would it be possible to pick up fifty chance comers and yet enjoy perfect immunity from anxiety on the score of pilfering?

When it came to truthfulness the difference was greater. The Tibetans and allied peoples tend to be extremely accurate, while the Indians are inclined to romance, more from a desire to please than from any wish to deceive. There is much truth in the tale of the tired English traveller who asked the distance to the next village. "Not far," was the answer. "What do you mean by that? Is it about three miles?" "Yes, your honour."

26

But the Englishman still entertained some doubts. "Are you sure it's only three miles? Or is it six?" "Yes, six, your honour." Losing his temper the Englishman cried: "What the devil do you mean by saying it's three miles and then six? Don't tell me any more lies, which is it, three or six?" "It's as your honour pleases."

The headmen were as good as their word; at the appointed hour the new coolies duly paraded for their loads. Physically they looked equal to any call; but their faces struck us as rather vapid, with a dash of that peculiar brand of slyness which goes with low intelligence. They were much better clad than the Mussoori men, for their hand-woven garments contrasted favourably with the heterogeneous collections of European misfits which have been adopted by a great number of the hill Indians. This regrettable practice cannot justify itself on the mere plea of cheapness, for the local cloth, still worn by women even when their husbands have discarded it, is spun and woven at home from the wool of their own sheep and costs them next to nothing. Furthermore, it is hard-wearing and warm as well as beautiful; made from it, even the rags of a beggar look dignified.

It did not take us long to discover how much we had been spoiled by our Mussoori coolies. As usual, having indicated the stage for the day, we left the men to their own devices, knowing that they were not yet in training and expecting them to follow slowly. After going some miles, I sat down for rather longer than usual and began to wonder why nobody had yet put in an appearance. Having waited some time, I walked back to a commanding point, but not a soul was in sight. Slightly concerned, I retraced my steps; but I had to go a long way downhill before I encountered Jai Datt, who had been retained in his office of leading porter, and who announced that most of the men were dawdling miles back. Some time later we came upon them all sitting down, their loads off, taking turns at puffing their charcoal pipes, and to all appearances settled there for ever. When we started to protest some of them stood up sulkily and raced a few steps uphill at an absurd pace, only to collapse once more. Out came the pipes again quite blatantly. This performance was repeated at intervals all the afternoon, and we reached Bhaironghati, the resting-place for the night, with frayed tempers. It was dark before the rearguard slouched in at last; not a good outlook, for we were still following a

27

path, whereas the next day we were to enter trackless country. Working out that day's rate of progress, I made it not much more than one mile an hour, as compared with the normal two and a half miles.

In the morning things at first looked a little more cheerful: there was a perfumed freshness in the air that left little room for worries. Towards ten o'clock the temple of Gangotri, the end of the pilgrim road, came into view, a pleasantly-proportioned domed building of grey stone that did not look very old; I should have guessed no earlier than eighteenth century, though this may not be quite accurate. It stands on the river bank, against a background of noble deodars. We were received by a priest who offered to show us round. We gave him a small present, and, following the ancient custom of feeding a specified number of poor Brahmins, we distributed alms to the neediest-looking of the pilgrims. In front of the temple steps we removed our shoes and were then permitted to approach near enough to peer vaguely into the dark interior. A tray with sweetmeats that had stood in front of the image was brought out and we were each invited to taste a piece, and then our foreheads were marked with powdered sandalwood, to the accompaniment of triumphant shouts from the bystanders led by Jai Datt. Sight-seeing, lunch, and a long rest filled a couple of hours before the signal was given to continue the march.

At once a chorus of moans rose from the porters, who had evidently been counting on our readiness to accept the few miles between Bhaironghati and Gangotri as the equivalent of a day's work. Wringing their hands they whined: "Please, please don't make us go farther to-day. There is no path, it is a terrible wilderness full of leopards and bears. We shall be killed by falling stones, and there are no camping-grounds!" At length, having exhausted themselves in vain lamentation, and seeing that we were not to be moved from our purpose, they lifted their loads with an ill grace and started off. Several truants hid among the temple outhouses, hoping to be overlooked, and had to be rounded up by Jai Datt and the forest ranger who, uninvited, accompanied our column.

The wild Gangotri gorge, the passage from the temple to the Cow's Mouth, is crossed at that season by huge drifts of compacted winter snow which bridge the river and allow free crossing to and fro. In summer, these get washed away and the approved route follows the left bank and crosses to Gangotri by a bridge. The other side is blocked by formidable cliffs lashed by the torrent which boils against their base. When we came down in the monsoon, though the main body took the left bank, two of us, ignorant of the obstacle, followed the right bank and only just got through, after a strenuous day's rock-climbing along ledges and up cracks, all the time haunted by the fear that in the end we might find ourselves cut off.

The porters soon began to repeat the previous day's tactics, but with even more frequent halts, a policy which was favoured by the abundance of cover. Every inch was contested. Sometimes a man would move not more than twenty paces and then subside under a bush and slip his arms out of the loops of his carrying-rope. Poor Jai Datt lost his head completely and showed abject irresolution before his men, while the ranger, being made of sterner stuff, preferred futile threats to entreaties. At last, when we had crawled a couple of miles, things came to a head. A ringleader, ordered to get up from behind a boulder where he was crouching, refused. Abandoning his load he declared that he could not go a step farther. Thereupon Ted Hicks snatched up the package and slung it over his own shoulders saying: "If you are too weak to carry this light box, I can do it myself." The man was utterly taken aback by the unprecedented sight of a sahib actually doing a job of work; he sprang up and rushed after Ted begging to be allowed to take back his load. A general stampede followed and before we knew where we were, we had gone quite a distance. For the moment we were in control of the situation; but it was doubtful how long the emotion which had befriended us would last, so as soon as I saw a possible site for a camp I called a halt. It was elementary generalship to be the first to offer, indeed to order, the very thing which the other party was still screwing up its courage to demand.

At tea-time we held a council of war. It was evident that we were facing a crisis; for had the discontent resulted in a strike and the dumping of our baggage, it would have taken us days to extricate ourselves from the mess. Gangotri is not a village; we could only have sent back for fresh porters to Harsil, the very place from which the present lot were drawn, and we should have been more than ever in their power. Nor would the monsoon have stayed its hand for our convenience. A loss of time at that moment could not have been made up later. As things turned out, it would have meant utter disaster, for the rains came on a full three weeks before the expected date, so that we only had a bare month on the glacier. In addition, we had visions of the sarcastic comments of those prophets who had shaken their heads over the imprudence of five amateurs venturing to run an expedition without an experienced transport officer. Heroic remedies were obviously called for.

The first move was to get rid of Jai Datt and the officious ranger; their presence as intermediaries was only adding to our difficulties. After that, remembering my army training, I worked out a new order of march, by which a slow but unflagging pace was to be imposed on all, on the fast few as well as on the many loiterers; they were to keep in one body, with official halts at stated intervals. We went the round of the camp-fires that night and explained the morrow's plans; we found everyone in better humour and more ready to listen to us in person than to Jai Datt's hysterical appeals.

We pointed out to them that at the present rate we were never going to reach Cow's Mouth; and that this rushing on a few steps and then stopping was actually the most tiring method imaginable. We pointed out that they were mistaken in thinking that we did not intend them to have time to rest; we promised, on the contrary, to arrange regular halts and they would see for themselves how much earlier they would make camp and how fresh they would feel. We said that the next day no one would be allowed to go fast, but all must go at a set pace; every half-hour there would be five minutes' halt, after an hour ten, after two hours a long rest. They were not to sit down except at a given signal, nor to start without another. Between the halts they must keep moving at an even pace. We assured them that they would thank us in the end, when they realized how much less tired they were. The men seemed disposed to respond to this appeal to their reason; we retired to bed still anxious, but somewhat more optimistic, and blessing the extra time we had spent on linguistic studies, without which such complex explanations would have been impossible.

After breakfast we lined up the men facing the loads and called the roll, so that the day might start in an atmosphere of calm. When all were ready, we formed them in single file, placing two of our party at the head, two at the tail, and one to act as liaison in the middle. Then we set off; but, at first, success hung in the balance. Several men attempted to sit down and had to be hooked up with ice-axes by their girdles. As soon as the hands of my watch pointed to the half-hour I called a halt and sat down. This seemed to affect certain notorious sluggards with an irresistible enthusiasm for going on; they had to be forcibly restrained and made to rest.

The next period went better; by the end of the second hour, when a lengthy pause was due according to schedule, we knew we had won the day. The coolies had caught on to the idea; their step had become springy and their whole manner changed. We had no further trouble with them, and during the next two days in the gorge everything went smoothly. At the finish, the tables were turned; for when we had nearly arrived in sight of the glacier snout the porters could no longer be restrained, and one and all raced off at breakneck pace across the slopes, so that we hardly knew them for the feeble creatures who, three days earlier, seemed hardly capable of putting one foot in front of the other. The whole episode was a valuable lesson to us, our first real experience of porter management: the story may make the hard-bitten traveller smile, but to five novices it seemed no small adventure.

Some little distance short of the Cow's Mouth and separated from it by an expanse of clean sand we camped in a leafless birchwood, surrounded by long drifts of snow. Ahead loomed the vast glacier, measuring a mile across, its rubbish-covered surface broken up into mounds, which turned out to be hillocks quite a hundred feet high. Peaks rose on every side in wildest confusion; not even in Sikkim have I seen anything like the mountain scenery round Gangotri. Dominating all was the glorious group of the Satopant'h peaks, a magnet for our ambitions during our stay there—one of them was eventually scaled by two of the party—but it is useless to try to describe the grandeur of the scene: there are perfections about which the only eloquence is silence.

During the following three days the baggage was transferred on to the glacier, to a spot close under the left moraine which had been chosen for the Base Camp. Across the opposite side, in a branch valley, a slope covered with low bushes of juniper provided plentiful firewood. After we had settled in, the majority of the porters returned home, leaving only the chosen four to keep us company. We now split up into pairs and began exploratory forays and to look for climbable peaks; we rejected at sight a nightmare version of the Matterhorn that overhung the camp. I do not propose to enter into minute details of our mountaineering round this region, for it is now old history, as an Austrian expedition has since explored the Gangotri district. But briefly, one small, one large and three medium peaks—not to mention two abortive attempts—were climbed before the warm rains descended upon us prematurely, to the accompaniment of a barrage of falling stones and avalanches, and put an end to operations.

The highest as well as the most formidable of these excursions was the ascent, previously mentioned, of Central Satopant'h [1] by Kirkus and Warren. Of this a full description will be given in the next chapter, written by C. F. Kirkus himself. At the time when the account first appeared it did not, to my mind, receive the general attention which it deserved. The ascent was not only a fine piece of mountaineering, but it afforded a triumphant vindication of the theory that Europeans were capable of carrying out such enterprises without the help of porters. In this case the two climbers did the whole of their portering on a difficult mountain, involving several bivouacs, unaided from start to finish, and at the height of 21,000 feet negotiated a rock pitch which would have counted as severe at sea level; it is this difficult rock-climbing at a high altitude that makes their achievement so outstanding.

[1] As a result of the Austrian party's explorations there is now reason to believe that the peaks known to us as *Satopant'h* should be named the *Bhagirat'hi* group.

CENTRAL SATOPANT'H

(BY C. F. KIRKUS)

ON the afternoon of June 14th Warren and I arrived at our advanced base, a pleasant camp at a height of about 15,000 feet, pitched on turf. It would have made an ideal Base Camp if only our transport arrangements had enabled us to get all our equipment up the extra seven miles of glacier.

We were still undecided about our next move. It was a warm and sunny day, the kind of day that inspires one to make bold plans for the morrow, and until the morrow comes, to relax in delightful idleness. Across the glacier to the east was the great rock mass of the Central Satopant'h Peak, 22,060 feet. Its face was a fearsome yellow cliff, crowned by a snow-capped ridge of red rock. This looked possible on the right where it sloped down to a col and, providentially, a long, curving easy-looking ridge led up to this col. We wanted to climb a big peak but we wished for no more slopes of endless, heart-breaking snow. The gleaming snow and silvery rock of Central Satopant'h standing up so boldly against a sky of deepest blue, proved quite irresistible and we decided to start the attempt on it next day.

There seemed to be two doubtful stretches on the route we had planned—a rock tower on the col and a vertical step in the ridge immediately above. This step was several hundred feet in height and looked formidable enough to stop us unless we could manage to turn it. The whole peak, in fact, looked definitely difficult and we were not too optimistic about our chances.

We set off at eight o'clock next morning, stumbling and cursing across the mile-wide glacier. Never is scree so villainous as when it is resting on ice; never are the limpid depths of glacier lakes less appreciated than when one is faced with the prospect of falling into them. We each carried a sack weighing about twenty-five pounds, containing sleeping-bags, bivouac tent, a week's supply of food (chiefly pemmican and boiled sweets), solidified spirit cookers and a Primus. Everything had been cut down to a bare minimum. A very pleasant slope of grass and grey boulders, with scarcely any snow on it, led us to

CENTRAL SATOPANT'H

a ridge, clustered with grotesque pinnacles of red rock. Soon afterwards we had to rope for a fascinating arête of grey rock, which reminded us of Snowdonia, wonderfully firm and rough and technically quite difficult. It made us feel almost homesick and was altogether an exhilarating interlude in this rather grim business of Himalayan mountaineering.

We had to traverse off finally, to avoid a wall that would have given good sport in gym shoes, but we had no trouble in getting back to the ridge again. We pitched Camp I at about 17,500 feet, right on its jumbled crest. The only flat place was a miserable patch of snow, four or five feet square; this we had to build up with stones until it was big enough to take our 4-foot by 6-foot tent.

As usual, it came on to snow in the afternoon and a bitter wind harried us. I kept my self comparatively warm by building a cairn and a wall worthy of the old Romans. By the time we went to bed there was half a gale blowing and we were afraid that our tent might be swept off its precarious platform.

It was still horribly cold in the morning and the tent was

frozen stiff as a board; we had to wait for about an hour before it was soft enough to pack. We had to rope very soon for a small pinnacle and then were forced off the ridge on the left, across a slope which looked from a distance like snow, but proved to be composed of small prickles of ice, about three feet high, frozen on to rock. Then we got on to slabs, smooth and holdless and covered with snow wherever snow would lie. The route-finding was very tricky and the climbing difficult and insecure, with a great scarcity of belays. All the time we were getting farther and farther away from the crest of the ridge, with less and less hope of regaining it. And this was the part that we thought would be an easy scramble up to the true peak above the col.

I came round a slabby corner and to my joy saw that an easy snow gully led right up to the ridge. Here we made some tea and basked in the sunshine. We were now 3,000 or 4,000 feet above the glacier, which looked like a great sweeping river of speckled grey and white. An astonishing array of peaks surrounded us. There was the huge pinnacle that we called the Matterhorn, half spire, half tower, red rock at the bottom, snow-powdered yellow at the top; beautifully alluring, hideously inaccessible. We unroped with profound relief and made our way across a slope of mixed snow and stones on the right. This was made necessary by a curious kink in the ridge, where it almost ceased to be a ridge at all. We climbed easily upwards by interesting rock pitches and little knife-edges of snow. I felt well and happy and was able to enjoy the noble scale of the scenery. Especially impressive was a weird and shadowy ice-valley, dizzily far below on the right, into which a hanging glacier, perched on top of 2,000 feet of cliff, rained showers of ice-splinters.

Then followed two towers, the second rotten and snow-sprinkled, after which a descent of a hundred feet or so brought us, still unroped, to our longed-for col. It was an ideal spot—flat, slatey ground with convenient stones all ready for the tent flaps. And there was even a water supply where a stone had melted a hole in some snow and left a small pool. One could not hope to find a better spot at 19,500 feet; it was amazing luxury not having to camp on snow. A full vertical mile below was our Base Camp and the whole dreary ribbon of the glacier. In front was the face of our mountain—3,000 feet of the smoothest, sheerest yellow-silver rock, almost luminous against

35

soon stiff and numb. At high altitudes I always feel sick and weak in the morning for the first two hours. This, coupled with the bad conditions, made even the first pitch seem much more forbidding than it had done the night before. And now we were standing under the final wall which was to decide the fate of our venture. We were in a vertical corner of red rock. The holds were flat but not incut and very rotten, and at the top there was an overhang of at least two feet.

With Warren belayed some forty feet below, I climbed up to this overhang, having first divested myself of my rucksack. The overhang seemed hopeless, but on the nose on the right was a projection like a wafer, about two inches thick, jutting out horizontally a yard or so. I pushed off the top layer, which was obviously loose, and then looked at it. If I could trust my weight on it I could cheat the overhang. Three days of grim and anxious effort could not wait on one doubtful hold. I stood on it—it had to be near the edge for me to keep my balance—and it held. That was the only time on the whole climb that I was really frightened. The pounding of my heart was not due entirely to the altitude. Another anxious step— only just in balance—and I lay panting on the scree above.

An easy slope of slates and snow led to a little tower and we were able to see what lay ahead. The ridge was narrow and very serrated—not at all the solid smooth slope it had looked from below. Quite close was a great snowy rise; behind, dimly seen through the mist, a shadowy pinnacle; steep snow on the left; almost vertical rock falling for thousands of feet on the right. We climbed the pinnacle. At the top the snow turned to ice, and, after a good deal of step-cutting, we had to take to the awkward slabby rocks on the left. We reached the top of the pinnacle at 11.25 a.m., rather tired, dumped our loads and decided to make an attempt on the summit that day. It looked very close, but I was dubious; things are always three times as far away as they seem in the Himalaya. I thought it would take us at least two hours.

Before starting out we made some tea. Water boils at about 175° F. at this altitude (about 21,750 feet) and all the tea-leaves floated, so that we had to drink them. It was about the most unpleasant tea I have ever tasted, but it had a marvellously refreshing effect. We started off again at 12.25, without our rucksacks, feeling fit and excited. We had to ascend a narrow ridge of snow, corniced on the right above the great rock cliffs and dropping very steeply on the left. The cloud shut off every-thing except the immediate foreground; we seemed to be very much alone on the crest of the world. We moved one at a time; it is safer that way, and the rests are welcome.

At 1.15 p.m.—surprisingly soon—on Sunday, June 18th, we stood on top of the Central Satopant'h Peak, 22,060 feet above sea level. It seemed an eternity since we had left the advanced base camp three and a half days before. I felt very little elation —altitude deadens all emotion—only a great relief; for I had been very much afraid that we should not succeed. We had no view. There was thick, depressing cloud all round.

We could just make out the other summit, marked 21,991 feet on the map. We decided we ought to include this, so after ten minutes' halt we set off again. There was an ice-cornice on the right and a steep ice-slope on the left leading down, as we knew, to 3,000 feet of cliff. Between the two, the cornice and the slope, was a little snow-filled crack. We walked on this to save step-cutting, which does not appeal at 22,000 feet. Even so we had to cut some steps. The other summit was about 500 feet away. We still moved singly, but led through. The actual top was such a narrow point of ice that there was room only for one at a time. We solemnly stood there in turn, then retreated without a word. We regained the higher summit after an absence of one hour.

It had grown colder now and the weather was threatening. As usual I felt weak and empty when descending, and pro-gressed in a curious bent-up attitude. We regained our ruck-sacks at 2.15 p.m. and descended the big pinnacle to an ideal shelf of flat snow, just the right width for a tent, at its foot. Here we pitched Camp IV (about 21,700 feet) under a large sheltering rock, at 3 p.m. It began to snow just as we got in. I had a very poor night with a violent headache and thirst. We had not enough fuel left to melt snow for drinking at odd moments. Also my pillow was most uncomfortable. This pillow consisted of my rucksack containing boots and an air cushion. When the boots came uppermost I rarely had a good night.

We set off at 8.15 a.m. on a perfect morning. It was a long and tiring day; we were rather short of food and again I felt weak and empty. On the ascent I had been keyed up with the urge to get to the summit; now a reaction of listlessness had set in.

When we reached the crux of the climb, the great rock wall,

we roped down it, cutting a loop off our line. I went down first and then Warren let down my rucksack with the ice-axe insecurely attached, with the result that it fell out, but luckily it stuck in the rock. As I was going to get it, a large piece of rock which I had grasped, began to slide. I held it up as long as I could and then jumped to the right, luckily landing on a ledge. The rock crashed down the other way and did not hit me. As if that had not been enough, the buckle got torn off my rucksack and I was just in time to save the tent. Our position would have been very unpleasant with only one axe and no tent. I was shaken by the incident and found relief in several minutes of continuous cursing.

We reached the site of our old Camp III (20,900 feet) at 9.50 a.m., made some tea and left at 10.15. Against Warren's counsel I decided to try the snow-and-rock slope on the left. We soon found it quite hopeless—loose snow on ice and sliding stones—and had to make an awkward upward traverse back to the ridge. A lot of snow had melted and the ledges were covered with slippery mud. One just had to hope that all the handholds did not give way at the same time as all the footholds. Climbing down the red rock tower without a rucksack proved to be much easier than I expected. Then we were faced with the problem of finding our way off the ridge. We found vague signs of our old footmarks and followed them. The snow was in a wickedly dangerous condition. We managed with a fair degree of safety by leading through in short run-outs, and, after a good deal of difficulty, found the top of our gully. We also found avalanches sliding into it. Most of them were small, and stopped at the top of the gully, but the stones were more serious. They came down in bounds of 400 feet at an incredible speed, and hit anywhere in the gully with terrifying cracks. We did not stay here longer than was necessary. Now that the monsoon had arrived, the Himalayan snow-slopes were certainly justifying their reputation.

We found an easier traverse back to the col than the way we had taken on the ascent. We kept a little lower and avoided the steeper rocks. We were so tired that we continued to move singly, leading through. I still remember what a blessed relief it was, when all the rope had run out, to sit down and wait for Warren to pass me, and what an effort it was when I in turn had to move. I have two recollections of this traverse—one of Warren, far ahead on the skyline, signalling to me to come on; the other of rounding, interminably, corner after corner and always seeing an endless distance between me and the col.

We finally reached the col (19,500 feet)—our Camp II of the ascent—at 3.15 p.m. very tired. Although clouds hid the sun, even at five o'clock it was warm enough to sit outside. I had quite a good night in spite of a headache. At five in the morning it started to snow; at dawn it looked quite hopeless. There had been only 10° F. of frost in the night and we realized that this must be the monsoon, in which case it might go on for days. The outlook was distinctly unpleasant; it certainly seemed as though we should not get down that day. We had only one tin of pemmican and a few biscuits left, two days' provisions at the most. Added to this, Warren was partially snow-blind, from having left off his goggles the previous day, and was in some pain. I put my head out of the tent and dug the Primus stove out of the snow. It was nearly empty and would not work at this altitude. After nearly setting the tent on fire several times, we barely managed to melt some snow and had to content ourselves with a cold drink.

About eight o'clock the other side of the glacier became visible, although it was still snowing, so we decided to descend. It was quite warm and, once we were outside the tent, not nearly so unpleasant as we had expected. Several inches of snow had fallen and we had some trouble in unburying the odds and ends which we had put outside the tent before going to sleep. However, we managed to start off by 9 a.m. It stopped snowing at ten o'clock, but the cloud remained, making route-finding rather a problem. We cut out a lot of the difficult traversing by an awkward descent on a double rope and managed to miss the lower rocks altogether. We finished down the turfy slope which we had left nearly a week before. Now streams of crystal-clear water were flowing across it and little alpine flowers were springing up all round in soul-satisfying contrast to the grimness above. There could hardly have been a more idyllic ending to our climb.

We reached the advanced base at three o'clock. Warren had to remain there for an extra day because of his eyes, but there was not enough food for me to stay as well, so I put some drops of cocaine in his eyes and left him with the remaining food and fuel and thirteen matches. I got lost in the mist and finally reached the Base Camp and a long-dreamed-of meal at 6.30, just before dark.

Chapter Five

THE GANGES–SATLEJ WATERSHED

THE last days of June found the party on its way down the Gangotri gorge, between mountains which hid their snowy heads under a pall of impenetrable mist. Nature, which still slumbered when we had passed upward five weeks earlier, was fully awakened now. The woods were gay in their mantle of young leaves. We had to push our way through thickets of pink ramblers which barred the gaps between the huge birches. Many unfamiliar shrubs were in flower and mingled their honeyed perfume with the incense of cedars. In open spaces banks of white lilies proclaimed the return of spring.

An interlude of several days at Harsil, where the surplus baggage had been deposited, passed in pleasant uneventfulness. Unstinted fresh food and sleep was all that glacier-weary men asked for. Two of the party, Hicks and Kirkus, who were now due to return to England, packed up, leaving the other three of us to make the crossing of the divide between the basins of the Ganges and the Satlej, into the country of Kunáwar known to readers from the pages of *Kim*. Its own people call it Khunu, a name which I like better than its Indianized variant. A fresh troop of porters, drastically reduced in number, was engaged. This time there were plenty to select from, as all the Jadhs had come up to the summer pastures: also a number of Tibetans had crossed the frontier seeking work. We were therefore able to confine our choice to these two races, and to exclude doubtful or troublesome elements.

From the moment that we began to have dealings with the Tibetans, we felt ourselves in sympathetic company. Though no one could then have foreseen the far-reaching effects fated to spring from this fresh contact, we felt from the outset that here was something entirely new, and that we had stepped right out of the circle of influences that had enclosed our lives hitherto.

Most of these Tibetans were drawn from the district of Sarang, just across the border. Their clothes, even those of the

It should be noted that only the principal mountain chains have been indicated; most of the area shown, however, is mountainous.

At Khyárkuti we passed beyond the birches, but stunted willows still formed diminutive woods. Higher up, nothing that could be called a tree was found, though dwarf willows crept in and out of the stones. The large-blossomed rhododendrons too had been left behind and replaced by a small lemon-yellow variety which covered the slopes just like the familiar "Alpine rose" of Switzerland. Immense auriculas of the deepest purple, ten inches high, grew under the bushes and three kinds of fritillaria, one with a speckled green bell shaped like the hood of a cobra, another white, and a third delicate mauve. There were, besides, asters similar to the Alpine ones, and wherever snow had just melted, tufts of golden kingcup. We were surprised not to find any members of the carnation tribe—but there may have been a campion—nor did we see any gentians or saxifrages, though various unknown rock plants abounded. The most conspicuous plant of the district, covering some slopes like a white sheet and over-topping the yellow rhododendrons, was an anemone with a circlet of flowers on a fleshy stalk. Judging from photographs and published lists the flora of our valley must be very similar to that of the Bhyundar glen, in Eastern Garhwal, made famous by Smythe under the name of *The Valley of Flowers*. From the extreme localization of such rich assemblages of flowers it seems evident that even in this latitude, sheltered places alone favour dense concentrations and multiplicity of species. The perpetual cold draught of the greater glacier valleys is probably discouraging to plant life and partly neutralizes the advantages of sub-tropical sun and generous rainfall.

The next day's march was a very short one, only three hours; but we had to halt near the limit of firewood on this side of the watershed because there was not time to cross from Khyárkuti to the corresponding point on the farther side of the pass in one day. We camped near a small green lake with tiny icebergs floating on it, not far from the end of a long moraine that leads conveniently to the foot of the actual pass. Two of our porters were Baspa men and knew the route, which is used to some extent by the local people. The mountains were more Alpine than anything we had yet seen, long jagged rock ridges enclosing combes filled by icefalls.

The Nela pass itself is long and monotonous: it is advisable to make an early start, as the snowfields lie steep enough to let their angle be felt to the full, but not sufficiently steep to help one to gain height quickly. In the heat of the day, after the snow has begun to soften, the walk up the airless trough is tiring, nor is the scenery interesting enough to make one forget fatigue. Unfortunately, being inexperienced in the psychology of porters, we let them dawdle at the start; the weather was dull and inclined to rain and porters hate to move before the sun is up. We also found out later that they had not bothered to cook a proper meal, although they knew that it would be an unusually long carry over the 18,000-foot pass. They are happy-go-lucky and never carry food to provide a snack at halts. It is a mistake to leave such questions to the porters' own initiative, and the person in charge must himself supervise every detail. Lack of food made them slow and when we stopped at the rocky rib which marks the real pass we became convinced that the next firewood in the upper part of the Baspa valley could never be reached before dark. Snow began to fall, turning to rain lower down, so we decided to pitch camp in an unpleasant spot on loose stones and wait for the stragglers. Night had fallen when at last they drifted wearily into camp. Though it was not part of our agreement to provide shelter for the porters, we thought it only fair to pitch all our tents and squeeze into a single one ourselves, so that, with some shelter, the night might be less miserable for them. That same day one lad narrowly escaped frostbite and three men were affected by snow blindness, a painful, though temporary ailment, from neglecting to shield their eyes against the glare.

While descending the Baspa valley some little trouble was experienced in crossing torrents in spate; in fact we had to camp on the bank of one of them, waiting for the flood to abate in the early hours of the morning, when the melting process on the parent glacier had slowed down. The porters excelled at this game of torrents, fearlessly threading a way through the swirling eddies and jumping from foothold to foothold; but in the worst places a rope had to be used. There was one porter, a native of Nesang in Upper Khunu, called Ts'hering Tendzin, an elderly man of dignified appearance, who had a special flair for detecting a practicable passage. He had slanting Tartar eyes and a pointed beard and wore a short double-breasted tunic of white wool with a cap to match. He looked like one of the Mongol archers of the twelfth century just stepped out of a Persian miniature. Djun Singh, his nephew by marriage, also used to treat torrents with complete disdain, plunging in headlong with no apparent precaution. In fact he became somewhat conceited about his skill. At last we reached the edge of a broad stream, across which some of the more timid of us, myself for one, after taking soundings with axes, worked out an intricate zigzag route; but Djun Singh, with his habitual recklessness, leapt straight into the middle, and having chanced this time on a deep hole, suddenly disappeared under the flood, while his load, which contained tents, was seen floating away towards the Baspa. Fortunately, his uncle was on the watch and hauled him out by the hair, while another excellent porter called Naranhu, whom we later kept on as a permanent climbing coolie, retrieved the precious bundle. Poor Djun Singh emerged from his chilly bath, suffering even more from chagrin than from the cold; we gave him dry clothes from our rucksacks and rubbed him back to warmth; but his pride received a damping from which it took days to recover.

Chitkul, the first village after the Nela pass, is built amid glacier boulders in a magnificent situation backed by a great curtain of fiercely sharp peaks. We had reached the birch line only just before; but below the village, forests of deodar cedar occurred again, carpeted with pale turquoise Aquilegia. A peculiar race inhabits Chitkul and its sister villages of Raksam and Sangla, whose affinities I have not been able to ascertain. There is no trace of the Mongoloid in their faces, neither do they look like Indians. They are tall, powerful and strikingly beautiful. I have seen no other race to compare with them for looks, except the Khambas of Eastern Tibet.

One of them picked up the load of one of our porters on two fingers exclaiming scornfully, "That's not a man's load, anyway!" We met men and even children carrying enormous logs on their backs, yet the people seemed to preserve their physique to an advanced age, for all their heavy work. The men had long flowing locks and short beards trimmed like those of ancient Persian kings; their dress was a grey homespun tunic girded with a violet sash. The women were like Greek goddesses; even quite elderly women had an unwrinkled complexion and a full contralto timbre of voice that would have been the envy of many of their younger sisters elsewhere. The young girls, merry and rosy-cheeked, invited us to fall head over heels in love at first sight. By their dress they recalled Tanagra statuettes, with a flat round cap and a shawl fastened with a brass pin, its design also reminiscent of ancient Hellas.

The children were little angels of beauty, but they had impish smiles; their bearing had the dignity found everywhere among those accustomed to spend much of their time alone in the wilderness.

I remember particularly two people whom we met at Chitkul. The first was a young man who would surely have put Adonis out of countenance. He knew it too; but this cannot be called conceit, for who could be the possessor of such supreme comeliness and pretend not to know it? In his dress, there could be detected an extra care in the choice of material (white wool instead of the usual grey) and a distinctive jauntiness in the way he wore it. On his finger we noticed a ring of unusually fine craftsmanship. It was the work, so he told us, of the best smith in all Khunu, whose fame had spread throughout the province. He dwelt at Sugnam beyond the Satlej, more than a hundred miles away and his products were everywhere in demand. Later, we met the artist himself.

The other person who lives in my memory was a woman, wife of one of the elders. She was middle-aged, but still possessed a rare beauty, shadowed by obvious signs of suffering; for she had a cancer of the breast, not uncommon in that district. It was tragic that nothing could be done for so sweet a creature.

Chitkul is almost entirely built of wood, and every house, as well as the principal temple, is adorned with notable carvings, in which, unlike the woodwork observed in the Ganges valley, Mughal influence is hardly apparent. The style of design is based on square forms and seemed to us to have a connexion with that of the older Hindu and Jain temples of the north of India. The temple was a masterpiece of the woodworker's craft, with rich floral devices, elegant verandas and pierced panels. A small detached pavilion, standing in the open space close by, was still more perfect. Round it hung a fringe of wooden drops, which produced a curious soft jangling in the wind, like the ghost of a xylophone.

Chitkul divided its allegiance between two Traditions. The temple already described, which was dedicated to the *Devta* or local divinity, was nominally Hindu; but there was another newer temple, looked after by a ragged and unprepossessing lama—a regular tramp—which was Buddhist and built in Tibetan style. To the first shrine we were not admitted for fear of pollution; but the second, like all Buddhist places of worship, is open to strangers. This contained some crude mural paintings that nevertheless had a certain liveliness. In particular I remember the figure of a huge slate-coloured Warden brandishing a sword, a St. Michael barring the way to Heaven against the wicked. The Tibetan influence appears to have been brought to Chitkul from the adjoining valley to the north, over the Charang pass.

The central part of the Baspa valley is friendly and park-like, with stretches of fertile farming, alternating with belts of conifer and groves of walnut. In places we found wild apricots bearing small but quite palatable fruit. Sangla, the richest of the villages, is a station of the Forestry Service.

Below Sangla the scenery becomes rather uninteresting: we hurried past it impatient to see the Satlej. That great river, which at this confluence has already run over three hundred miles of its course, is so impressive that it seems immediately to reduce the Baspa to the status of a minor tributary. There is something awe-inspiring about the Satlej, which many other rivers do not share. Man is not alone in feeling its secret power, for according to certain authorities, Nature herself recognizes it by making the river into an easterly boundary of the kingdom of the goats. The horned species that are to be found farther east of that line, despite their goat-like appearance, are all sheep or antelopes, with the one exception of the *t'har*. The ibex, whose range extends even as far west as Spain, when he comes to the Satlej, hears a mysterious voice whispering in his ear: "Thus far, but no farther!"

Chapter Six

THE HINDUSTAN–TIBET ROAD

WE crossed to the right bank of the Satlej by the *jhula* or cable-bridge of Paori. Such bridges are frequent in all Tibetan countries and are rather amusing to negotiate. The passenger or baggage is fastened on a wooden platform suspended from the main cable which is then drawn across by means of a second rope. Ferrymen are deputed to work the *jhula* from each end; at Paori there were ferrywomen too, real Amazons, who pulled as vigorously as the men. While doing this job they wore their jewels, and their appearance would not have disgraced a wedding. Pack-animals were slung by a girth passed under their bellies, and then hauled across, dangling over space. Ponies seemed rather nervous of this passage and began to kick when they got near the landing-place; but donkeys faced the ordeal with stolid unconcern, never moving until all four feet were safely over the land.

Opposite Paori the path zigzags up a long rise to Chini, winding through dry and open fir woods with occasional cornfields in the clearings. We had now said good-bye to the monsoon and rain troubled us no longer, though clouds still clung to the mountain tops. At Chini there is a post-office and a delight-ful Forest Bungalow with a terraced garden planted with apples, plums and every sort of English vegetable, commanding a surpassing view across the Satlej towards a splendid group of mountains, the Chini Kailas.

Chini is also an important post on the Hindustan-Tibet road, which connects Simla with the trade-mart of Gartok. All along it, bungalows have been erected at convenient intervals by the Public Works Department; we were glad to use them, for they are comfortable and invariably placed with an excellent eye for a commanding view. Staying in these houses we gained additional enjoyment from being able to have regular chamber music every evening, playing on two viols, treble and alto, which had accompanied us so far without our having found an opportunity for using them.

String music that sounds complete in two parts, needing no accompaniment, is not easy to find. Our great stand-by was the book of Two-part Inventions by Bach which, though composed for the keyboard, transcribe excellently for viols. We also had a set of fantasies in two parts by Thomas Morley which are authentic viol music. Finally we arranged a number of sixteenth-century English and Spanish tunes in such a way that, by the generous use of double stops, they sounded like a full quartette. It often happened that, unperceived by us, a little group of porters would gather quietly round us and listen intently. They formed a perfect audience, unobtrusive yet seeming to possess the true faculty for listening.

On quitting Chini the woods begin to thin out rapidly and the country takes on the character of semi-desert, with patches of cultivation only at points where the waters of snow-born torrents can be tapped for irrigation. Here the beauties of the landscape are quite different from those of the wooded regions with open views and especially vivid colours. We felt sudden stirrings of emotion each time we came to greenness after hours of walking through parched country. The combined effect of dry air and an average altitude of about 8,000 feet is extremely exhilarating. The flora changes to the arid type: thyme and other aromatic herbs and various thorny plants are scattered sparsely over the hillsides; only high up, close to the melting snows is there any grass for summer pasture.

Such a climate suits the apricot: orchards surround each village, and the trees appear from a distance like little dark green islands in a golden sea of barley. The houses are well built and the general aspect of the villages is more prosperous than in Garhwal. As one approaches the frontier of Tibet, timber becomes scarce, and the chalets and carved wooden temples with their high-pitched roofs give way to an exclusively stone style of architecture with flat roofs. The roofs are used for drying piles of apricots, which do not rot, but are turned by the sun's rays to every shade between orange and deepest crimson. When dry, they form a staple winter food.

On entering a village, the road passes through a gateway something like a lych-gate; under its pointed roof is placed a *chhorten*, the Buddhists' emblematic monument which replaces the crucifix of Catholic lands. *Chhorten* means literally "receptacle of offerings" or "reliquary": some of them do shelter relics of saints as a protection against the entry of evil influences; others again are cenotaphs. The interior of the gateway consists of a shallow dome from which rows of saints of the Tibetan calendar peer down gravely upon the traveller. These paintings are excellent and probably of considerable age, though, judging by the freshness of the colours, some of them have been renovated in modern times.

Besides *chhortens*, each entrance to a village is marked by a *mendong* or *Mani* wall, a low cemented breastwork upon which innumerable flat stones carved with sacred texts in low relief have been laid, the accumulated offerings of local piety. The commonest text is *Om mani padme hum* from which the name is derived. Its significance will be explained later. Where such a wall occurs the road divides, leaving a free passage on either side of the *Mani*, so that passers-by, whether men or beasts, are enabled to walk on its left side, that is, turning their own right sides towards it. It is an invariable rule in Tibet that any sacred object must be passed on the left; neglect to do so is considered both disrespectful and unlucky. There is a popular saying: "Beware of the devils on the left-hand side." To turn the right flank is a sign of assent to the doctrine inscribed on the stones or enshrined in the *chhorten*; the left side is turned towards the devils, personifying sins and errors, in token of defiant rejection of their blandishments.

The basic food of the people in this land of Khunu is barley, first parched and then ground into flour; in this form it is consumed. It is called *tsamba*, and takes the place of bread in all countries of the Tibetan group. Frequently it is eaten mixed with buttered tea to form a kind of stiff porridge; when dry it is not unlike sweetened sawdust—an acquired taste! Along the Satlej excellent potatoes are also grown and a sort of white radish, the size of a turnip. Rice is imported and a little sugar. Very little meat seems to be eaten: the chief, and almost the only source of fat, is the butter melted into the tea. To this list must be added apricots fresh or dried. On this diet both men and women maintain a magnificent physique. Their teeth are invariably excellent and likewise their eyesight, except in cases where there is definite disease.

On July 28th we reached the important village of Kanam, notable as the place where a systematic study of the Tibetan language by a European first began. A Hungarian, named

Csoma de Körös, arrived in Western Tibet about 1825 and settled at Kanam, where he resided several years. The ostensible object of his researches was the origin of the Hungarian race and language, over which there was controversy. Like ourselves he immediately fell in love with the character of the Tibetans and in consequence found no difficulty in adopting the hypothesis that a people so endowed with charm and intelligence could not but be cousins of his own Hungarians. He pursued his studies most conscientiously, living exactly like the people and assimilating their ideas by the one method which, to my mind, is likely to yield reliable results, namely, by steeping himself in the life of the country, and by seeking information only from those who, by their own traditional standards, were qualified to impart it.

Csoma must be hailed as the Father of Tibetan studies and at the time of our visit his lamasery was being drastically reconditioned, having become rather dilapidated. We were fortunate in seeing the work in its early stages. The temple had been partly pulled down and the walls had only risen again to half the intended height. Round the courtyard, which was encumbered with timber and stones, the residential buildings were arranged; cells occupied the upper story and access was gained to it by a "ladder," that is, by a tree trunk with nicks cut in it, more alarming than many a rock-climb.

The work was being directed by a tall and dignified-looking person in a long robe, with a silver chain round his neck, from which hung a cylindrical charm-box. His beard was sparse and his hair gathered into a pigtail. Across his forehead were scored three parallel wrinkles as straight as if they had been drawn with a ruler. He was introduced to us as a painter from Ladak who had been engaged to be the *capo maestro*; under him senior monks acted as foremen, whilst for labourers he had juniors and peasants of both sexes who were giving their spare time as an act of devotion. Thus it could be claimed that the entire labour employed was amateur, except for the director. But it must not be forgotten that the practice of building is common in this country: most people would have done such work at some time or other on their own houses, so that it would be false to describe them as unskilled. The masonry and woodwork were excellent. It was probably the artist's intention eventually to line the walls with paintings. It was indeed exciting to witness the same process by which our own cathe-

54

drals and parish churches were built in the Middle Ages, when technicians, the laity and ecclesiastics could each contribute to the final edifice.

The painter invited us to follow him up the ladder, into an upper chamber supported on pillars and furnished with some elegance. He was using it for a workshop and a number of unfinished figures of painted wood were drying in a corner. We were also shown a scroll-painting of the type found universally in Tibet, and called a *t'hanka*, in brilliant colours on cotton impregnated with lime, and mounted on Chinese brocade, with a baton at either end so that it could be rolled up like a map.

One fact puzzled us at first: whereas on the *t'hanka* the colours, though vivid, produced a harmonious effect, the wooden images stared at us from under a coating of shiny and rather offensive pigment. How could the same eye and hand have produced these two incompatible results? Suddenly the explanation dawned on me and I said to our host, "Surely those are not Tibetan paints which you have used for the images?" "That is true," he replied. "I bought some foreign paints for doing wood, but I always employ Tibetan paint for pictures."

There is little doubt that he had sometime been tempted into buying factory-made chemicals of cheap grade to save the trouble of grinding up his own paints. Once he had accepted this compromise with his artistic standards, his senses, in their turn, had duly registered the result and become correspondingly coarsened. His taste was now partly vitiated, remaining sound when doing pictures, but over-tolerant when painting statues, probably for no stronger reason then because the amounts of paint necessary for the latter are large and tedious to prepare.

It was at Kanam that we had our first taste of tea made in the Tibetan way. A broad-leaved kind is used, compressed into bricks, and brought mostly by yak caravan from Western China. The Tibetans have such a preference for this sort of tea that even when living on the south side of the Himalaya, where Indian tea would be cheaper to obtain, they go to no end of trouble to import their favourite brand. In preparing the infusion the leaves are put into cold water and then brought to the boil. When the proper strength has been reached, salt, with a pinch of soda, is added, then butter, whereupon the whole is thoroughly mixed in a churn. Finally it is warmed up again and served from the teapot.

The two best silversmiths of Khunu belong to this neighbourhood. The first lived at the village of Sugnam, a few miles up a side-valley, where Richard Nicholson went to visit him. Assisted by his son, he was working to supply a very wide market, chiefly with silver clasps and trinkets for the country women, who delight in jewellery. His colleague, who came to call on us, lived quite close to Kanam, in an outlying hamlet called Labrang, conspicuous for its old watch-tower. They both were men of fine presence, typical of master craftsmen the world over. That profession, with its happy blend of head and hand, the intellectual and the practical, seems to include some of the best types of humanity, and its members might well style themselves the "salt of the earth." Their extinction, under the pressure of the modern industrialism that is overrunning the Orient, must be regarded as a social, no less than an artistic, disaster.

Metalwork is the craft at which the Khunuwas excel. Teapots in brass, decorated with silver and copper bands *appliqués*, are in common use: the combining of several metals is typical of Tibetan work. Handles are usually made in the shape of dragons, which exhibit almost endless diversity of detail, but fall roughly into two generic types, the fish-like, and the pure dragon type with horns, related to Chinese models. The spout issues out of the jaws of a monster rather like an elephant, but said to inhabit the sea; it is called the *Makara*.

Ornamental woodwork is also to be found in the better houses and temples, happily combining both boldness and grace; but this craft is seen at its best in the villages of Lower Kunáwar, in the well-timbered tract between Chini and Simla.

The next halt after Kanam is called Poo. We had been listening to tales about the wonders of this place for weeks before we reached it, because Ishwar Singh, or to give him his proper Tibetan name, Odsung, lived there. We had recently appointed him head-porter, as he had proved exceptionally reliable and intelligent. "The sweetest potatoes come from Poo." "Apricots! you don't call these apricots: you wait till you get to Poo and then you will learn what's what." "Woodworkers? The ones here all overcharge; besides not one of them can hold a candle to the carver at Poo!" This became a standing joke; but to do our friend justice, his home village did

SATOPANT'H PEAKS (*From Camp below Gaumukh*)

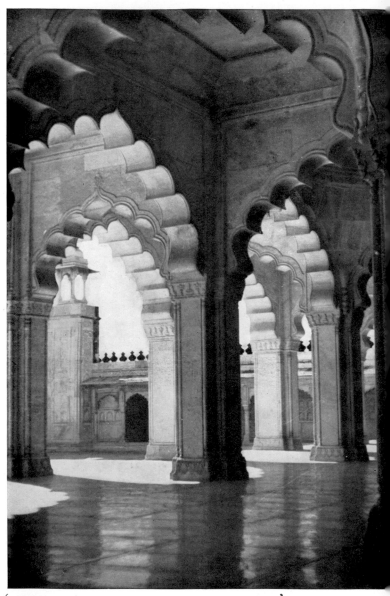

'INCOMPARABLE MONUMENTS OF MUGHAL ART'
The Pearl Mosque (Shah Jahan's) in Agra Fort

not fall far short of his claims: it was a charming place, with quite the most succulent apricots, the tastiest potatoes and the most intelligent inhabitants in the whole district.

The first sight of the village is dramatic. The road descends to the edge of the Satlej, follows it for some miles through an extremely hot gorge: then suddenly quitting the bank, by a sharp rise to the left, it takes a sweeping curve round a combe to a small pass between the main hillside and an isolated knoll above the river. On this pass stands a conspicuous *mendong* that, even from a distance, makes one feel as if something exciting is about to appear. From this gap one looks straight across a ravine to Poo, with its terraces of well-built stone houses relieved by elegant wooden balconies, and surrounded by barley fields and apricot orchards. At the edge of the village stands the pleasant little rest-bungalow in a garden full of hollyhocks, probably introduced by the British. When we arrived, the loaded apricot trees were being stripped by boys who had climbed up into the branches and were beating down the fruit with poles. It was then gathered into baskets by their mothers and sisters. The caretaker of the rest-house, one Namgyal, seemed like an old friend before we had been an hour under his roof.

The people of Poo are well-to-do peasants, and the cultivated land is shared out among the various families. Besides tilling the fields and taking their flocks up the mountains to graze, they also do a certain amount of trading, especially in the autumn when a series of great fairs is held, at which merchants from Ladak, Garhwal and other distant places gather to exchange their wares, first at Gartok in Tibet itself, then at Kanam and, lastly, at Rampur, capital of the State of Bashahr, of which this district forms a part. The Poopas lead a well-balanced life, free from strain, which has its times of leisure as well as hard work. Ready money is scarce, but they are well provided with food, clothes and good housing. The artistic influences emanating from independent Tibet are apparent in the high quality of most of their possessions.

We were invited to supper in Odsung's home. The family consisted of his mother, a widow, and numerous brothers and cousins whom we never quite managed to identify, since the term "brother" is indiscriminately applied to both. Their house, which was two-storied and built round a court, was planned on generous lines. The chief living-room was left

C

half open on one side, commanding a magnificent view down the Satlej to the snowy summits of the Kailas. Our hostess at first refused to come and sit with us at table, till I got up and pleaded with her, saying: "If the mountain will not come to me, then I shall have to go to the mountain."

The old quotation, thus adapted, gains additional piquancy on being turned into Tibetan, because the words referring to the other party—the mountain in this instance—can be placed in what is called the honorific language, while to oneself only common terms are applied. To give a rough paraphrase of the sentence, it reads something like this:—"If the honourable mountain will not deign to proceed to me, the insignificant fellow (myself) will have to go to the mountain."

It should be explained that the Tibetan language reflects in its vocabulary the nicely-judged grades of feudal society. For every noun, pronoun, or verb, and for many of the adjectives, not one but two words must be learned, a common one which applies to ordinary folk and an honorific which must be used when speaking to or about persons of quality.

In the evening the Poopas invited us to watch an entertainment of folk-dances performed by torchlight and accompanied only by drums. The dancers provided their own music by singing songs at the same time. These dances are rustic in character, simple ring groupings, which reminded me of the old Scotch Brawl. One of them was broadly comic. A huge circle was formed, half of men and half of girls, turning clockwise. Suddenly one group of men, without warning, would violently reverse the direction, causing a general collapse, which was greeted with shouts of laughter.

We were sorry when the time came for us to leave Poo, but time was slipping away and we wished to tackle the last item on our programme by attempting the highest peak of Khunu, Riwo Pargyul. Crossing the Satlej by a bridge, we made for the last village on this side of the frontier, Namgya. Before we left, Odsung's mother, with many tears, committed her son to our care. The country now became barren and stony, even the river's margin showing no trace of green. We passed the junction of the Spiti and Satlej, where the rock had been eroded to form a chasm of such depth that the water was not visible from the path. Namgya is a beautiful village with many fine houses and carvings. We camped on a terrace of stubble in an orchard: all night long we could hear a soft patter on the tent-roof, as the trees, gently shaken by the wind, rained down ripe apricots.

Fifty yards along the terrace some other tents were standing, guarded by a terrifying Tibetan mastiff, a regular Cerberus, all snarl and fang, who strained furiously at his chain when we approached. We found that this camp belonged to one of the ablest scholars of the day, the Italian professor, Giuseppe Tucci. He had just come down the Spiti valley on his way into Tibet, accompanied by one companion, Captain Ghersi, who filled the twofold function of doctor and photographer. Professor Tucci kindly invited us to share his dinner, so we sat down with him to an appetizing meal of five courses. During the meal, the professor kept up a running lecture in excellent English, on archaeology, history and art, out of his inexhaustible fund of scholarship and enthusiasm; at the same time he carried on whispered negotiations in Tibetan, spoken *prestissimo e sempre accelerando,* over the purchase of an antique ceremonial apron made from carved plates of human bones, joined by strings of beads of the same material, such as are used in certain rites. It was being offered for sale by a mysterious person hovering in the background.

Over the coffee, we were shown photographs taken in the ancient temples of Spiti, which contain some of the most precious relics of Tibetan art. The professor explained that the unusually perfect examples which existed at Tabo were in considerable danger of disappearing. The prosperity of the country, and consequently its culture, had been declining steadily in the last century and the upkeep of ancient monuments was lapsing. The school of painting to which the Tabo examples belong is unique, so perhaps some authority may devise measures to protect them. It is often only a question of blocking up a few cracks which, if neglected, will eventually let in the weather. In other respects this dry climate is the most perfect conceivable for the preservation of antiques.

From Namgya the path once more descends to the Satlej and crosses a bridge to the right bank, whence it rises again to a small grove of willows, below Tashigang, the see of the presiding Lama of all Khunu. From there a track rounds the spur which fills in the angle of the two rivers and the Spiti valley is entered at a height of about 12,000 feet. The rest of the way to Nako, our base of operations for the mountain, is about level, rising to 13,000 feet at times.

At first the hillside was devoid of vegetation. From far above us some big stone-falls, that looked as if they could not miss the path, came crashing down with a thunderous din. Round the corner, we came to plants again. First there were enormous rose bushes, covered with pink flowers, that grew out of crannies or climbed up the face of the cliff. Then a patch of vivid violet revealed the presence of a magnificent bushy delphinium among the stones. Later, in the Spiti valley, the path was bordered with Alpine flowers, speedwells, harebells, rock-roses and saxifrages that reminded us of Switzerland.

Nako is built among the boulders brought down by old glaciers, and a walk through its "streets" involves constant scrambling. Behind the village extend the endless scree-covered slopes of Riwo Pargyul, which, when we arrived, hid its head under a cap of cloud. On the outskirts numerous *chhortens* and *mendongs* look as if they have sprouted like mushrooms among the stones. At every street corner there are prayer-wheels containing cylindrical paper rolls inscribed with prayers which are set in motion by passers-by. The best place to camp is on the edge of a small lake fringed with willows, which are among the few trees that survive this altitude. It is too high for apricots, but not for barley, which is supposed to be of special quality when grown at this height. There are three big tracts of cultivation, to which water is conducted through a leat from the Riwo Pargyul main glacier stream.

Our baggage had been brought from Poo on ponies, the first pack transport we had used. It was pleasant to notice how well the animals were cared for. The local people, like most Tibetans, were devoted to their animals and did all that was possible for their comfort; they never thought of settling down to cook their own meal until saddles had been removed and fodder distributed. They carried rounded sickles in their girdles, and in this barren country they often had to go some distance before they found any grass to cut. The clear emphasis laid on the position of animals in Buddhist teaching undoubtedly influences the people in the right direction.

Though we were intending to set out for the mountain next day, we found time to visit the ancient temple, ascribed to a famous saint of the tenth century called Rinchhenzangpo. He is surnamed *Lotsawa* which means Translator or Interpreter: it is a title accorded to a few scholars, in honour of their having made the Indian sacred books accessible to their own country-

60

men. The same sage was the founder of most of the Spiti temples.

A Translator, in the sense recognized by the Tibetans, is not to be taken for a mere scholar who, aided by dictionaries, turns a certain text from one language into another and leaves it at that. A text interpreted according to the whim of every reader, however uninstructed, is a public danger, since the seed of a whole crop of errors may be sown which, in their turn, engender new errors, which again, in course of time, may themselves become invested with the prestige of acknowledged authority.

An elementary example will serve to show how easy it is to slip into this pitfall. There is a popular proverb in Tibetan which says that, "without the Lama no man can be delivered." Europeans have quoted it with indignation. "See how the lamas try to keep the people in subjection!" was their comment. "Here's priestcraft for you, here's jesuitry!" Actually they have been betrayed by a slight yet crucial inaccuracy over the word *Lama*. The word, which means "exacted," should, strictly speaking, be applied either to a Teacher, "one's own Lama" or personal spiritual director, or else to eminent members of the clergy. This is a simple case, typical of countless similar ones. The real interpretation of the proverb quoted is "without a Teacher, no man can be delivered." It refers to the fact that, in common with all Orientals, the Buddhists regard study at the feet of a Teacher or Lama as the normal and virtually indispensable prelude to "entering the current," that is, imparting to one's spiritual aims a definite direction towards Enlightenment.

To return to the real Translator: his task was indeed a formidable one. His first duty, before putting pen to paper, was to seek out some adept of the doctrine expressed in the treatise which he wished to translate and be properly instructed over a period probably lasting years. Then, having experienced the meaning of that doctrine in his own person, he was prepared to turn the Sanskrit text into Tibetan with more than mere verbal accuracy. That task completed, he carried back the manuscript to Tibet and proceeded to reverse the process he had himself followed by expounding the doctrine in all its aspects to his own disciples, at the same time placing the text in their hands. Thus the tradition was truly imparted. Several divines besides the Nako founder have been accorded the title of

Translator; one of the most renowned was Marpa, tutor of Tibet's ascetic poet, Mila Repa, about whom much more will be said later. Even nowadays, as the Lachhen Lama emphatically declared, it is useless to try to read sacred books except under the guidance of a competent teacher. According to this conception the word "read" begins to mean something more than skimming through so many pages.

In former times Nako and the whole Spiti valley belonged to the kingdom of Gugge, which attained an extraordinary degree of civilization. Since the extinction of that kingdom there has been a steady decline. Cultivated areas have shrunk, populations have dwindled and the sands of the desert are invading the surviving settlements. Gugge was the province of Tibet first visited by European missionaries in 1624. Portuguese Franciscans established a mission in the capital, Tsaparang, the modern Chabrang Dzong. They were received by the king with all the honour that Tibetans are ready to accord to the bringers of unknown doctrines. The friars, at one moment, had some reason for hoping that they were about to effect a royal conversion; but it is also possible that their optimism may have been somewhat exaggerated. The Tibetans are always ready to offer worship to any sacred object, and do not necessarily confine their homage to the more familiar forms. They do not feel that by so doing they are tacitly admitting the superiority of the foreign Tradition or showing infidelity towards their own. They will bow as naturally before the Crucifix as they would at the feet of a Buddha, whereas our own people, accustomed to the sectarian exclusiveness of Europe, usually feel that by offering reverence in a church with the tenets of which they disagree, they are condoning its errors. The Hindus have a special term for that section of mankind, regarded by them as spiritually immature, who are unwilling to honour anyone's gods but their own. They are called *Pashu* (from the root *pash* = bound) and are supposed to be blind to the larger Unity of the Godhead, though within the parochial limits they lay down for themselves, they may be worthy of all respect and praise. They are described as men in whom a tendency towards obscurantism is strong, who exaggerate the distinctions of mere form or name; this makes them all too prone to speak contemptuously of the beliefs and practices of others. Far superior to the *Pashus* are the men who fall into the class known as *Viras* or heroes. They are those who recognize that though modes of

62

thought are many, yet metaphysical realization, wherever obtained by direct intuitive identification of the knower with the known, is one and only. It is that which counts; it is that truth which underlies all symbolism and is the object of every traditional ritual. The Buddha Himself counselled His followers against abruptly curtailing the gifts which they had been accustomed to offer to the Brahmans: that spirit still prevails to-day. One young lama told me that they were taught from childhood not to speak ill of other religions, but on the contrary to treat them with every respect. Similarly, along the Chinese-Tibetan border, it is said to be conventional at any chance meeting of strangers for one to ask the other, after the first greeting, "Sir, and to which sublime tradition do you belong?"

RIWO PARGYUL

THE peak which was to be the last objective of our journey possessed a topical interest in that it had been ascended to a point well over 19,000 feet quite early in the nineteenth century by two enterprising Scotsmen, the brothers Gerard, who travelled all over the country of Khunu and published a diary which shows them to have been honest observers. In those days, when travel was more of an adventure than it is now, doubtless only those attempted it who were impelled by a keen curiosity to see and learn. Considering the early date of their expedition, when only thirty years had elapsed since the first ascent of Mont Blanc, and when the Pillar Rock in our own Ennerdale was still virgin ground, the height which the two Gerards attained is a highly creditable performance, though that does not imply that they went in for any serious climbing. The snow-line is very high and a number of subsidiary points could be reached in a couple of days' laborious plodding over scree, without setting foot on snow. But for all that, to have braved such an altitude involved real enterprise at that time.

Many legends connected with Riwo Pargyul exist, for in common with all permanent snow its twin peaks are regarded as sacred by the Tibetans. One of the chapels in the temple at Nako is dedicated to the genius of the mountain; but it is now derelict, devoid of an altar and all furniture. On a rock near by, the imprint of the god's huge foot is pointed out.

There are even tales of early ascents: a pious lama, so it is rumoured, had actually climbed to the summit long ago. In more recent times a party of four villagers ascended the mountain in quest of sapphires. When they reached the highest pinnacle they found it to be formed of a huge sapphire about a foot across and worth millions of rupees. They managed to dislodge it and were already well on the way down with their booty when a terrible storm arose and overwhelmed them all. Exactly how the accident to the second party came to be

64

reported with all its details is unexplained! There are other legends too; at Poo we witnessed a folk-dance performed to the strains of a ballad in which Riwo Pargyul figured prominently; but we were unable to secure a copy of these verses.

On the evening of our arrival at Nako we started to sort out the miscellaneous things required for the assault on the mountain, and made them up into forty-pound loads. There was food for the body, and food for the soul in the shape of Chaucer's *Canterbury Tales*, and paraffin for the Primus which, by some silly miscalculation, was measured out short, and all the usual climbing apparatus.

Two Jadh porters, Djun Singh and Naranhu, were chosen to come high with us, while three men from Poo were told off for the initial carry to a camp just below the snow. After following the main road northwards a mile or two, we veered sharp right up the valley of a torrent which we believed, correctly as it proved, to issue from the central glacier basin between the two main peaks. The lower slopes are a chaos of old glacier debris, waterless save for the leat, fringed with gentian-spangled turf, which brings the main water-supply down to the village. Higher up, from about 14,000 feet, patches of grazing occur, and low thorny bushes, the inhabitants' only source of fuel. Between 15,000 and 17,000 feet, some way below the zone of melting snows, lie the summer pastures, which support quite a number of cows and sheep. There is a fairly rich Alpine flora, which was only just coming into flower when we passed on the upward way, but had reached full bloom by August 11th. We saw two or three kinds of blue gentian and a light mauve delphinium with large rounded blooms, growing in clumps among the stones.

For the last couple of hours before approaching the terminal ice of the glacier at a height of some 17,500 feet, we passed along a succession of boulder-covered moraines. A drearier landscape could not well have been imagined, for lateral ridges confined the view to a crumbling world. These containing walls of the valley were no more than great rubbish-heaps, an aimless accumulation of rocks piled one upon another; only at the lower extremities of the ridges, where they faced outward towards the Spiti, their tips were still sheathed in a carapace of slabby rock, like the rams of some monster ironclads still standing in mock defiance long after the rest of the hull had rotted away.

65

A Tibetan, hermit in search of a place in which to rest in meditation, as so many do, on the great principle of Death and Impermanence, would have found these surroundings peculiarly appropriate. "The Universe is running down . . . down . . . *tout passe, tout casse, tout lasse*" seemed to be whispered by a thousand expressionless voices. "Where's the glacier now, that viscous flood which once upon a time overran all these slopes? It was active then, look where it reached to; but now it's getting old, and one day it will die, there will be no ice to melt and the water will dry up, then the gentians will be dried up too and the crops of the people of Nako, and the men also will die out. The stones which remain, they too are gradually dying; death is not an appanage only of the apparently living, nor are they alone in being subject to death; in this is to be seen the pattern of all things." Thus would muse the hermit—a faint whisper of this message reached even our own ears—and a great love and pity would be kindled in his heart for all the deluded creatures blindly chasing the will-o'-the-wisp of happiness, trying to fix it firmly, now in this life, now in the next. Not to realize this, say the Tibetan sages, is to remain the plaything of ignorance and of the suffering born therefrom, but to know it, is reality and freedom, which is called Buddhahood.

We pitched our second camp—for we had taken two days to approach the glacier—in a hollow, and then walked up to a point whence we hoped to obtain the first view of our mountain; but its face was veiled in mist. Though Riwo Pargyul has a very low rainfall and is considered to stand outside the monsoon's influence, the proximity of rain-clouds at that season is enough to produce constant mist, hanging round the mountain tops though not falling in actual showers. Beyond that point the moist vapours are cut off sharply by the dry Tibetan winds. One of our principal hindrances in climbing the peak was our inability to obtain any save the most fleeting glimpses of the upper parts of proposed routes. In the end we had to hazard a partial guess in making our choice. There is evidence that this mountain does not enjoy very good weather as a rule, for other travellers have remarked on it. Possibly the fact that it stands considerably higher than anything for many miles around may account for this, for it seems to collect all the weather.

In the evening the miscalculation over the paraffin was brought home to us, for when we set about cooking a meal for the porters on the Primus we were not long in finding out that a single boiling of rice used our meagre supply of fuel at such a rate that it threatened to jeopardize the commissariat arrangements. Something had to be done without a moment's delay, for time was precious. An anxious debate ensued, after which it was resolved that one of the men should be sent down, next day, to Nako, to collect more paraffin from the big carboy left in charge of Odsung, while the rest of us, to make doubly sure, were to postpone the pressing reconnaissance and to go down to brushwood level and lay in enough fuel to stock the camp for two or three days. A man named Djambal, a strong and willing young fellow with flowing locks, volunteered to run down with the message. That night we retired to bed feeling rather depressed over the bad management that had caused the waste of a day.

Next morning we all trekked off downhill again, bearing empty rucksacks and ground-sheets, not at all relishing the idea of having to retrace our steps across the unending screes. But luck favoured us in an unexpected way; we had gone but half the distance and arrived at the upper pastures, when Djun Singh, with an exclamation of joy, pointed to some droppings of cattle scattered about the slope and dried hard by the sun. "Here is good fuel," he cried, "and lots of it. It's what we always burn in Tibet." So we set about with a will stacking the dung and filling our sacks, taking care to reject any that was still at all damp. By afternoon we were loaded up and on our way back to camp, cheered by the knowledge that we need not raid the precious store of paraffin for at least three days. The dung was found to yield quite a fair heat, smouldering like peat and surprisingly free from unsavoury smell; but it is rather difficult to coax it into a good fire and, in default of bellows, Djun Singh kept up a steady blast from his lungs.

We had prayed that the sun would shine on our efforts to reconnoitre the approaches to the peak, but mist continued to harass us all day long, hanging disobligingly round the 20,000 foot level, now tantalizingly lifting a little, now threatening to ring down the curtain over the whole scene. The party had agreed to split up, two men going into the main basin, while I explored a snowy col on a ridge uniting the west flank of the north peak to a small spur. Nearer portions of the mountain had already been ruled out. The south peak, which consists of a long rocky ridge bristling with pinnacles, looked as if it would

67

offer good sport; but as it was slightly the lower of the two we felt more drawn to the north peak, which was of an entirely different character, a huge rounded white mass, portions of which looked ominously grey, suggestive of ice and hours of step-cutting. A great shoulder not easily attainable in a day indicated a pitch for an upper camp, but the sides seemed badly exposed to stonefall; even if we had got up that way it would hardly have been justifiable to have let porters return down it alone. So we decided to look farther afield.

In the afternoon we foregathered again to compare notes. Those who had been to the glacier had drawn a blank. They found no practicable col on the ridge connecting the peaks, as the basin was walled in by forbidding cliffs of mixed rocks and ice. I was able to give a better report, however, of the snowy col on the west side: the approaches were gentle and the ground was safe till quite close under the col, where there was a lake of the purest azure and one or two crevasses that had caused me, being alone, to restrain my curiosity to look over the other side. As to the route up the west flank, it seemed promising, since it consisted entirely of snow without a trace of rock. The only snag was an icy bulge on the skyline just below the mist, which looked as if it might either be easily contourable or else might indicate a row of formidable ice defences: but it was well worth chancing. All voted in favour of adopting this route and we sat down to await the return of Djambal and the paraffin; nor were we kept waiting long, for he soon turned up with a bulging pack, looking as if he had been out for a stroll instead of having raced all the way from Nako over bad ground with a heavy load.

Eagerly we undid the package—"Ah! I see Odsung has sent some extra biscuits, thoughtful of him. Butter? Well, I should have thought we had enough, but no matter—all is grist for the mill. Chocolate—matches—that can't be all? Look here, where's the paraffin?" Djambal turned on us an uncomprehending eye. "The paraffin, the paraffin! Why on earth——?" But it was useless to go on lamenting—the awful fact was there: a misunderstanding had occurred and the wrong stores had been sent. We were as far as ever from getting on to the mountain.

There was no help for it; we must face another delay. Who would go down next day to Nako, while we carried on with pitching a camp on the western col? The stout Djambal was the

68

first to jump up and offer his services a second time for the tedious errand; this time, however, to make doubly certain, Richard Nicholson, who was not intending to come beyond the next stage, thus leaving two for the final dash, offered to descend at once and see that no further blunder occurred. As there were still some hours of daylight, they started immediately. The two of us who were left, retired to our tents, chafing at this new delay, for time was getting short and the weather did not promise many extra chances in case of initial defeat.

The job of carrying stores and a good-sized tent as far as the col occupied the next day. The camping site proved to be excellent, a few minutes from the west flank of the north peak. Looking northwards, a great glacier (the Chango Glacier) lay outspread, possibly for the first time, to human gaze, surrounded by serried rows of peaks of every kind, easy ones and hard ones, snowy ridges and forbidding needles, first cousins of the Aiguilles of Chamonix. How we wished that half the season were still before us; we could even discern, on a flat piece of moraine across the other side, the exact spot for a Base Camp; and there were some enticing passes that beckoned us over into Tibet. We slept on the col that night, sending back the porters to the lower camp, where our two Jadhs were ordered to collect the paraffin and bring it up with all speed. The Poo men were dismissed, as there was not enough work to keep them busy.

The following morning passed in enforced idleness; but in the afternoon the porters returned with the eagerly expected supplies of paraffin. At last all was ready for the start and even the weather began to show signs of clearing up. This promise was fulfilled, for the morning of August 8th was sunny. We started off in good spirits, but had not climbed more than a couple of hundred feet before we found that the snow was turning into pure ice, though luckily not of the toughest black variety which occurs so frequently in the Himalaya. A long spell of cutting lay ahead and it was evident that we should be unable to reach the upper shoulder, where we hoped to bivouac, in a single day, unless the ice gave way to soft snow higher up, which at the time seemed unlikely. This day had therefore to be devoted to the job of cutting a well-graded staircase to a point as far up as possible that would serve as a jumping-off spot for completing the ascent afterwards. So we started in an unhurried manner and worked our way upward, chipping

69

careful steps in the ice-slope, equally safe for descent and ascent. We were, however, unexpectedly lucky, for just below the ice-bulge, past which we could not yet see, we discovered a tiny platform, barely wide enough to take our bivouac but not a bad pitch, if rather airy, with clear ice-slopes leading the eye down in all directions and with the bulging cliff of ice blocking the upward view. It was a blessing to have found any flat ground at all at such a convenient level, so we called it the site for Camp IV and retreated to the col in an optimistic frame of mind.

Unfortunately, we were reckoning without our host, Riwo Pargyul himself, and his reputation for storms. At about nine o'clock that night, a tremendous blizzard suddenly arose, driving hard from the north across the ridge. It was so furious that we were afraid lest the fragile-looking bivouac-tent, that we were to use at Camp IV and in which the porters were now sleeping, might have been torn away from them. So we got up at midnight and shouted to inquire if all was safe. Contented, sleepy voices answered that they were quite snug.

The sight of our lovely staircase so laboriously cut, or rather the sight of the place where it had been—for it had disappeared under a coating of fresh snow—was not the best of morning greetings. The hurricane had blown itself out, but the weather still looked ominous and another day of impatient waiting confronted us. If things went on at this rate, it was important for supplies to be made to spin out to the latest possible moment, so we resolved to dispense with porters' help even at the cost of making our loads to Camp IV heavier than was pleasant. Our men were therefore told to join the others at Nako and to await us there.

Towards evening, the sky began to clear and pessimism gave way once again to rising hopes. Packs, weighing about thirty pounds each, were hastily shouldered and off we went towards the old steps, which the wind, once it had ceased to bring snow with it, had cleared as if to atone for its earlier misdeeds. The bivouac was successfully pitched on the platform and we were soon inside consuming an energizing brew of pemmican. We did not sleep very much during the night, partly from excitement, and partly because we were listening anxiously for signs of a return of the storm. The earlier performance of the tiny tent should have made us confident, but the fact that we were pitched on hard ice, not dug into snow, and anchored with the

70

spikes of our crampons in the absence of stones, in a very exposed situation, left little margin for accidents.

August 10th dawned radiantly; zero hour at last. Bolting our breakfast, we set about dismounting the tent by withdrawing the two ice-axes, which with their bamboo extensions served as poles, one of our several dodges to save weight. Prospects of reaching the top that day seemed so bright that we felt it was worth while to go light and take only one rucksack with spare clothes and the utensils for brewing fresh tea.

We were, of course, expecting to have to continue hewing out steps, and we also had the bulge to negotiate: but our luck held; the bulge proved innocent enough, being only part of a small isolated projection on the mountainside. To the left of it the passage was clear and, still better, free from ice. A splendid slope of hard snow, in which the points of our crampons gripped safely, extended before us into the distance. We happened to notice that down on the left there was a labyrinth of crevasses which showed that our line of ascent had been the best possible one. This observation was to prove useful later in an unexpected way.

Some hours of walking in wide zigzags eventually led us on to a huge plateau, "the shoulder," from which we could see the sharp crest of a ridge, continuing steeply upwards, perhaps the final lap. It was now just after noon, and we were thirsty, so we chose that moment for rest and the making of tea. It was so hot that we debated whether to climb the last bit in shirt-sleeves; but Charles Warren, being a prudent mountaineer, said that on these high places one never knows what abrupt changes are in store and that it would be wiser to take spare clothes, leaving the rucksack behind. We were full of excitement trying to imagine the view which awaited us on top; it must surely be one of overwhelming grandeur, since Riwo Pargyul is not only the highest point of vantage for a wide tract of country, but stands midway between groups of still higher peaks. Without being quite sure of the lie of the land, we thought of the Karakoram to the north-west and our own Gangotri range to the south. But most of all, we were looking forward to our first sight of Tibet; our recent contact with its people, their fine sturdy character and their ideas had forged a bond between us and Tibet which was destined to influence us in the future more profoundly than we dreamed of. A longing to pass within its closed gates had taken possession of our hearts; already it would be a milestone in our pilgrimage to look into the promised land. With such thoughts to urge us on, we advanced towards the foot of the ridge.

The giant was taking his noonday siesta when he was awakened by a slight tickling on the shoulder. Looking to see what was the matter he perceived two minute dwarfs just starting to climb up his neck, making for his head. "What, at it again?" he exclaimed, "wasn't the drubbing I gave you the night before last good enough to teach you manners? You just wait and see this time!" So speaking, he shuffled off to his cave as fast as his legs would carry him. The four winds who were imprisoned inside were holding a rehearsal of the chorus *Zerreisset, zersprenget, zertrümmert die Gruft,* by Bach.

"Zerreisset!" they yelled, as they battered on the door. "Just hold on a minute, my hearties," growled the ogre, "till I unfasten the padlock." Then out they charged, driving black thunder-clouds before them, till the whole mountain became enveloped so that the world was blotted from view. Back and forth they lashed, snarling round corners and whistling athwart the ridges, while the thunder-spirit added his counterpoint, now decrescendoing to a low growl, now administering a succession of *sforzandi* that would have roused the envy of a Beethoven, now coalescing into a roar like a continuous barrage, now taken up in canon by a choir of echoes.

We looked at one another. To advance or not to advance, that was the question. "Let's go on a few more steps up the ridge." Sss . . . sss . . . sss! "What's that?" One of us had waved an axe and it emitted a prolonged hiss. From the direction of Tibet came up an icy draught. We drew on our windproof suits and caps, and as we did so our hair crackled uncannily. The axes by now were sizzling: it sounded as if the storm were drawing nearer. It seemed unsafe to keep hold of steel, so the axes were planted in the snow on the crest while we cowered some way off to leeward. Again we debated whether to persevere or not, for we dared not leave the descent until too late.

Every mountaineer knows the difficulty of such decisions. The confronting of an insurmountable obstacle, as happened to us on Simvu three years later, leaves no choice and therefore no sting; but to turn back for bad weather always involves doubt whether one might not have pushed on with a little more firmness of purpose. No worse dilemma could be imagined than that of a climber who had reached a point say 200 feet below the summit of Everest and saw the weather changing or realized the danger of becoming benighted. If he turned back he would, probably rightly, be praised for moral courage; but most climbers would suffer cruel searchings of heart or they would not be climbers at all.

The storm, with occasional threats to revive, did indeed seem to draw away from the ridge, though the blackness was as dense as ever, save for brief moments when glimpses of ghostly glaciers appeared away in the depths. The axes, though still sizzling occasionally, were growing more silent and we judged that we might try our luck by pushing on a few steps. We agreed, however, on a time limit of three o'clock after which, if the top was not in sight, we must retrace our steps at all costs. To ease the strain we took it in turns to lead on short stretches. Fortunately the snow on the ridge kept good and firm. Suddenly, two black specks appeared ahead. What could they be—rocks? But when we caught sight of the upper part of the ridge earlier in the day we had noticed that there were no rocks save on the very top. We must be there! A moment later and Charles Warren stepped on to the summit and saw the other two main ridges disappearing into the mist below. Nearly 3 p.m.: but the mountain had surrendered; the whole of Riwo Pargyul's 22,210 feet lay under our feet. "Thou shalt tread on the lion and the basilisk."

No view was vouchsafed us, and Tibet might have been the Atlantic Ocean for all we could see. It was no time to linger, not even to hunt for sapphires, for already the first stray snowflakes, harbingers of the blizzard, were drifting over. We turned and hurried down the ridge; but by the time we had got to the rucksack, snow was falling heavily and all trace of our footsteps had vanished, so that the problem of keeping direction on the featureless slopes was not easy. As we made our way down, trusting to a sixth sense more than anything else, we were pursued by periodic bursts of hail, like volleys of pins. It was strange that with so much wind, the mist could remain so unmovingly opaque.

We had come a good way down but were beginning to doubt our bearings, when we saw close under us the margin of a huge crevasse, then another, and then a third; we were certainly off the route and in that weather there was but a poor prospect of setting ourselves right. We wondered, if we were benighted, whether one of the crevasses might offer us shelter, only temporarily, we hoped. But surely we had noticed a crevassed area on our left when we started out in the morning? If this was it, we ought to contour, with a faint downward trend and then might strike the proper route. We altered direction accordingly, crevasses were swallowed up in the mist and we found ourselves again on open snow. Then something loomed ahead, ice pinnacles; were we approaching another crevassed system—in which case we had miscalculated in the first instance? But surely there was something familiar in the shape of that bulge! Could it be *the* bulge, the one above Camp IV? Yes, it must be, and beyond it was a black speck marking the dismounted tent. Snow had not fallen densely here, the mist too was thinning.

Thankfully we came to the tent, all anxiety now dispelled. We had finished with the mountain and the last item on the expedition's programme could be ticked off. In a flash our thoughts were homeward bound, speeding across the seas. The tent and the second rucksack were hastily packed and all unnecessaries were sent spinning down to the glacier; then, leaving the last traces of the snow-storm, we walked down the ice staircase and by 6 p.m. found ourselves back on the col by our big tent. Fatigue began to steal upon us, and made us feel too lazy to cook, so we contented ourselves with a cup of Horlick's, and then curled into our sleeping-bags.

Indescribable was the fury of Riwo Pargyul at having allowed his prey to checkmate him. All night long he raged impotently, like a blinded Cyclops, lashing the upper parts of his mountain with storm after storm: but we, peacefully sleeping, knew nothing of this, till, on waking up rather late in the morning, we found that masses of snow had piled up against the sides of the tent. Looking out we saw a wintry landscape extending some thousand feet below us. The weather, too, seemed to have broken again decisively: it was evident that the only possible day for the climb had been the one chosen by or rather for us.

74

Thinking back now, one can see that the north peak, under reliable conditions of weather and if free from ice, would not be a difficult mountain; but for all that, it was a grand adventure.

Having struck the tent and gathered whatever of value was left, we started down the 7,500 feet that separated us from Nako. By the time we and our excessive burdens had struggled across the wilderness of boulders and at last reached the road, we felt thoroughly tired and longed to be relieved of our loads for the last mile. As if in answer to a prayer, as we rounded a bend within view of the houses, two figures sprang up and came running towards us. We felt a sudden lightening as the loads were whisked from off our backs, and our strength seemed to rush back to us in that moment. Our two faithful coolies, who had been watching for our return, were overjoyed to hear of the success of the climb and spread the news among the villagers standing near. Someone made a joke, evidently at our expense, the tenor of which eluded us, and the whole company burst out into uproarious guffaws.

BACK TO " CIVILIZATION "

Now we walked the last few miles of the Hindustan–Tibet road towards the corrugated-iron-roofed summer capital of the Indian Empire. The trek back from our mountain on the frontier ridge of Tibet had been sheer joy. Nothing to worry about, the entire programme accomplished without serious hitch, everyone feeling fit after four months of an ideally healthy life, lovely country to traverse, a perfect climate at the enlivening height of 8,000 feet.

Our favourite coolies, who had been with us from start to finish, were still in attendance. There was little for them to do, so we treated ourselves to the hitherto forbidden luxury of walking unloaded and handed our personal rucksacks over to them with instructions that they should keep close at heel in case of a sudden call for camera or notebook. The first time I stopped, my heel landed on someone's toe; as I turned abruptly I collided violently with one of the faithful coolies, who had interpreted his orders with literal exactitude.

The first few days we passed through familiar country. From Nako, at the foot of the mountain, we plunged down the steep side of the valley to the stony banks of the Spiti river, which we crossed by a rope-bridge to the prosperous fields and orchards of Li. Then over a pass covered with Alpines, to the Satlej again and our beloved Poo. After this came Kanam with its monastery and the joy of the first woods, and the taste of ripe apples as good as Ribston pippins in the garden of the delightful Forest Bungalow of Chini. There we beguiled the evening playing over the old English and Spanish airs on our viols which, judging by their tone, shared our pleasure.

From there we began to tread new ground. The Tibetan language and Buddhism were now things of the past and the village *devtas* belonged to the Hindu Pantheon. But the Kunáwari peasants with their long hair and beards and homespun gowns with purple sashes were still with us and their artistic

76

talents were in evidence, now that timber was plentiful, in the decoration not only of temples, but of ordinary houses, on which the carvings were of great boldness and originality. There was not a veranda or window-frame, beam or rail or string-course which was not appropriately beautified.

Gone, however, were the laughing, self-confident faces of the women of Upper Khunu; their sisters here looked shy and rapidly ageing, and the golden rings they wore in their noses made their wizened features look all the more dejected.

After Urni we entered the zone of rains again; the monsoon was sending down the last few drops from its bucket. All kinds of butterflies were flitting to and fro in the river gorges; some looked like huge orange-tips or brimstones, yellow, white and red; we also saw fritillaries and swallow-tails, some of them velvety black and others the commonest species, dusted with golden green powder and with an electric blue mirror on the hind-wings. They settled on moist patches of the road, and rose in clouds when disturbed. Numbers of large grey-green lizards lurked on the rocks, lying in wait for the yellowish grasshoppers that swarmed everywhere. Having seized their prey, they carried it off struggling in their jaws to a hole, before gulping it down.

In the more humid parts the forest rioted in tangled luxuriance. Balsams, pink, yellow or white, bordered the track and in one place a rock that oozed moisture was half hidden behind a curtain of pink begonias. The ground was covered with a thick carpet of ferns and selaginella.

At Sarahan we were received in audience by H.H. the Raja of Bashahr; we welcomed this opportunity of thanking him for his kindness and all his subjects for their willing help. Our head-porter, the man of Poo, on this occasion suddenly shed the character of Odsung the half-Tibetan Buddhist and appeared again in the guise of Ishwar Singh, the complete Hindu, with a sash and a turban like a monstrous onion, in which his flat Mongolian features were comically framed. Thus attired, he paraded before his ruler to the accompaniment of many bows and claspings of hands; we always thought he would have made a perfect Vicar of Bray.

Then down from the woods we went to another dry valley, along stubbly hillsides dotted with euphorbias looking like weird candelabra, and so on into hot and stuffy Rampur, the capital of the State. After a night spent in the Raja's guest

77

bungalow, we continued our way to Nirt'h with its graceful temple spire, which seemed to tell us that we were really back in India, and then, after bidding good-bye to our old friend the Satlej, we climbed again to 8,000 feet and the frontiers of British India at last. We were now all impatience to get to Simla and its luxuries. The expedition was over, and long unheeded cares and desires, like an elbowing throng of ghosts come to life, began to jostle us.

We arrived at Narkanda in a heavy shower and stood rooted in horror gazing on its hutments covered with old kerosene tins hammered out flat. For nearly three months we had not looked on an ugly thing and had begun to take the beauty of the world for granted, even including the works of man. Now the unclean hand of encroaching slumdom had reached out to welcome us home even here in this glorious situation.

The dak-bungalow's charges, though perfectly normal, struck us as terrific. For a single man's meal we were expected to pay what had hitherto sufficed for the expenses of the party for a whole day. When the caretaker quoted the price, our porters turned on us such a look of reproach that we simply could not face it. We managed to find cheaper lodgings in a house that had, so we were told, belonged to some missionaries, but had now been abandoned and converted into a private hostel. The house was of wood, shockingly put together; not a decent joint in it, every window-frame warped, cracks in the plaster, furniture both uncomfortable and unsightly, and a few irrelevant ornamental details on the mantelpieces, that could be traced back to some obscure Roman source. Tea, black as pitch and bitter as gall, was served. We hated to sit down or to touch anything. That night, for the first time for weeks, under the influence of these distressing emotions, it took me more than a few moments to drop off to sleep.

As I lay restless on my bed, I heard a curious scurrying and snapping going on as if a pair of huge rats was at work gnawing behind the wainscoting. I prayed that they might be successful in rearing a numerous progeny to collaborate with them in their useful and civilizing efforts.

After Narkanda, continuing along the ridge, we entered the devastated belt, though the valleys on either side looked fair enough still. Rickshaws turned up and the coolies offered to draw us to Simla. The inhabitants were now all dressed in the cast-off reach-me-downs of Europe mixed with loin-cloths and turbans in all sorts of unlikely combinations. Once, however, when we halted for lunch, we came across a young shepherd with an extraordinarily spiritual face and the body of an athlete, comely in his peasant dress of grey wool. He was amusing some children who played around him with shouts of merriment. How did he manage to keep himself untainted in such sur-roundings? Or had we been speaking unwittingly to Lord Krishna himself?

Lastly came Simla itself, with its inevitable thoughts of luxuries long untasted. The spell was broken : "civilization" had claimed us, at least for the time being, filling our minds with conflicting desires and impressions.

We still had a few days left before catching the steamer at Bombay, so we decided to spend most of them at Agra, visiting its incomparable monuments of Mughal art. At Kalka junc-tion, where the narrow-gauge railway from Simla joins the main line, we said good-bye to the two Jadhs, Djun Singh and Naranhu, who had continued to attend upon us in the hotel. In fact there had been some difficulty in persuading them that Simla was not a nest of robbers and that it was really needless for them to lie across our threshold at night like watch-dogs. We had suggested to them that they should walk back to Mus-soori by a high-level route, instead of descending to the plains and going round via Dehra Dun; but Djun Singh, who, if so commanded, would have gone alone across 500 miles of Tibetan desert without turning a hair, absolutely declined to risk him-self in this tame bit of British territory, declaring it to be swarm-ing with crooks and brigands! Ishwar Singh, alias Odsung, re-fused to be parted from us till the last possible moment and accompanied us as far as Bombay, whence we saw him off on a return train, the day before we sailed. When the coast of India began to fade from sight, though we were full of excite-ment at the prospect of home, we could not help feeling some twinges of regret, which made us realize how hopelessly we had lost our hearts. The Himalayan germ, once caught, works in-side one like a relapsing fever; it is ever biding its time before breaking out again with renewed virulence. Dr. Longstaff had warned us when we set out, "once a man has found the road, he can never keep away for long." "It is certain you will return," had declared Professor Tucci, over supper, that even-ing at Namgya: to which I could only answer "Amen" in all sincerity.

Part Two

SIKKIM

(1936)

THE ANTECHAMBER OF TIBET

MARCH, 1936, found us back again in the Himalaya, as the prophets had foretold; or rather two of us, Richard Nicholson and myself, for of the other members of the old party, Ted Hicks and Colin Kirkus were not free to join us, while Charles Warren had been yielded up, grudgingly, to the Everest expedition.

Our return into Occidental society, after having spent some months separated from it, made it possible to examine in a new and critical light many things that had hitherto been taken for granted. Indeed, reversion to the old conditions came in many ways as a shock, for the restless, noisy daily round seemed strangely futile after the manageable pace to which we had accustomed ourselves. We missed the quietness and the physical well-being of the mountain life, and we looked round in vain for any adequate substitute for that sense of poise which, more than anything, distinguished the people among whom we had lately stayed.

As soon as we began to make definite plans for another visit to the East we invited two more climbers to join us, J. K. COOKE,[1] a very able mountaineer with whom I had been associated both in the Alps and in Wales, and F. S. CHAPMAN of Greenland fame, a keen field ornithologist, who after leaving us, accompanied the Political Officer of Sikkim to Lhasa as private secretary, and finally capped his varied adventures with a first ascent of the lofty peak of Chomolhari. The medical officer's place was filled by Dr. R. ROAF of Liverpool who, though he had done but little mountaineering, shared many of our other interests, especially the artistic ones.

The projected expedition was to be divided roughly into two parts. First, we wished to attempt one or more of the peaks situated near the margin of the Zemu glacier in Sikkim, before the arrival of the monsoon about June. In the second half

[1] He was killed at Dunkerque in 1940, while serving with the Navy.

Cooke and Chapman were to be free to continue climbing in the north of Sikkim if they wished, while the other three of us devoted ourselves to Tibetan studies. Permission to enter Tibet proper was solicited from the Government of India, who promised to take an early opportunity of forwarding our application to the Lhasa authorities. The district for which we required a passport was called Hlobrak, which means Southern Crag. It is a valley adjoining the north frontier of Bhutan and is reputed to be both of extraordinary natural beauty and to contain a number of ancient monasteries of great interest, in one of which we hoped to be allowed to stay and receive instruction.

Hlobrak is famous as the birthplace of one of Tibet's great divines, Marpa, who, like the founder of the Spiti temples, earned the rare title of Translator, from having brought back doctrinal books to his country from India. He is still more renowned as the spiritual guide of Tibet's most popular saint and national poet, Mila Repa. The latter had started life as a notorious sinner. When his father died, his uncle and aunt seized on the inheritance and drove Mila and his mother out into penury. The widow vowed vengeance and called on her son to show himself a man by exacting a cruel punishment from the usurpers of his patrimony. But his uncle only mocked the youth saying, "If you are many, declare war on us: if few, cast spells on us!" The young man took them at their word and went in search of a sorcerer able and willing to teach him the art of black magic. Eventually he found his man and became initiated into the mysteries of witchcraft. When he felt his powers sufficiently matured, he made his preparations and launched spells against his uncle's house, condemning all who dwelt there to perish except two, his uncle and aunt, who were to be spared so that they might experience the anguish of their loss to the full. At that moment a feast was in progress and the horses belonging to the guests were stabled on the ground floor of the house, as is still customary in Tibet to-day, while the family entertained their friends on the first floor. A maidservant, sent down on an errand and deluded by the spell, imagined she saw a scorpion as big as a yak tugging at the central pier that formed the main support of the building. Unhinged by terror, she rushed shrieking from the stable, and her alarm communicated itself to the horses; upon which all the stallions hurled themselves madly upon the mares and a terrible

84

fight ensued. The whole house was shaken so violently that it toppled down, burying all the company under the ruins except the wretched aunt and uncle.

The news did not take long to reach the ears of the old widow, who hastened to the scene of the disaster and added her triumphant gibes to the sorrows of the hapless pair. To escape the consequences of his crime Mila Repa had to flee the country; but in exile he began to be tormented by remorse. His highly sensitive and spiritual nature craved to understand the true meaning of life. A chance acquaintance happened to mention to him the name of Marpa the Translator, and Mila instantly experienced, as many young Tibetans still do, a conviction that he, and he alone, was the Master to lead him into the Path of Truth. He set out at once for Hlobrak where Marpa, who is represented in pictures as a rather stout, choleric-looking man, already expected him, having sensed his approach through second sight. Mila offered himself body and soul to his Lama, and prayed that he would impart to him his special doctrine. "What!" cried Marpa, feigning anger. "Do you think I am going to hand over secrets which I brought all the way from India at great trouble and risk, to the first comer, to one moreover who is a wicked sorcerer, the slayer of I know not how many human beings? It is only after a long probation that I may, if I see that you are really in earnest, instruct you in the doctrine." Mila, having agreed to Marpa's terms, awaited his commands.

One of the first measures taken by Marpa will perhaps astonish my readers, though to a Tibetan it would seem more natural. He ordered Mila Repa to use his magic arts to coerce the people of a village who, so he said, had offended him in some way. Mila, who was by this time consumed with shame for the murders that he had perpetrated by his sorcery, crimes which he now appreciated at their true worth, suffered the pain of realization a hundredfold, now that he had to repeat them in cold blood; but, like a true pupil, he never for a moment dreamed of disobeying his master. The strange-sounding command was really a means of bringing home to Mila, in a way that no mere precepts could have done, the real enormity of the sin of violence, revealing it to him in its true colours. The sole object of a genuine Lama's training is realization; whatever does not conduce to that end is a waste of time. Innocence, if due to nothing more than unconsciousness of evil, is considered of little worth. Not the new-born baby, but the experienced sage is the Tibetan ideal. It must be admitted that in the history of these events, Marpa got out of a difficulty by restoring to health the men, rats and birds that had suffered from his so drastic experiment. He then invented a fresh series of tests. He ordered the building of a house on a certain site and specified the exact design. Mila was to erect it unaided, bringing every stone with his own hands. When after unspeakable toil it was completed, Marpa came along and said casually: "Who ordered that absurd building to be put up there?" "It was your Reverence," answered Mila. "I must have been crazy when I said it. Pull it down and re-erect it here." This episode, with variations, was enacted again and again. Mila was even made to replace the stones where they had come from, miles away, carrying them on his back.

At last when the young man had proved that, though pushed to the limit of endurance, his steadfastness was utterly unshakable, his formidable tutor relented. Mila could hardly believe his ears when he heard the news that the coveted initiation was to be his at last. Then, in the centre of a *Khyinkhor*, or Sacred Circle, Marpa admitted his favourite pupil into his spiritual family, while foretelling for him a most glorious achievement.

Then follows one of the most moving episodes of the whole story, the description of the parting of the old Lama from his beloved disciple. After the stern lesson of Mila's cruel labours, the poignant tenderness of this farewell is strangely affecting.

Mila Repa's autobiography, which he dictated later to one of his own pupils, is the great masterpiece of Tibetan prose and has fortunately been competently translated into English, and into French still better. It gives a clearer impression of how the Tibetan mind works than any other book that I know, and as a picture of daily life it holds good to-day, though these events happened about the time of William the Norman.

Mila Repa became one of the greatest saints and by his extreme power of concentration, succeeded in telescoping into the space of a single earthly life all the stages that must precede the Supreme Illumination of a Buddha. He spent most of his remaining years in reclusion in caves, some of them not far from Mount Everest, where one can still meet a few of his spiritual children. There he meditated upon the Truth for the good of all creatures. The Order of Lamas which Marpa and he founded on Earth is called *Kargyudpa* or Verbal Tradition

Order. It hands down, in golden succession, doctrines which perhaps represent the richest manifestations of the Tibetan spirit. The saint has revealed his most intimate musings in a collection of poems, characterized by an extreme succinctness of expression. The autobiography is also a model of brevity; the style is vigorous and free from padding and the dialogue is vivid in the extreme.

It was to the scene of St. Mila's apprenticeship, to the mountain valley hallowed by his footsteps, that we hoped to go, perhaps to receive there some faint reflected glimpses of the teachings which he had dared to face in their dazzling effulgence. After an uneventful voyage we landed at Calcutta, buoyed up by hopes, little dreaming that we were fated to be thwarted in every single item of our programme: that we should fail on our peak, and be unable to set foot in Tibet; that our arrangements would work less smoothly than when we came out, quite inexperienced, three years before; and that luck would only turn at long last, when we had left our chosen ground, and migrated to the opposite end of the Himalaya, where, at P'hiyang in Ladak, a spiritual descendant of Marpa of Hlobrak would instruct us!

At Siliguri on the edge of the plain, we packed into a car driven by a Nepali chauffeur, and sped off along a road bordered by dense jungle, said to harbour tigers and elephants. A sharp turn into the hills, and the river Tista, flowing between banks overgrown with luxuriant tropical foliage, came into view. There we saw the polished leathery leaves of wild banana and of the indiarubber plant, palm-like cycads that called to mind remote geological ages, the light fronds of bamboo, screwpines or *Pandanus* and creepers in amazing variety. The trees, covered with ferns and orchids, exhibited the characteristic phenomena of damp tropical vegetation; fine air cables like telegraph wires, buttressed roots and subsidiary trunks growing out of the ends of branches so that a whole grove might really consist of but a single tree. Monkeys played overhead, and here and there huge butterflies, known hitherto only from collections, flitted past.

After crossing the Tista, the road winds upwards in numerous bends to a ridge 4,000 feet high with the bazaar of Kalimpong straggling along its crest. This place, which once belonged to Bhutan, forms part of a district annexed to British territory in 1865; it owes its commercial importance to its position as a

87

terminal of the Lhasa-India trade route. Thousands of mules and ponies come and go, bringing the wool of Tibet to India and carrying in exchange cotton, manufactured goods and also silk and other Chinese products. In Kalimpong's rambling street of shops many races rub shoulders, Bengalis and merchants from Marwar celebrated for business acumen, neat little Nepalis and high-cheeked Tibetans, lanky bullet-skulled Bhutanese in short striped tunics, heroic-looking Khambas with their broadswords swinging from their belts, lamas trading on behalf of their monasteries or intent on a visit to Buddh Gaya in Bihar, where the Victorious One obtained His final revelation. The best shops, neatest, cleanest and most tastefully arranged are those kept by Chinese; the smiling faces of their owners strike a friendly note as one walks through the bazaar.

The presiding genius of Kalimpong at that time was The Very Rev. Dr. J. A. Graham, sometime Moderator of the General Assembly of the Church of Scotland. Having come out as a missionary, his attention was drawn to the crying evil of unwanted children of Anglo-Indian parentage, who, like Kim of old, hung about the streets of India, deserted and neglected. Dr. Graham came to their rescue and, starting from small beginnings, built up a wonderful organization to deal with the problem, including a school where the boys and girls are fostered, educated and eventually placed in suitable trades or professions. Many firms, as well as private persons, have recognized the great public benefit of this work by becoming regular subscribers to its upkeep. It was a moving experience to visit the Homes in company with the saintly man who acted as father to this huge family. The unfeigned joy that lit up the rows of faces, as he pushed open the doors of successive class-rooms, the general atmosphere of health and confidence, the pleasant cottages among which the children had been subdivided into small groups instead of being allowed to grow up under barrack conditions, all these things made the St. Andrew's Homes deserve the much-abused name of Charity.

During my stay at Kalimpong I spent every available moment, in trying to improve my Tibetan. Having picked it up in the western provinces, and gone on building upon that foundation, my ear was not attuned to the dialect and accent of Lhasa, which is the lingua franca of educated Tibetans everywhere. I had several teachers at Kalimpong, one of whom, an elderly layman, used to come and coach me on the hotel veranda. One day, as

88

THE ROUND OF EXISTENCE

TIBETAN TRADER

we were sitting at our lesson, I happened to see an ant crawling up the hem of his gown and picked it off and put it on the grass. "You have done well," said the teacher. "I rejoice to see that you did not unthinkingly squash the ant. You must be familiar with the doctrines that enjoin respect for life however lowly." "Yes," I answered, "I have heard the popular saying that any insect one sees has probably been at some time one or both of one's parents." This is a way of expressing the idea that all beings are continuously passing from one state to another, according to the actions which consciously or unconsciously affect them, so that all living things are brothers, and all things whatsoever, one. This doctrine will be explained in detail in the chapter on the Round of Existence.

While at Kalimpong I had many opportunities of investigating the attitude of the Tibetans towards animals, as not a day passes but long trains of mules or ponies come and go along the caravan route. I think one is safe in declaring that genuine cruelty is uncommon and that in their relation with the animal world, the Tibetans might serve as an example for most other races. Wild animals are in consequence often very tame. Feeding of birds and fishes is considered a pious act. Meat-eating, though general because of the scarcity of other kinds of food on the plateau, is indulged in as a regrettable necessity but never defended, and the stricter lamas and any others who abstain from it altogether are much respected.

In view of what has just been said, the reader must be warned against misinterpreting the motives that govern the Tibetans in their attitude towards cruelty. Their treatment of animals, in which their standard is above average, must not lead one into ascribing to them an extreme tender-heartedness or an inability to witness pain without repugnance. By no stretch of imagination could they be called humanitarians, even when their acts conform to the humane code. With us the chief objection to cruelty is the actual pain inflicted: not so with the Tibetan, whose powers of enduring pain without flinching are great, and who can also look unmoved upon suffering that would horrify us. For him, the feeling of hostility, which leads to the doing of an injury, is far more serious than the pain involved in the cruel act. The two points of view differ profoundly, even if they sometimes approach in their results.

The Buddhist takes for his starting-point the rights of all his living fellow-creatures, rights which he recognizes in theory,

D

whatever may be his own practice. The sinfulness of ill-treatment lies in the ignorant denial of those rights and in the indulgence of anger or self-interest. For our part, we make a marked distinction of principle between the rights claimed for man and those accorded to animals. The latter can vary between moderately full rights—sometimes marred by a patronizing attitude—slight recognition, and non-existence. On the other hand, our objection to pain is extreme. We fear it greatly for ourselves and, by a projection of our own highly-developed sensibility, we recoil from the idea of inflicting it on others.

The Tibetans, on the other hand, take little stock of pain as such. A man who would not commit a cruel act himself, could be unmoved by the severest torture suffered by either man or beast, provided he were convinced that it was inevitable or deserved. If it were purely the result of chance, he would probably feel no strong impulse to seek a way to remedy it. A man who would put himself to no end of trouble in order to spare his animals, might experience little horror on witnessing an accident to one of those same animals; even a deliberate act, such as a painful penalty decreed by the criminal law, would not stir his feelings.

The virtues of the Tibetans in their relations with animals they owe chiefly to their Buddhist principles, which remain unquestioned, even if they are not always applied consistently. Were such to be the case, indeed, it could not but bring about the abolition of all cruelties. But of objection to pain for its own sake there is little, and inhuman practices hallowed by custom, such as the slaughter of animals in certain districts by suffocation, do not stir the public conscience.

One of my pressing duties after my arrival was to go over by car to Gangtok, the capital of Sikkim, and introduce myself to the Political Officer, Mr. B. J. (now Sir Basil) Gould, who controlled the issue of passports into Tibet. He had very bad news for us. A report had arrived concerning an untoward incident on a different part of the frontier which, it was feared, had annoyed the Lhasa authorities. In consequence the promise of forwarding on our application for a permit to go to Hlobrak could not be fulfilled. It was a great blow: all our plans were in the melting-pot. There was, however, nothing to be done now but to carry on with our immediate programme of climbing in Sikkim. We spent several days at Gangtok organizing transport.

By far the most interesting of the sights at Gangtok is the new temple attached to the palace, which has only recently been completed by the reigning prince. Both the structure and the interior decorations and fittings are new. It is significant that a work has been carried through in this little Himalayan principality which would nowadays be well nigh impossible in the capitals of the richest countries in the world. Externally the building is plain, built in two stories like all Sikkim temples. The nave, well proportioned and resting on pillars with the usual Tibetan bracketed capitals, is lined with mural paintings by the best contemporary artists from Tibet. Symbolical figures, illustrating metaphysical doctrines, scenes from the life of the Buddha and from local sacred history, together with bands and panels of conventional foliage, have all been executed with precision and in animated style. The colours are clean and well blended.

Unlike so many Hindu and Moslem rulers, the Maharaja and his Court invariably wear their traditional dress. This wise and salutary practice, in keeping with the dignity of a prince, is unfortunately not copied as it ought to be by the officials of petty rank. Postal servants, overseers on roads and, most serious of all, schoolmasters, are frequent offenders. This last case is specially regrettable because of their influence upon the character of their youthful and uncritical charges. I used to meet the schoolboys returning home in the evenings with their satchels: some of them looked in the picture, but far too many were got up as grotesque travesties of European children. There is no law I should welcome more than one which made it a duty of every employee of the State to wear his national costume. The same rule should be applied to school children. Designers of school buildings and Government offices might follow this principle, so far as is practicable, in regard to the style of the architecture and furnishing. It is only long after people have relinquished their heritage that they begin to feel regrets; but then the attempt to reconstruct the past is only too liable to result in a mere romantic affectation, like the Gothic revival in Europe.

I believe that this question of costume, external though it may appear at first sight, is a crucial one for India, China, Japan and other nations too. It has become a symbol of something far more deep-seated, a touchstone by which the traditional and anti-traditional souls can be distinguished. That I am not alone in thinking so, is proved by the actions of those to whom, in this matter, I feel most opposed. I call to witness the inveterate

Occidentalizers, Kemal Atatürk and his Persian and Afghan imitators, for they, though from diametrically contrary motives, came to the same conclusion as myself. They wished to uproot tradition, for they too felt the power of symbols; that is why they persecuted all the outward signs of native culture and forcibly imposed trousers and bowler hats, Romanized architecture and jazz orchestras. They accepted, for a criterion of civilization, conformity to the Western model, and that alone. In their eyes such an object as a typewriter was more than a useful tool to do a certain job; it became invested with mystical qualities, like an emblem of progressiveness in the new era. Their ideals matched their outward trappings. Militaristic nationalism, identification of propaganda with education, hatred of religion and denial of the private authority of conscience, above all the exaltation of feverish action over thought in every sphere, these were their ideas of culture.

A general reversion to the traditional costume on the part of male Indians, and Chinese and Japanese of the educated classes, especially students and officials—women seem usually to have more courage and sounder instincts in these things—would, in my opinion, earn general respect from Europeans. Self-respect is the first step towards friendship with others. Slavish imitation is the way to get oneself despised, when all talk of equality or reconciliation becomes merely futile.

DEFEAT ON SIMVU

THE valley of the Tista, approached by a short descent from the Penlong pass, is the ordinary route from Gangtok to North Sikkim. It is a sylvan fairyland which should have inspired poets; but its name has been more often associated with the unpleasant topics of malaria and leeches. True, the disease is common in the lower parts of the valley, especially during the rains; but the upper reaches, along which the path of expeditions lies, are, except for one stretch, free from it. It is only in the rainy season that certain sections are overrun with leeches; at other times of the year they are only found in large numbers in some unusually moist side-valleys.

When our caravan marched up the four stages between Gangtok and Lachhen, at the gate of the Zemu glacier valley, the drought had not yet broken and vegetation was not showing at its best. There were few insects or flowers; only here and there a vivid purple splash indicated a plant of Dendrobium orchid perched up in a fork of the branches. I will leave more detailed description till our return in the monsoon when everything had come to life again. In the space of a few days on our outward journey we went through the gamut of the year's seasons in reverse, starting from the perpetual high summer of the sub-tropical zone, passing within a few hours into an evergreen sub-temperate summer, then gradually rising to temperate spring, till finally, after climbing abruptly on to the much higher shelf, where stand the pretty chalets of Lachhen, we were back again in a landscape of leafless trees, except for the conifers; the first touch of spring was just showing in the red of tree rhododendrons, the waxy white blooms of magnolias, and the mauve of primulas dotted over the brown turf. When we reached the glacier, after a brief stay in the village, we had taken the final step back into a wintry, snowbound world.

Lachhen stands on a minor caravan route leading into Sikkim

93

*It should be noted that only the principal mountain chains have been indicated;
most of the area shown, however, is mountainous.*

from Tibet, which has been followed by several Everest expeditions. The Zemu torrent, which feeds the Tista with the drainage of a huge group of snow mountains, culminating in the gigantic massif of Kangchhendzönga, comes out some two miles beyond the village, which thus occupies a strategic position on the path of parties intent on climbing in these parts. The villagers, who provide a good deal of the porterage, are well aware of their power to hold the climbers up to ransom; they do it with some show of rustic cunning, though quite good-humouredly. These people are all born pleaders. They will talk interminably before they accept your terms, but once an agreement has been made, they will not try to violate it; for they are not educated to the ways of the great outer world and have yet to learn that one can always find a loophole for wriggling out of one's pledges.

The village runs its affairs largely on a co-operative basis. Property is privately owned; but all take their share of work that affects the community as a whole. Rules have been made which aim at preventing one family from getting an unfair advantage over the others by such means as an early sowing, or a reaping of the crops before the date laid down by the commune, which meets to debate in the *agora* on the edge of the village. Regulations having this end in view are often enforced with unimaginative rigidity, not taking into account whether a field faces the sun or has a different kind of soil. Madame David-Neel, who spent several years near Lachhen, tells some amusing stories of how the principle is apt to be interpreted. She was herself nearly forced to accept a whole pack of hounds, because a family which sold her one dog, was considered, by so doing, to have tried to steal a march on its neighbours.

Above the village there stood a small monastery, of not more than twenty lamas, which nevertheless had acquired considerable fame through its abbot, a most remarkable man, who styled himself the Lachhen hermit. He occupied a thatched cottage adjoining the temple and had gained his title by spending several years in meditation in mountain retreats. He was considered to have advanced very far on the road to Buddhahood.

We naturally felt a wish to make his acquaintance, so we sent word to ask leave to come and pay our respects. When we arrived at the monastery, we were told to wait a few minutes as the abbot was not quite ready to see us. While we stood outside, several lamas rushed hither and thither in a feverish search for five chairs, considered indispensable to the proper reception of

95

the party. After four stools had been carried into the abbot's room, a fifth one, a wicker armchair, was produced; but the door was too narrow to admit it. As the lamas struggled to force it through the entrance, I tried in vain to explain that so much trouble on our behalf was unnecessary. When once a Tibetan has made up his mind that politeness demands a certain course of action, no power on earth will turn him from his purpose. The guest may be made to wait all night out in the cold, but that is preferable to insulting him.

We finally stepped into a dimly lit room, furnished with altar, lamps, scrolls and books. On a rug by the window, turned so that the disturbing rays of the sun should not fall directly on his face, a rather fat man in orange robes was seated, Buddha-fashion. His face was broad, with twinkling, humorous eyes, his hair long and wispy; from his ears hung a pair of large gold rings. The great thickness of his neck was increased by a prominent goitre; the whole effect might have been comic but for the aura of power which seemed to radiate from his person, making one feel at once that here was no ordinary mortal. Actually, I have never looked on a more impressive face, despite its grotesqueness.

We presented a ceremonial scarf and were then invited to take our seats in strict hierarchical order, with myself in the armchair. After this there followed a brief and formal conversation, during which I asked him to be so kind as to bless the porters before we started up the Zemu. On the following day the stage was set for the blessing ceremony on the open space before the temple, where a high seat was installed for the abbot and facing it, five lower ones covered with small Tibetan rugs for us. The porters, both Lachhen men and our nucleus of Darjeeling Sherpas, gathered round, and then the hermit, attended by his lamas, mounted the dais. He was wearing on his head a queer hat of papier mache, shaped rather like a top hat and secured under the chin with a string, which made him look even more peculiar.

Before the service began, offerings were presented on behalf of ourselves and our party. The porters gave him a white scarf, which is as indispensable in Tibetan social intercourse as a visiting-card in nineteenth-century England, and a silver coin, while I handed him a large *t'hanka* of the green Dolma, a divinity who plays a part analogous to that of the Blessed Virgin in the Christian religion. It had been sent to me from North China and we had brought it out to Sikkim in accordance with our

96

policy of giving as presents only those things that would fit in with their surroundings in every sense of the word. For gifts to temples I had brought three such scroll-pictures and two silver lamps made in Greece over a century ago; for highly-placed personages there were rings and a pendant made by my gold-smith brother. We had, besides, a number of semi-precious stones, unset, such as garnets and amethysts, cornelians and lapis lazuli; these were suitable for persons of medium status, while for people of higher rank we had reserved a few aqua-marines and tourmalines. Stones, being endowed with an intrinsic beauty that cannot be affected by time or fashion, provide an easy solution to the whole problem of presents.

The abbot's benediction differed entirely from that of the lama who officiated for us at Harsil in 1933. The Lachhen prelate remained seated throughout, and let us file up one by one to receive from him a few drops of a strange decoction. We sprinkled our hands with it and sniffed a little up our noses, after which he gave us an equally mysterious pill to swallow. Then, to the accompaniment of an invocation, rice grains were thrown up into the air and the service concluded with a distribution to everyone of small muslin scarves, knotted in a peculiar manner by the abbot himself. As he handed out each one, he said: "May your stay in the mountains be fortunate."

Rather late on our last evening, I wandered out alone by the path that led to the entrance of the Zemu valley; the others were still busy packing. As I was returning homewards I saw a pathetic sight. Two men were approaching from the side of the village, weighed down by bulky burdens, at least eighty pounds apiece. One of them walked ahead at a brisk pace and the second, who was blind and tied to him by two bits of string, arm to arm, followed without hesitation over the irregular ground. "Where are you bound for?" I stopped to ask. "We are going over the Kongra pass to Kampa Dzong"—that is, over a pass 17,000 feet high across the mountains at a season when snow was still lying quite deep! "Alas," cried the blind man, "woe is me; for twelve years I have not seen the light. Who is there to take pity on me?" I felt much affected, but could think of nothing to say. I saluted them and had moved off a few paces, when I suddenly recalled a story in Madame David-Neel's book about her famous journey to Lhasa. She tells how she met a dying man by the roadside and found a way of comforting him. I turned and ran after the pair, who were walking away rapidly.

I nudged the leading man's arm and he turned round in surprise. "Listen, friend," I said, "to the possessor of the eye of the doctrine there is no darkness. In the Western Paradise of the Buddha who is named Boundless Light the sun shall rise for you once again." A flash of joy chased the blank despair for a moment from the blind man's face, while his comrade thanked me with a touching look of gratitude.

Next day the whole party set out by the same path on which I had met the blind man. Before we had gone a mile I noticed that the Lachhenpas were walking badly, advancing a hundred yards at excessive speed and then putting down their loads and starting to gossip. The symptoms were unmistakable: I saw the ghosts of the troublesome porters at Gangotri rising again. But this time I was no longer a raw hand. If they were working for a prolongation of marching time in order to earn more days' pay, we could manoeuvre for position too. One thing to do was to pick out the willing elements and play them against the malcontents, and another, to anticipate intended halts and rush the men quickly past attractive camping-sites on to ground where a stop was not so alluring. At each inviting spot I was ready for them and managed to hustle a few beyond it, without betraying my feelings. The men were argumentative but friendly and often a jest was enough to keep them on the move.

Our three days' trek to the Zemu passed off quite satisfactorily in the end, though it required constant vigilance to control the troublesome elements among the porters. In the evenings, the leading trouble-makers used to harangue us eloquently on the scarcity of camping-grounds and fuel for the next day; we countered this by proposing an exceptionally distant place as the end of the following march, in language no less rhetorical. This little game was played without ill-feeling, and the compromises that we reached worked out about right.

The Zemu valley is richly wooded with conifers and mixed rhododendron scrub. In April the tall red variety is flowering: to see the vast number of smaller kinds one must wait till the end of May. On our upward journey we found great snowdrifts lying on the path under the trees; the ground underfoot was often quite hidden by masses of primroses, like the English ones, except that they were mauve instead of yellow.

Trees ceased near the snout of the glacier. Beyond that point the whole country lay under snow and at night it was very cold.

We followed a trough between the left moraine and the mountainside, making for the "Green Lake" where former parties had camped, opposite the side glacier coming down from Simvu, the mountain that we wished to attempt. In the end, however, we chose another spot about three miles lower down, a sheltered bay that caught all the sun, where a patch of grass had already been thawed clear of snow. The Lachhen men then left us, promising to return when the camp had finally to be struck. We kept on five Sherpas and our old friends Odsung and Djun Singh who had been with us in Garhwal days. We had only intended to retain four of the Sherpas, but one man, called Ang Babu, had so set his mind on going up the mountain with us that we had not the heart to send him away. He turned out to be the keenest of them all. He had a monkey-house face, an asset in his chosen part of professional humorist; he kept everyone continually amused with his sallies.

Weather favoured us for the first few days on the Zemu, which were spent in finding out the lie of the land and in surveying routes up Simvu from neighbouring heights. Two lesser points on the left bank of the glacier were climbed, one evidently a Bavarian peak, judging by the neat masonry of the cairn found on the top, suggestive of German thoroughness. The other peak was new (Point 19,420 feet) and consisted of a pleasant rock-ridge, giving out on to a rounded cap of pure ice, with a diminutive crevasse right on the very top. We felt in a hopeful frame of mind, for acclimatization seemed to be proceeding satisfactorily for everyone; this was proved by the absence of signs of distress when walking up to 18,000–19,000 feet and confirmed by certain tests carried out by the doctor.

Optimism about the weather turned out to have been premature, however. After a week, when we were just thinking of making a move towards our mountain, the wind changed its quarter and blue skies disappeared behind blankets of grey mist; this was followed by snow soon after midday, which drove us under cover. Late at night the sky cleared again and hopes revived; but next day brought the same order of changes, and the next day after that; and so it continued, till we began to lose count of the days, and passed from a mood of chafing to one of blank resignation. The only useful work that could be done was carrying stores across the glacier and making a dump on the moraine that led up towards Simvu. After that there was nothing to do but to be patient and reflect that if this was purgatory, the

Everest party on the other side of the mountains must be having hell—a doubtful consolation.

A protracted period of waiting is trying for the nerves, especially in the case of people of athletic temperament, with much energy to spare. As day after day passed with the same tedious routine of early morning sun, followed by mist and then snow all the afternoon, ending in a tantalizingly clear spell after eight o'clock at night, everyone began to feel the strain of inactivity, which translated itself into a curious sense of guilt, as if we ourselves somehow were to blame for the delay. Our company was an extremely good-tempered one; but a similar experience in a large, ill-assorted party, must be most unpleasant.

One morning, we had just finished breakfast and were settling down to yet another wasted day, when suddenly we noticed that something unusual was happening to the mist across the glacier. A rift opened in the clouds and the graceful Gothic pinnacles and flutings of cathedral-like Siniolchu appeared, glistening against an azure background, a sight which, at that hour of the day, had long been denied us. Then in ten minutes, as if under the stroke of an enchanter's wand, the mists dissolved into nothingness and on every side the peaks stood out clear and sharp against the sunlight. We leaped up, galvanized into instant action. Orders were shouted, lists hastily consulted, kit was packed, and in less than a couple of hours we were ready to start. The porters, in their green windproofs, gathered round a big boulder outside the camp before shouldering their packs and kindled their ritual fire, on which they piled branches of juniper and sweet-smelling azalea, with shouts of "*Hla gyaló!*" (The Gods conquer!).

I do not propose to give a lengthy description of our attempt on Simvu, nor to tell how we worked our way up the great snow-slopes towards our ridge. Successions of camps, numbered or lettered, are familiar to readers of climbing books. Their unavoidable repetition can only be compensated by the conquest of the peak. When that is not achieved, it is wiser to cut short that part of the story.

We spent ten days on the mountain, and established three camps, the highest being placed at about 20,000 feet close to the foot of the north-east ridge. The promise of good conditions on the day we started was not fulfilled, and we reverted to a slightly improved version of the previous weather. The mornings were usually sunny till about eleven; then mists began to swirl over from the south, followed by a cold wind which brought snow in the early afternoon. Thus every day counted but half its normal length in climbing hours, and this made upward progress extremely slow.

Except on the crest of the ridge itself we never touched good snow. It was always quite soft, even early in the day, so that the carrying of loads and the kicking of steps was a laborious business. We often used to sink up to our thighs in the snow and a good deal of care was required to keep clear of hidden crevasses, for when sounding with an axe one could rarely touch bottom even on safe ground.

From the Upper Simvu Saddle, where we established our principal depot, we saw, through gaps in the mist, an overwhelming panorama of peaks, culminating in the monstrous mass of Kangchhendzönga. To the south, on the other hand, across the steamy Talung valley, source of the bad weather, a sea of trees extended as far as the eye could reach; we knew that it only ended at Siliguri, on the edge of the Bengal plain, where passengers for Darjeeling were even then sitting in the station restaurant consuming their coffee and bacon and eggs. Looking back, we had before us the terrifying Talung face of Siniolchu. It looked a most inaccessible mountain and it was a great surprise to hear, in the autumn of 1936, that it had actually been climbed, by a dangerous route from the Zemu side, by that most dashing of parties, Paul Bauer and his Bavarians. The men who climbed Siniolchu certainly earned their glory.

But there was something else which, in the clear hour after daybreak, drew our gaze even more than that icy spire. To the left of it, through a distant gap in the mountains, we could just make out lines of rolling purple hills that seemed to belong to another world, a world of austere calm, of deserted plateaux and colourful downs, which made the snowy Himalaya seem strangely young and assertive. It was a corner of Tibet. My eyes rested on it with an intensity of longing. I sometimes wonder whether I shall ever be privileged to approach the vision any closer. Tibet is well guarded, as it should be. The issue still lies on the knees of the gods, and what is still more formidable, on the knees of the officials of two Governments, who do not always find it easy to distinguish between the genuine seeker after knowledge and the charlatan or the sensation-monger intent on "getting into Tibet," merely because of its reputation as a closed and mysterious land.

The final assault on our peak occupied two days. First we tried a side of the ridge from a point about 400 feet above our highest camp, where a steeply inclined snow-slope led through a breach in the formidable ice defences which ring the mountain. Had the surface of this slope been hard, it would certainly have led us out on to the higher part of the ridge; but it was found to consist of shallow rotten snow, adhering precariously to a substructure of pure ice, and ready to avalanche at the slightest provocation. We pushed on as far as we could; but eventually even the most daring among us voted emphatically for retreat.

Early next morning we explored another line of weakness, a similar slope starting level with the camp, but it was no safer. One can deal with pure ice if one has time enough, but that disintegrating film of snow, ready to part company with its glassy base at any moment, was more than nerves could stand. We proceeded to work along the bottom of a quite vertical curtain of ice cliffs, of the purest white and conspicuously layered, till we came to the very steep nose of the ridge, which fell away into hazy depths that looked bottomless. I happened to be walking behind when I heard a shout: "Come on quickly! We've found the passage!" I rounded the corner of the cliff and saw that we were close to a comparatively short ice-slope, free from snow, which joined the crest. Everyone put on spiked crampons and I led out on to the ice.

We had often, in Switzerland, spent off-days practising making steps up and down the steep pinnacles of glaciers; but we had never yet been called upon to tackle ice at such a steep angle on an actual mountain. I still remember that slope as one of the most exhilarating bits of climbing of my life. I worked my way in a wide zigzag, out over the abyss into which the ice-chips went sliding down with a silvery tinkle. I graded my steps with the same unhurried precision that I would have shown on a purely experimental pitch. Not having specially strong arms, I did not try to cut fast, but I was glad to note that accurate aim, with its consequent economy of strokes, was resulting in sufficiently speedy progress. Our long enforced spell of idleness at the Base Camp had brought about a very complete acclimatization, and we felt a mastery over our movements, without any greater strain than we would have experienced on a Swiss peak. Having cut a long course to the right, I returned on the left tack and suddenly felt the dancing resiliency of the ice give place to a dull "plop," as the head of my axe buried itself in snow. A few steps higher and I stood on the ridge and had plunged the stem of the axe into firm, deep snow. Attached to it by a loop of the rope, I was in a position to hold a whole party. Everyone followed up speedily and then unroped, for before us the ridge extended upwards broad and easy. We felt that the first trying obstacle was behind us, and that we could relax a little before tackling the summit ridge some 1,000 feet ahead, which, though it looked jagged, did not suggest insurmountable resistance.

We sat down to lunch in a hollow. Then, without roping, we advanced once more over the next bump. To our amazement we found that we were gazing down into a huge gulf. A crevasse, as broad and deep as a castle moat, cut off all communication between our part of the ridge and its continuation. Up and down its lip we walked, looking for a bridge, but the harsh truth was not to be charmed away: the upper part of the mountain was cut off from us.

We had no alternative but to retreat. The situation was rather comic: there was no arguing with stark impossibility. We descended to the head of the ice-staircase and only took a few minutes to reach the lower slopes again. As we drew near the camp, the first flakes, harbingers of the usual blizzard, began to eddy round us. The rest of the day had to be spent in our sleeping-bags.

A day sufficed for us to clear the upper camp and descend to the Zemu. Tufts of a tiny mauve azalea, the first moraine plant to open to the sun, caught our eye from afar, by sheer brilliance and purity of colour. The spring—and the monsoon—were at hand. That same night we crossed to the Base Camp and celebrated our defeat by lighting the plum pudding, a festivity to which the Sherpas were also invited. We hid a rupee in it and there was great excitement when one of the porters unearthed it from his slice. The honest fellow, doubting his luck, came round after supper to ask if he was expected to return it.

Had more time been available we should have continued climbing on other peaks; but the weather was showing by unmistakable signs that the season of rains was beginning. Word was therefore sent down to Lachhen to arrange for the collecting of our baggage, while we and the Sherpas enjoyed a brief rest at Tset'hang, a beautiful clearing in the Zemu forest.

Sikkim at the end of May is famous for its rhododendrons. They are of every conceivable size and colour, from tiny white or purple varieties found above the tree line, to showy bushes covered with huge tufts of blossoms, which make up the tangled undergrowth of the woods, and colour the slopes mauve and white or, most wonderful of all, yellow. On the way down from the snout of the glacier we kept discovering fresh species. For variety, the primulas almost equalled them; there were mauve ones, and deep purple, and yellow ones on all the grassy banks. Blue *Meconopsis* poppies were also at their best, but the great yellow poppy which we had been hoping to see was not yet out and only showed as a rosette of leaves. In the forest, festoons of white clematis bound tree to tree.

At Tset'hang we parted company from two of our friends, Cooke and Chapman, who were intending to go up north into the Lhonak valley and continue climbing. They were joined there by a third friend and, in spite of poor weather, managed among other things, to make the first ascent of the difficult Fluted Peak.

The last few miles before Lachhen brought more changes in the plants. Among the new kinds of rhododendrons, there was one of a fiery scarlet with flowers hanging down like bells. Another species, in its efforts to evade the competition of its neighbours, had ingeniously made its home forty feet above ground, as an epiphyte on old and mossy pine trees, which it adorned with bunches of snow-white flowers. There was an orchid also, on the same pines, called *Pleione*, tinged with a delicate mauve. Bushes of orange azalea flamed round the entrance to the torrent valley.

THE ROUND OF EXISTENCE

PERHAPS our defeat on Simvu was symbolical. We climbed no more peaks of ice and snow on our travels, for we were led into a different world. We became pilgrims of the Tibetan Buddhist Tradition; but before I tell of these adventures of the spirit, it is necessary to explain a few fundamental teachings of the Doctrine, so that those who read of our journeyings may realize the nature of the quest, and may share in the treasures that are to be found along the Path.[1]

None of the great Traditions can be enclosed within the narrow framework of a school of philosophy. Nor ought an explanation to be over-simplified in the vain hope of bringing it within the effortless comprehension of all men; facile diffusion of an idea can only be achieved to the detriment of its purity. It is not for the Doctrine to abase itself to the common level, but for those who can, to exalt themselves to its height. That is why a doctrine spread by organized propaganda is liable to be reduced to a hollow shell, empty of the essentials. The Truth may be likened to a difficult mountain peak which, though free of access to all mankind, is yet actually scaled by a chosen few, by those who are willing to pay the price in self-discipline, steadfastness and risk. Though it is no one's private preserve and all have an equal right to possess it, yet all do not attain it simultaneously, for there are those who feel no urge to seek, and those who suffer from vacillation, doubting whether the quest is worth the trouble. Others again must measure painfully every step on the Path, inch by inch, over an indefinitely protracted period of effort. A few rare souls find it possible, like

[1] For a more general account of the Buddhist doctrine the reader is advised to consult A. K. Coomaraswamy, *Hinduism and Buddhism*, (New York Philosophical Library, 1943). This exposition is masterly in its conciseness and can be accepted as perfectly accurate both factually and traditionally (which cannot be said of most books in European languages); the same applies to the section dealing with the parent tradition of Hinduism.

Mila Repa, by supreme concentration, to compress into one the several stages which ordinary flesh and blood must needs take successively. That road is known to the Tibetans as the "Direct Path"; but it is not for faint hearts to think of braving its perils.

It is therefore not without misgiving that I have decided to include the present chapter; for I may, in spite of these warnings, be luring someone into rash generalizations, not warranted by these gleanings from my own elementary knowledge. Nevertheless, it seems imperative for me to try to clear up certain basic ideas; otherwise many of the illuminating talks which I had with the lamas may not be fully understood, since terms will have to be used and references made which are unfamiliar to the reader though common knowledge among Tibetans. More than that, there is no phase of Tibetan life which is not pervaded by the subtle influence of the Doctrine, as by an ether; the whole Tibetan picture must be viewed in that light for it to become intelligible. It should be understood that I have had no first-hand contact with Buddhism except in its Tibetan form. When I speak of the Doctrine I mean the tradition that has come down through the Lamas. Of other schools, such as the Southern School of Ceylon, I know little, and that little is taken from books.

If some of the profound metaphysical teachings of the Tibetan Tradition are traceable to a Hindu origin, that in no wise invalidates them. The power of drawing on any and every source for the illustration of the Doctrine, and of pressing the most unlikely tools into its service, constitutes the "Note" of Catholicity, which unites all the authentic Traditions. However widely separated their viewpoints, there resides, under what, at a superficial glance, may seem like irreconcilable differences, one and the same metaphysical knowledge, which is allowed to clothe itself at will in whatever guise best suits its immediate purposes, without yielding up one jot of its reality or one tittle of authority. The origin of a doctrine or the historical personality of its author are trifling matters compared with its truth.

I have already made several allusions to the Round or Wheel of Existence. Facing page 88 is a picture of the conventional representation of this doctrine, as displayed in the porch of every Tibetan temple. It is said to have been first drawn by the Buddha Himself in rice grains on the ground, and it was
106

one of the very earliest lessons that He communicated to His disciples. Readers will find it helpful to refer to the picture frequently, for it is essential to familiarize oneself with this fundamental theme.

The Wheel consists of a circle subdivided into six sectors, with a small concentric circle in the centre and another of wider diameter outside, so that a continuous border runs round the main circle. The whole is a diagrammatic scheme of the principle of Multiple States of Finite Being. Existence is not conceived as a single episode in Time, affecting a basically fixed individuality and finally determining the future status of the being concerned. It is viewed as a connected series of changes, a continual passage from one state into the next, without a single

THE ROUND OF EXISTENCE

one of the participating elements remaining exempt from modification. Man is but one of an indefinite number of states of being. His earthly life is but one episode among many others. No special importance distinguishes the human state from the others, though it is legitimate to treat it as a mean from man's own point of view, seeing that he is located therein by definition and cannot escape viewing all other beings in relation to it. Therefore it is just for us, and for us only, to call any other being, which compared to Man is less limited in its possibilities "superior," just as the converse holds good for "inferior" beings which, in comparison with Man, are hedged in by narrower limitations. Thus a passing into one of the former or higher states may also be called an ascendant movement, while the exchanging of the human state for one of the lower degrees can be described as an obscuration or fall.

The agent which keeps the Round moving, and rings the changes between various states of Existence, is the force of Action. Its well-known Indian name of *Karman* means nothing else; it is wrong to translate it as Law of Cause and Effect, or Fate, though the two notions are closely connected. It is the play of complex activities which introduces the incessant modifications into every being and it is legitimate to say that no existence preserves its identity for two successive moments: change in one part entails corresponding variations in all the others. There is nothing but ebb and flow, continual reshuffling of the cards, continual Becoming.

A circle is well chosen as the symbol of this unending process. The Wheel is a misnomer, for when a wheel turns it is as one solid whole, whereas in the Round it is the contents which remain in motion, a tangle of orbits entering at every moment into new permutations, as the Existences, planet-like, collide, split, cohere, grow or dissolve. A whirlpool is perhaps the best simile of any.

The Round is described as of indefinite extension, reaching backward into the impenetrable dimness of the past and, in default of Deliverance—that is, of an interruption in the Action which provides the motive power—extending equally relentlessly into the future. The question of Deliverance will be discussed later, however. As the Round includes the state of existence in which we are situated ourselves here and now, it calls for detailed consideration before we turn our attention elsewhere.

The flux of endless change involves each being in accessions of strength and onsettings of weakness, entries into stages marked enough to receive a new name, and exits from previous states; these are what we call youth and age, birth and death. They are signposts, imaginary but convenient points of division in a process that, nevertheless, remains fluid and uninterrupted. So we live out our lives, as corks, playthings of the waves on the ocean of Activity, or as pebbles ground against one another under the poundings and buffetings of the eternal tide.

We must now consider Action under some of its aspects. It comprises a great deal more than the manifestations that we normally call acts, attributable to beings in virtue of their individual existence. First there is Cosmic Activity, the sum total of effects (themselves already on the way to becoming new Causes) of all the Causes that have occurred throughout the Universe. These include effects of Will, recognizable as such, and the interplay of so-called inanimate forces. Then there is Localized Action, bound up with the conditions that prevail in any subdivision of the Universe considered separately. There is also Racial Action, the united causes and effects definable as Heredity. Finally there is Personal Action, individual acts and thoughts, with their chains of results. Any one of the many series of causes and effects can be discussed in isolation; but in reality they are all contributors to the General or Cosmic Activity and have no proper existence outside it.

The effects of Action on a given being may be direct, or indirect and produced by unsuspected causes at the other extremity of the world. No series develops in a continuous line like a bundle of endlessly extensile threads: it forms part of a network, throwing out filaments and gathering them in from all directions, beyond hope of unravelling.

Every activity is the result of previous activity, or activities, and bears in it the seeds of future ones. This is one of the fundamental postulates of the Buddhists, summed up in the sentence:—"Every effect springs from a cause." Creation, if taken in the sense of something expressly fashioned out of nothing on a certain occasion is foreign to their ideas. They will admit indefinite combinations and dissociations, changes advantageous or harmful, simplifications or increases of complexity, but never out of relation with the general idea of causality. All that is, whatever its nature, can be referred back to causes in the indefinite past and points forward to effects in the indefinite future. It follows from this, that nothing can fail to produce some effect or other, since the merest thought, devoid of observable results, does introduce instant and inescapable modifications in the general Activity of the whole world. This doctrine will be found to have important ethical implications, since it does away with the possibility of a totally ineffective action. No right action, however Quixotic it may seem, can be called useless; no foolish action can be excused as harmless. Every activity, be it the most trivial or apparently purposeless, sets in motion, as cause, a new series of effects, which even if they are incalculable to us, are none the less strictly determined.

If the Round depends on Action, Action viewed as a whole is the product of Desire. Every being, even the most inert, must be credited with some form of Will. Attachment or repulsion, which are the same thing viewed under two aspects, are inherent to all existence. Volition may be conscious or reflex or so faintly energetic as hardly to be recognizable for Will; but some response to the impacts of other Existences is there all the same. In a conscious being, attachment is the aspiration after pleasant experience and its repetition, repulsion the avoidance of the unpleasant and of its recurrence. Each attempt to catch and hold and repeat the former produces a new chain of Action; so does every endeavour to change painful or disadvantageous experience: and so the Round goes on turning.

But the argument can be carried back another stage. What is it that prompts Desire or Attachment? That is declared to be none other than Ignorance, the want of realization of what things really are and how they really work. If the search for the pleasant and the shunning of the disagreeable only results in going round in a circle, if the action planned to that end as a result of those desires, is not, in fact, calculated to yield the results aimed at, then that action of seeking and shunning is unreasonable, based upon false information, on a failure to fathom the mechanism of the Universe. It deserves the epithet "ignorant." Were true Knowledge to be present, assuredly a totally different method would have to be followed and with quite different ends in view. No one, in that case, would go on doing exactly those things which were bound to perpetuate his wandering in the Round; he would devote his energies rather to *Undoing*. Therefore so long as Ignorance, unawareness of the true constitution of the World and of oneself, persists, so long must be postponed any hope of breaking the Vicious Circle. Obstinate attempts to cure disastrous Activity by still more Activity, Desire by fresh Desire, are as futile as the babblings of those who would make War to end War or cast out devils in the name of Beelzebub.

"By Action men enjoy happiness," says the book called *Great Liberation*, "and by Action again they suffer pain. They are born, they live, and they die slaves of Action ... As a man is bound, be it by a gold or an iron chain, so he is bound by his Action, be it good or evil." It must never be forgotten that the Action referred to is always associated with some degree of Ignorance. Everything can be changed by real Knowledge.

Activity and War have something in common; both are largely remedial in intention. If there is nothing to be set to rights, no livelihood to be gained, no want to be supplied, no loss to be made up, then there can be no incentive towards action, even the most creative and altruistic action. The fiddle that is guaranteed to play eternally in tune, does not require any turning of pegs. Peace or Harmony belongs to Non-activity. The cessation of action will result in peace: but how is such a pacification to be brought to pass? So long as Ignorance is still there, it must remain a dream; there is no cheating the inexorable law inherent in the very nature of things. Ignorance, teeming womb of Desire and Action, supplies the power which keeps the wheels turning, as in a factory where the machinery must never be allowed to stop day or night. All else depends on this: were Ignorance to be interrupted for a second, the Round would automatically come to rest.

The world passeth away and the lust thereof.

We must now return to the examination of the diagram of the Round of Existence. We have already noticed that there are six compartments, corresponding to six groupings or classes of beings. The number is arbitrary: it should really be indefinite, for they merge into one another imperceptibly; the classification is a mere matter of convenience, a symbol. Attention must be drawn to one omission. All the six classes that we are about to name can be termed Animate beings. Ought not inanimate existences such as stones or air to occupy a class also? Logically speaking they should, for no sharp boundary is really admissible; but those who devised this symbolism for popular use, like their colleagues of other faiths, gave most of their attention to those beings that showed affinity with the human, and treated all that was inorganic, and even plants, as so much furniture. Nevertheless, they ought to recognize the omission; though I once had difficulty in persuading a lama to admit that plants were alive in the same way as animals. This slight crudeness is in the iconography, not in the theory. That the more profound thinkers were in no two minds about the essential Oneness of everything, can be proved by a quotation from a Japanese sage who declared that "the very mountains can become Buddha."

The six classes are named respectively:—

1. Gods } higher than man.
2. Non-Gods or Titans
3. Man
4. Animals
5. *Yidags* or tantalized ghosts
6. Tormented beings in the purgatories, } lower than man.
   including devils

Popular belief which, all the world over, tends to a literal interpretation of the external symbol and to an overlooking of the principle symbolized, makes of these six classes so many closed realms, entered by successive individual rebirths. Similarly, it has read into the Universal law of Causality, a law of Retributive Justice and turned those effects which flow from Action as its unavoidable continuation—a fruit inherent in the seed—into so many moral sanctions punishing the wicked, and so many rewards, earned by the merits of the virtuous, on a basis of a strictly kept profit-and-loss account. This is the commonest attitude everywhere; but it need not imply that the symbolism fails in its purpose. As was said before, it is for those who can, to raise themselves to the heights of the Doctrine. Symbolism is the ladder and some may never climb farther than its lowest rungs. But the other rungs are all there, in proper succession, so that the climber may pass, according to capacity, from what is crudely external, through stages where the spiritual is half seen, till he rises to the height where the Doctrine dawns on him in its universal applicability.

For the ordinary man the abode of gods is a delightful kingdom into which suffering does not penetrate and where all wishes—and whims—will be gratified. Thousands pray for rebirth in that sphere and look no farther. They are content to enjoy its pleasures—while they last. As with us, the heavenly scene may be spiritualized or gross, according to each person's mental development; but in any case it is an *individual* enjoyment that is imagined, as in our own popular conceptions of Paradise—that is to say, an enjoyment which is the fruit of Desire and in which Ignorance continues to play its part. Such joys, therefore, contain all the elements that perpetuate the Round, which will, in due course, bring back change and pain.

A word should be said about the use of the name "gods," since it is liable to cause misunderstanding. The gods here referred to are not immortal and self-sufficient deities, but simply beings of an Order higher than ours, possessed of wider powers than man's, such as longevity, unfading beauty, and freedom from pain, except at the last when they are about to cease from being gods and turn into something lower; for then their charms begin to wither and their fragrance turns to stench so foul that their goddess-wives flee from their presence. Having set their minds on nothing but pleasure, and felt no incentive to listen to the Doctrine, their end is a miserable one. When they suddenly become aware of this, it is too late. Confused by the Ignorance which they have done nothing to diminish, they flounder helplessly and fall even into hell. "Many long-lived gods are fools," said a lama to me. One cannot help comparing this with *Paradise Lost*, where Milton makes Lucifer, after his fall, deteriorate by imperceptible degrees from a hero, still endowed with personal beauty, a noble address, and several of the conditional virtues such as courage, until he turns into Satan, repulsive, crafty, wholly evil. These changes are not punishments imposed on him by a sentence of the Divine Judge, so much as self-imposed consequences, fruits of his own wrong-headedness or, as the Buddhist would say, of his own Ignorance.

It would have saved some confusion if we could have called these gods "supermen" or "angels" or some such name. Technically speaking, they should have their full denomination of "Gods of the Round" (to worship whom is idolatry), to distinguish them from true Divinities, those who are free of the Round, Buddhas and high degrees on the road to Buddhahood. In common speech, Tibetans employ the same word *Hla* to denote both kinds, leaving the context to explain itself.

Non-gods are another sort of supermen, more powerful than ourselves, but portrayed as warlike and ambitious, discontented with their many advantages because they envy the superior felicity of the gods. Titans is a good name for them.

Next comes mankind, occupying but a small number of places among the innumerable existences of the Round. Man, though he possesses no privilege over the others, is naturally of special interest to us as men. Likewise a cockroach, in drawing the Round, would doubtless have created a special class for cockroaches, probably including man in one of the other sections.

Man is spoken of as an enviable state, and many are those whose aspirations do not go beyond a hope of rebirth into a world of men. It is claimed that man's life is, on the whole, a fairly happy blend of joy and pain: not enough joy to dull the senses, as is apt to happen to the gods, and not so much pain as to induce perpetual self-pity, as occurs in hell; both fatal distractions from the problem of looking for a way of escape from the Round.

Animals, the fourth class, are creatures for whom the gaining of their daily food is a dominant care, so that they have little leisure to spare for higher things. Their intelligence, too, operates as a rule within a restricted circle. They are objects of pity, because generally they cannot live without preying on one another, a characteristic that they share to some extent with Man. Animal life is therefore counted as the most tolerable among the states called "sorrowful," because the margin for modifying such existence in a favourable sense is necessarily narrow.

Yidags or tantalized ghosts are beings in whom Desire has taken the upper hand. They are pictured as having huge bellies, but pinpoint mouths, so that though their hunger is insatiable, their power of satisfying it is minute. When they drink, the water turns to liquid fire inside them; when they eat, the food swells like undercooked rice and brings on acute colic. Under this imagery, we see a state of Desire so overweening, that every attempt to pander to it only serves to make its pangs more consciously felt. One lama, who was telling me about the *Yidags*, said that sometimes they see a refreshing spring or a table set for a feast and hasten towards them, but, just as they are about to seize the food, guardians appear, harpy-like, before them, armed with swords, spears, bows and arrows and rifles —a delightful modern touch—and drive them back. People often perform a rather touching rite and consecrate some morsel of their own food for the benefit of the poor *Yidags*. A special prayer is said over the offering which is supposed to counteract any painful results.

Lastly come the purgatories, both hot and cold; to call them hell is really a misnomer, because that word, to the Westerner, denotes a hopeless state, without a chance of eventual escape; whereas in the Buddhist view, torments however prolonged, must surely, by a turn of the Wheel, when the effects of their evil causes have played themselves out, give place to some other kind of existence, as surely as the paradise of gods will also be exchanged for a less happy State. Inmates of the purgatories, are not deemed incapable of good impulses, and even devils, that is to say beings who have sunk into a State of utmost malignancy, are able to rise in course of time.

To the eye which troubles to look further than the symbols, all these States are simply corollaries of various sorts of activity. He in whom Desire has become an overmastering passion, sees all things in the light of his desire; for him the World is as *Yidags* see it. To the being who has given way to hatred, all the world is spiteful; what is a pleasure to others becomes his torment, and the whole Universe transforms itself into a hell. Man is a comparatively balanced State, with some surplus energy left, after satisfying physical needs, for paying attention to wiser counsels. But men, in this respect, must again be subdivided; for many are forced to lead lives in which the available surplus of free attention is reduced to a minimum. Their lot must be considered unfortunate beside that of their less enslaved neighbours. Rebirth in the humblest Station in Tibet offers fuller possibilities than life in a factory town of Europe or America, or even life in the manager's office of a great firm. In hell, suffering is so intense as to leave little time for serious thought; only by an exceptional effort can a being rise above the distractions of that dreadful environment. Gods, as we have seen, just because of the evenness of their life, are in danger of being lulled into unawareness, till one day their Stock of merit becomes exhausted and a change for the worse supervenes, an exact reflection of their mental State at the time, so that they may sink as low as hell itself.

So turns and turns the Round of Rebirth and Redeath. Suffering is inseparable from its process, for some of its classes are wedded to suffering by definition, and the others are ever dogged by it, as their cherished happiness ages and fades, as change and death remove from them the objects of their love; friends, possessions, one after another. Even in one's day of health, one knows, beyond question, that deterioration and disease, if nothing worse, are lying in wait.

> All that liveth impaireth fast.

Even the hope permitted to the damned is only a palliative, not a cure. If relief is gained for a time, yet the disease will, of a surety, recur some day. In the Round, real bliss is impossible; to seek it therein is self-deception. Our hope of heaven, the reward for well-doing to be enjoyed by individuals, as it is usually conceived, leads into the paradise of gods, but not to real freedom. The ruler of the Round is disappointment; each of its so-called joys bears within itself the seeds of insecurity, separation and sorrow.

Everyone has, at some time or other, in a moment of extreme well-being, in the contemplation of a sunset over an estuary, or while sitting silently beside a chosen friend, experienced that peculiar pang which is inseparable from intense joy, a drop of gall distilled into its honey. It is as if one were striving to hold up Time, to keep the vision immovable for just one moment; but even in the hour of rapture, in our innermost heart we feel its beauty slipping away, leaving us bereft. It is the pain of "Joy, whose hand is ever at his lips bidding adieu."

This brings us to Suffering, the real starting-point of the Buddha's teaching. The Tibetan books mention two kinds of suffering, to both of which I have alluded already. There is the Pain of the Round, found in the purgatories and the land of *Yidags*, and in the disease and death which afflict animals and men, and there is also the Pain of Happiness, the regrets brought on by change, the turning of youth into old age, of health into infirmity, the separation which brings friendships to their close, the dreariness which succeeds to a joy that is gone over.

SUFFERING is the FIRST of the FOUR TRUTHS or Pointers in which is summed up the message of the Buddha, His invitation to seek something less ineffective than the transient rewards of the Round. Suffering is the beginning of His whole argument, chosen because it is a truth which none could think of denying, which calls for no act of faith, since it is seen and experienced in the world around. The Buddhists make no attempt to explain it away by poetical sophistries, nor to neutralize it by offering compensations in another life. They regard it as inseparable from all states of existence, a thing not to be fled from but to be faced, here and everywhere. But the important thing is to discover the proper means, if such exist. The remedial activities of the Round are clearly inadequate. Buddhism is primarily a war on suffering, not on its symptoms but on its causes. When a disease has to be diagnosed, what must the good physician do first of all? He must find a cause for the symptoms. Till this is done he cannot treat the disease.

What is the cause of suffering? The cause of suffering and the cause of the Round are identical, Ignorance, which leads to ignorant Desire and ignorant Action. Already the SECOND TRUTH or Pointer is discovered. THE CAUSE OF SUFFERING is IGNORANCE.

Ignorance of what? Ignorance of the real nature of things, a mistaken notion of ourselves and our relation to other beings. It is more than an absence of correct belief; it is something entrenched in our nature which must be eliminated and replaced with Knowledge. Mere study is of no avail; there must be realization, bringing about a radical and *irreversible* change in our Being. It is not a question of Faith in certain propositions.

Understanding both the illness and its cause, the doctor reassures his patient: the illness is not incurable. This, incidentally, disposes of the rather silly accusation that Buddhism is "pessimistic," as if such words as optimism and pessimism have any meaning in an investigation of the Truth. As René Guénon has said:—"Truth does not need to be comforting; if some have found it so, so much the better for them." Nevertheless, though there are good grounds for hope, the treatment is not easy and must be carried out by the patient himself, who is apt to be his own worst enemy. The THIRD TRUTH or Pointer is discovered, the CESSATION OF SUFFERING; that is our aim and that aim is possible of achievement.

Now it only remains to find the remedy, that is to say the FOURTH TRUTH, the WAY LEADING TO A CESSATION OF SUFFERING. The Buddha tells us what it is. If Ignorance is the cause of suffering then the opposite, AWARENESS, is the remedy. Ignorance cannot live in the same heart as real Knowledge. Introduce the latter and Ignorance will die. The evil will be cut off at the root. When Ignorance has ceased, ignorant desires no longer can arise, nor the Action loosed by them. When useless activity is stopped, the Wheel is deprived of its motive power and stops turning. Action is no longer needed when once the harmony of Knowledge has been achieved. In real Knowledge there can be no action, because there is nothing to change or to improve. Change and imperfection go hand in hand. Once Enlightenment has been attained, the Wheel of Change comes to rest in Eternity, in which there is no action and no rebirth or death. Action breeds action for ever. Enlightenment breeds Enlightenment for ever.

The Four Truths are the quintessence of the Doctrine: all

else that may be said or written is only a commentary upon them. It is good to reiterate them in order to fix them in the mind:—

1. Suffering   } Diagnosis
2. Cause of Suffering }

3. Cessation of Suffering
4. Way leading to a Cessation of Suffering } Cure

Let us now return to the picture and look at the little circle in the middle of the Round. It contains three animals:—

A pig typifying Ignorance
A cock typifying Desire-Attachment (To define this as Lust alone, as is often done, is to miss the meaning completely.)
A snake typifying Anger

These three, commonly spoken of as the Three Poisons, are the basic evils to which all other evils can be reduced. In reality Ignorance is the only basic vice, for neither of the other two could occur without it. It always accompanies their every manifestation, and one of their results is a renewal of Ignorance. The immense stress laid on the duty of combating Ignorance distinguishes Hindus and Buddhists from Christians. Not that this theory does not also hold good for Christianity; but in practice there has been a great difference of emphasis. Charity, the central Christian virtue, is regarded by the Indian Traditions as the natural consequence of Knowledge. There are comparatively few overt allusions to Knowledge in the Gospels, though the implications are there all the same.

Ignorance is much more than mere lack of information on this or that subject. It includes every kind of sin against the Light, not only false beliefs, but unawareness, loose thinking, woolly-mindedness, obscurantism, and above all, indifference to knowledge, neglect of the duty of trying to be truthful and intelligent; a life organized in such a manner as to produce constant distractions, dishonest stifling of doubts, doubt as to the necessity of seeking knowledge at all, neglect of opportunities of listening to those who have a doctrine to teach, all these things fall within the scope of Ignorance. The pursuit of Truth must not be left to chance. No number of charitable actions can be a substitute for that primary need. So-called altruistic actions, if uninformed, are not quite what they purport to be.

118

In so far as they are founded on false premises, they remain ignorant actions and bring forth some of the fruits of ignorance. You cannot gather figs from thistles. Nor is mere Innocence, due to lack of opportunity rather than to a clear appreciation of the issues, accepted as a sufficient passport to heaven: indeed if it were so, the greatest blessing that one could wish for a human being would be death in infancy, before the child could experience a temptation to sin, and Herod should be acclaimed as the special benefactor of innocent children. Similarly, sincerity of motive, which is so often stressed among us here, is counted as no palliative for wrong action. The evil, in that case, is the expression of the innermost nature of the agent. Evil resides not so much in an act, as in the state of mind that makes the act possible. If the Ignorance of an evil-doer is invincible and he is thereby relieved from doubt, that is a matter for regret, since it holds out little promise of a change for the better. A hesitating sinner, whose conscience is alive, is far preferable to one who is misnamed a sincere, but mistaken, doer.

The second poison, Desire-Attachment, which includes repulsion, is taken in a much more radical sense than mere egotism. An *impulse to individual experience* is the nearest definition I can offer: it has sometimes been expressed by the one terrible word "Thirst." This trait must be taken as appertaining in some degree to all things, though one commonly treats it as if it were only synonymous with conscious volition as found in sentient beings. That is the form in which Desire interests us most directly; but it would be a great mistake to lose sight of its general applicability to the whole of Creation.

If we turn to the special case of Egotism, a sharp cleavage is to be noted between the usual Christian conception and that of the Buddhists. In the former it is taken for an overstressing of one's own importance, an arrogation of rights outside one's just limits, with a consequent invasion of the rights of others. Nowadays it tends to become more narrowly restricted to its social applications. The vice is then regarded as springing from an excess of a supposedly legitimate feeling of individuality. But the Buddhist argues that when we confine our condemnation to the examples cited, we are still treating symptoms only. The roots of Attachment lie deeper still, in the centring of attention in an individual self as such, and in the attribution to it of reality, permanence, and of the rights consequent upon those qualities. Self-denial, for the Buddhist, is literally a denial of self. The separateness which is ascribed to the "ego" is the error. "He is the rogue who playeth every sort of trick," and his Action which, to our eyes, seems like an independent development *in* the Universe, not *of* the Universe, keeps up a false relation of dualism between the self and what lies outside it. So are engendered the concepts "myself and others."

A Tibetan work, the *Powerful Good Wish*, says:—

Immersed in ignorance and obscured by delusion the Knower (Mind) was afeared and confused. Then came the idea "I" and "Other" and hatred. As these gained force a continuous chain of Action (*Karman*) was produced. The Root Ignorance is the abyssal ground of the knower's unconscious Ignorance. The other Ignorance is that which regards self and others to be different and separate. The thought which regards beings as "two," begets a hesitating, doubting state. A subtle feeling of Attachment arises, which if allowed to gain force, gradually resolves itself into strong attachment and a craving for food, clothing, dwellings, wealth and friends . . . There is no end to the Action flowing from ideas of dualism.

This duality is denied both by Hindus and Buddhists; but their expression of the doctrine takes somewhat different forms and has given rise to long discussions. The Buddhists, in particular, never tire of inveighing against the belief that the "myself" constitutes a true or permanent entity. For them the so-called individual is a bundle of activities, joining and dissolving, and passing into other activities. They do not, of course, contradict the obvious fact of some sort of quasi-individual existence within the phenomenal world of the Round. That would be absurd. But they deny its reality, saying that once its components are dissociated, the individuality also ceases to be, since no single one of those components has the right to act as its nucleus or to continue to bear its name. Selfishness is therefore more than an abuse of legitimate rights; it is an ignorant arrogation of reality to the "ego." What *we* call selfish is but a secondary product. So long as a craving for individual enjoyment and individual reward persists, so long is the root of selfishness kept alive, nourished by mistaken notions of "self." The Christian heaven, as popularly conceived, in which "I" is rewarded and preserved in perpetuity, is, according to the Buddhist doctrine, only a temporary state: its beatitude cannot be anything else, for in spite of good acts the root-error is still present, and it offers no more than a provisional salvation.

Many parables have been used to express the Buddhist doctrine of non-individuality. I have taken upon myself to invent my own simile, after the traditional style, which, I think, expresses the idea satisfactorily. The nature of a man or other being may be likened to a river of which the source is undiscovered. Activity is the water. As the river flows along seeking the sea, several tributaries, from tiny brooks to quite big streams, come in to swell its waters. The farmers along its banks have dug irrigation channels and drain some water off and spread it over the land. The Government, under a big inland waterways scheme, has also opened up canals joining the river to other river systems, flowing towards different seas. Part of its course takes it through hot desert, where evaporation is high. In summer the river becomes shallow and broken up into channels. In the rains it swells with the drainage of a huge area. Along its banks stand several modern manufacturing towns, which allow their sewage and all sorts of polluting chemicals to enter the stream. Close to its mouth, it becomes a tidal estuary and the water is brackish. Some of the water of the sea and of the river itself is evaporated and comes down in rain all over the land and into other rivers and lakes, and falls as snow on the mountains where is born the river's unknown parent glacier. The river exists: no one could deny that. Geographers give it a name and draw it on their maps. But which part of the water has the right to say, "I was and still am the river?" It might well be that hardly one drop which actually falls into the sea is identical with any other drop which formed part of the river when it was still a glacier torrent.

The river's existence is undeniable, but the phenomenon of its individuality cannot be called real.

Thirdly comes Anger. Here again we find a slight difference from the common Western notions of anger. When Christ denounced uncharitableness as the deadliest sin, Anger, driven from its first line of defence, entrenched itself behind the question of motive, and assumed a new name under which it hoped to remain unrecognizable. This was Moral Indignation, anger rightly directed, as it is supposed to be, in which case the violence is held to be respectable. The toleration of anger under this disguise has ended by making the Christian teachings of mercy and non-retaliation almost a dead letter; for

E

self-righteous people never fail to find an excuse to justify their resentment against those who, as they say, have not harmed them personally, but have injured other people, whom it is their duty to protect. It is considered unnecessary that such giving of protection should be a coldly-thought-out, passionless act, undertaken with a view to serving in the appropriate way the higher interests of both aggressor and victim. On the contrary all the sentiments of hatred, pent up as a result of the Christian veto upon them, have been able to find channels where they are allowed unrestricted scope. The Buddhists never recognized such a compromise. Anger, whatever its motives, remained anger in their eyes. When people showed hatred and violence, as men do everywhere, at least they were not to be allowed a loophole for self-deception. Hatred in a righteous cause should, logically, be regarded as more heinous than that prompted by pure selfishness, of which anger is, after all, but a natural expression. To degrade the service of Righteousness with such a weapon verges on sacrilege. If the judge must chastise, he must be a judge who weighs up all the evidence, and pronounces an unimpassioned sentence according to the law, free from Ignorance. If the reformer feels called on to fight an abuse, he must never forget that the cruelty of the tyrant is as worthy of pity as the groans of his victims. Moral Indignation is the subtlest form of Anger, which should not even be directed against Satan himself, for he too can become an object of compassion. Our hatred for him is the seal of his kingdom upon our foreheads. So long as the hatred of Satan is allowed to be an exception to the general law of Charity, so long will hatred continue to flourish in human hearts. Moreover it is but a step from hating Satan to hating evil-doers. If Satan is considered as a being incapable of redemption, it follows that we ought not to desire his salvation, for it would be contrary to the Divine Order. The Buddhist rejects the idea that any single being is unalterably evil, any more than it can be unalterably good. Good and Evil, belonging as they do to dualistic thinking (though valid at their own level), must alike be transcended before one can begin to speak of Knowledge in the absolute sense.

While I was writing these pages, an acquaintance with whom I had been discussing the alarms of the political situation in Europe, made the remark, half approvingly—so I thought—and half doubtfully:—"I see you take a very detached view of it all, as if you stood outside. But does that not prevent you from getting anything done? Can we really avoid attaching ourselves to a cause, or a party, and putting our enthusiasm into it, shutting our eyes to everything but the main issue?" There seems no valid reason why the detached person, the philosopher in the primitive sense of "lover of wisdom," should be any less capable of effective action than his more passionate neighbour. On the contrary, in so far as with him opinions are opinions, that is, based on all ascertainable evidence, and judgments are judgments, that is, formed after hearing both sides without prejudice, so also this same philosopher's action ought to be intelligent action, not a mixed bag of elements germane to his purpose, together with many irrelevant factors thrown in. The demands of this impartial approach to life are too exacting for it to make an instantaneous appeal. The plausible security of a label is dear to the slothful, whose passionate loyalties often mask an innate passivity of outlook. In any case, one must remember that visible results count for comparatively little. The fruits of Action cannot escape ripening somewhere, sometime. There are no such things as fruitless actions; though they may be temporarily lost from sight, they will be stored in the aggregate of Cosmic Activity, and will, beyond all question, become Causes in their turn. I have mentioned this example, which is my own, and not derived from a lama, to show the sort of way in which the general law of Action applies to a given problem. The partisan way of life exemplifies the action of the Three Poisons better than anything else. The root is Ignorance, evinced in an unwillingness to weigh up a question fairly, and in a readiness to allow the will to conform to a so-called opinion, based on evidence selected by methods which would not be followed by a genuine investigator unswayed by sentiment. Above all, in the anxiety not to weaken one's own devotion to the chosen cause, one becomes *indifferent* to accuracy, even more than a deliberate falsifier of facts. The latter state only follows on the former. Anger is represented by detestation of the opposition; this is true, irrespective of the rightness or wrongness of our cause. But it is Desire-Attachment in this case which incites us, and forms the substance of our loyalties and readiness for self-sacrifice. From a Buddhist point of view the whole business is corrupt through and through. The same ought to hold good no less from a Christian point of view, were it not for the fact that many of the Christian churches have been only too willing to make things easy for those who actually treat Attachment and Indignation-Anger as things worthy of encouragement and who, for the sake of obtaining speedy results, are willing to resort to the demagogue's appeal to Ignorance.

Every poison has its appropriate antidote. For Ignorance the antidote is Knowledge, Just Views, Awareness. For Desire-Attachment the antidote is Non-Attachment, including abandonment of ignorant belief in a permanent individual self. For Anger the antidote is loving-kindness and a consistent refusal to inflict suffering.

Love, Charity or Compassion is the first-fruit of Knowledge. We have seen how, in spite of moments of pleasurable delusion, life in the Round is lamentable. All find themselves in the same quandary, from the most carefree of gods to the most tortured of fiends. No one is favoured; to each one comes his turn. This, logically, makes us all fellows in trouble: there is not one corner of the Universe undeserving of pity. Whoever stops to contemplate the crowds frantically chasing the will-o'-the-wisp of happiness, or falling over one another as they turn and flee from a suffering which they believe to be external to themselves, cannot but be seized with boundless compassion.

"That which makes one weep," said St. Marpa, "is the thought that all creatures could be Buddha, that they know it not and die in suffering . . . If that is what you are weeping about, you should go on ever weeping without pause." So, also, wrote a Chinese sage: "With an understanding of the impermanent nature of all things, devoid of reality in themselves and subject to pain, rises the sun of true wisdom . . . Go on with hearts overflowing with compassion; in this world that is rent by suffering, be instructors and wherever the darkness of Ignorance may happen to reign, kindle there a torch."

There is a close connexion between the idea of Compassion and the teaching on the subject of "self-naughting." Mila Repa expounds this truth in three lines of one of his poems:

The notion of emptiness (absence of real self) engenders Compassion,
Compassion does away with the distinction between "self and other,"
The indistinction of self and other renders the service of others effective.

124

His sequence of thought is not immediately apparent and requires elaboration. His meaning is that once a being is aware of the impermanence of individuality, he is brought to the recognition of his one-ness with all things which before had falsely appeared to be external to himself. Their sufferings become his sufferings; their liberation becomes identified with his own; His service to others is no longer one-sided generosity, for the distinction between giver and receiver is no more. The Buddhist Tradition denies to "the Ego" any vestige of permanence, and refuses to recognize the real existence of a central thread of individuality on which the various qualities of body and mind are strung like beads. It declares repeatedly that the so-called individual soul is but an aggregate, temporary, changing and devoid of firm foundation, a play of forces derived from heredity, environment and a thousand other influences, as well as from the effects of its own actions, good and evil.

The aim of the intelligent life is therefore to reach complete Non-Attachment to self, the state which implies final abandonment of the partisan attitude towards life's happenings. The enlightened being perceives that he cannot monopolize the credit for his own acts of charity, because no act is entirely one person's doing, all beings having a share in the causes and consequences of every act. Everyone must likewise accept some responsibility even for the murderer's knife.

One who has realized his complete one-ness with all creation, and who has thereby become an initiate of the supreme Doctrine of Non-Duality, is called a Bodhisat, of whom Jesus might almost serve as an example, since He claimed no merit for Himself but suffered all sorrow, knowing that whatsoever belongs to one already belongs perforce to all others too.

An equable loving-kindness is the only reasonable outcome of the doctrine of the Round; it can accept no limits short of the entire Universe. To preferences and aversions, which are really nothing else than extensions of a false belief about self, it cannot stoop.

Now let us suppose that we have been successful in substituting the antidotes for the poisons and that Just Views have replaced Ignorance in our make-up. Being set free from our fictitious individuality, with its fixed idea of dualism, we are no longer forced to act as a cog in the Wheel of Existence. The Round ceases for us: we are Delivered or Enlightened. That is the state called Nirvana, which translated literally, means "Extinction." The word has given rise to a number of foolish interpretations—outside the countries of its origin—by which the Buddhist is accused of seeking mere nothingness, annihilation. The perpetrators of this error let themselves be deceived by the word "Existence" and its associations *for them*. What ceases to exist, so they argue—because for them existence and reality are associated—must be reduced to Nothingness. The Buddhist understands it in quite another way; for, in his eyes, it is the Existence of the Round which is the illusion, the veil over the face of the Real. Enlightenment is nothing to *us*, for it is the beginning of Reality, something utterly foreign to our present limitations. It is a waste of time trying to imagine that state; for whatever we think or say must perforce be taken out of our own experience of the world of phenomena. "When you will have understood the dissolution of all compounds," says the *Dhammapada*, "You will understand that which is uncompounded." At present one can only say of Nirvana what the Hindus say of Brahma, the Infinite; "Not this, not this."

The word Nirvana means extinction, something like the action of the fingers in snuffing out the flame of a candle. That which is extinguished is Ignorance and its train of consequences. A double negative—the extinction or annulment of Knowledgelessness—is our only way of faintly suggesting its positive reality. What Buddhahood, the state of having found Enlightenment, is, we simply cannot say. He who attains it, knows it. He who has not attained it can only speculate in terms of his own relativity, which do not apply to it. To be Buddha is not just one more degree in the series which we know, like an ascent to a higher existence within the Round. There is complete discontinuity between that state and the Circle of Existence, a great gulf fixed, that can only be crossed at a single leap.

To return for a moment to the diagram. We have still to mention the border, containing twelve little scenes, which runs round the outer rim of the circle. These scenes explain, in more detailed form, the process of rebirth under the influence of Ignorance. They are known as the "Twelve Interdependent Origins" and must be studied by anyone who wishes to enter deeply into the doctrine; but as they are really an amplification of the basic concept Ignorance—Desire—Action, it is unnecessary to analyse them here. They express, in more precise terms, ideas which we have already considered under those headings.

The remedy for Ignorance is Knowledge or Awareness. It goes without saying that by Knowledge is meant something more than ordinary discursive knowledge. Liberation is not to be compassed by attending courses at the University or by reading up manuals of philosophy. Rational knowledge makes its own useful contribution in helping to clear the ground of minor delusions; but Knowledge, the transcendent virtue by divine right, stands above Reason. It is the fruit of a direct intuitive experience, which is not so much a thing acquired by accretion, rather it is a thing which is already there from the moment that the obstacles to its realization have ceased to be. The effort of the seeker after this Real Knowledge is all along directed to the elimination of hindrances, to *allowing* the Knowledge to arise spontaneously, as it will do, the instant the necessary *undoing* has been effected. The presence of Knowledge is reflected in a radical alteration of the entire nature of a being; to know is to be, there is no other way.

Sound Method is inseparable from Wisdom. The Tibetans speak of these two as husband and wife, making Method into the male and Wisdom into the female aspect. They are symbolized, respectively, by the thunderbolt sceptre or *Dorjé* and the Hand-bell or *Ḍilbu*. These emblems appear everywhere. In pictures they will be seen wielded by the hands of Divinities and every lama possesses a pair for use in the temple rites and at his own altar. His prescribed movements, as he turns them about, represent the eternal dalliance of Wisdom and Method; even to think of divorcing them is to court disaster. "Just as one desirous of reaching a certain city requires the eyes for seeing and the feet for traversing the way, so doth one desirous of reaching the city of Nirvana require the eyes of Wisdom and the feet of Method." Method itself is sometimes made synonymous with Universal Love or Compassion.

The Buddha in one of His early sermons, explained the Method by which Wisdom was to be gained and suffering destroyed, under eight headings, known as the PATH WITH EIGHT BRANCHES. It is often compared in its scope with Our Lord's Sermon on the Mount. It therefore corresponds to the last of the Four Truths, the Way that leads to the extinction of suffering. The Eightfold Path is the Buddhist's programme of life, and comprises:—

Perfect Vision ⎱
Perfect Will ⎰ relating to spiritual direction

Perfect Speech
Perfect Action ⎫
Perfect Means of Livelihood ⎬ relating to fitting and
Perfect Effort ⎭ intelligent conduct

Perfect Attention or Awareness ⎱ relating to one-pointed
Perfect Meditation ⎰ concentration

It may at first appear strange that a method of which the
avowed aim is the acquisition of Awareness, should place Perfect Vision as the first item on its list, for by so doing it seems
to beg the question somewhat. Though Awareness, in a sense,
must be regarded as the end, from another point of view it is
also the starting-point, since were there not some measure of
Awareness at the outset, where would be the incentive to
embark on the Eightfold Path at all? An earliest vision tells us
that it is both possible and useful to seek the Way. As the
various virtues of the Path are perfected, so do inferior visions
give place to higher ones, of more universal applicability, leading at the last to Truth, the Changeless Knowledge of the Real
and the Infinite.

Similarly, the four branches of the Path concerned with conduct are both a result and a cause of Awareness. As we learn
to define our relation towards ourselves, our neighbours, all
creatures and the entire world more and more accurately,
so our conduct becomes more appropriate and enlightened.
The fruit of fitting conduct is an increase in Awareness, in
Realism.

Some degree of Awareness is therefore indispensable from
start to finish. If our actions or thoughts are to have the
slightest value, they must be fully responsible actions or
thoughts, designed and carried out for ends and by methods
which harmonize with the facts of the world and with the
relations which unite all beings, as far as it lies in our power
to ascertain them. Our actions and thoughts are the products of
our whole nature at a given moment, and become the causes of
its further development for good or ill. A nature which is still
mainly emotional, and not brought under proper control by the
intellect, is a weathercock turned by every impulse. In such
a condition of irresponsibility, even if an action happens to be
right, it is largely an accident; for, not being based upon

128

relevant motives, it is properly little better than a foolish action in masquerade. It must be one's constant aim to withdraw as much of life as possible from the power of outside influences and accidents and to bring it into subjection to one's informed will, so that each act may be exactly what it purports to be, no more and no less, each perception a genuine perception uninfluenced by anything irrelevant, each decision a judgment reached after due consideration of all accessible evidence.

It is as a means towards heightened control that the great Teachers so strongly recommend certain disciplines, aiming at bringing movements which are normally reflex under the partial rule of conscious volition. To turn matters of habit into deliberately controlled operations is considered highly beneficial. Conversely, the cultivation of an automatic response to external stimuli, by expedients such as marching in step or shouting slogans, the stock-in-trade of modern European organization, must, Buddhistically speaking, be reprobated as a disastrous abuse, leading to greater and greater irresponsibility and enslavement.

Attention and Meditation, the two last branches of the Path, are concerned with the cultivation of calmness and harmony of soul, the attuning of the whole being to the Word, the promotion of a state of perfect receptivity. Like a rippleless tarn in which the snows are seen so distinctly reflected that one forgets which is solid mountain and which the image, so is Meditation, the solvent of distinctions and the gate of the Real. It is an experience which the average person ignores; yet without it and its resultant mastery over self, Illumination cannot be achieved. A state of agitation always fosters Ignorance; therefore all the sages of the Orient counsel the cultivation of the habit of calm, unruffled meditation. In the highest degree, Meditation is the mark of the saint, the serenity which nothing can disturb, not even in the middle of the Round's eddy.

Concerning the branches of the Eightfold Path that deal with conduct, little need be said. Right speech, Right Action and Right Effort are indistinguishable from the same virtues as taught by Christ. Selfless Love and all it implies, Mercy and Non-retaliation for injuries, Gentleness, Reverence, in all these there is nothing to choose between the teaching of the Buddha and the Gospel. So striking is the similarity, that one lama gave it as his opinion that Christianity was simply an aberrant branch of Buddhism.

129

Right means of Livelihood deserves a word of its own, for though it is just as implicit in the Christian revelation as in any other, it is apt to be overlooked, and it has been especially disregarded by those subscribers to Puritanical tenets who played so prominent a part in the development of big business. According to the Eightfold Path, it is not enough that one's personal conduct should be apparently blameless, one must look further, lest one may be deriving sustenance from some practice inconsistent with the law of Mercy or Truth, from some brutality or exploitation of fellow-men or animals, or from some organization which is tending to hinder Knowledge and favour the growth of Ignorance. A Buddhist may not be a trafficker in lives, that is to say a slave-dealer or a butcher; worse than the actual killing is the failure to realize that animals are alive and sensitive—the unawareness is as bad as the cruelty. The calf led to the slaughter is not to be shorn of its pitifulness by allowing one's sensibility to seek shelter behind that handy word "veal." Neither may a man live by selling drugs (save for medical use), nor may he be an arms-manufacturer. Living in modern times, he should look to his investments lest he be the unwitting accomplice of commercial exploitation of the weak. It is obvious that a Christian ought to investigate the sources of his income with no less scrutiny, but on the whole this duty has been understressed.

We have now covered most of the ground. For the sake of completeness, mention ought to be made of one more detail in the picture of the Round, the fearsome monster who clutches the entire Circle of Existence in his teeth and talons. He is Shindjé, judge of the dead; in his horrible visage we see the true nature of the Round unmasked, and in his domination over the whole scene, we recognize the inexorable character of the Law of Causation, with which the Round itself is cognate. Shindjé must not be taken for a minister of retributive Justice. He does not dispense penalties in the name of offended Deity, nor do the consequences that accrue from good or foolish actions depend on his private pleasure. Neither gifts nor charms can buy his indulgence.

> I set no store by gold, silver, nor riches
> Nor by pope, emperor, king, duke, nor princes
> For if I would receive gifts great,
> All the world I might get;
> All my custom is clean contrary.

Shindjé's sole office is to operate the mechanism of cause and effect, in faithful obedience to its rules. "Every effect proceeds from a cause." The whole implication of this law is that every act will bring about an appropriate modification in the Universe, which nothing can hinder. Other actions may change its direction, neutralize it or transform it; but an effect as such can by no means be wiped out. Joy and pain are simply effects of causes, needing no bestowal of grace or word of condemnation from outside to produce them. They are symptoms of the state of a given being at a given moment. The present condition of the whole Universe, viewed as one, is what it is, because, with the history of causes and effects as they have been until now, it cannot but be otherwise than what it is.

In Buddhist countries, as elsewhere, the majority refuse to give up the simple idea of poetic justice. They measure merit as one might weigh potatoes; so many good acts against so much happiness, so many sins against such and such penalties. All those who, in spite of anything they may profess in theory, still show their belief in their own self-sufficient ego naturally continue to hanker after the delusions of individual enjoyment and advantage, in the form of happy rebirths. I remember one lama who told me that he did not feel equal to an immediate effort in the direction of Buddhahood, but he was at least making sure, by a nice balance of his acts, that he would earn rebirth as a man again, so as not to lose his coign of vantage for further progress later. He confessed that he was an inveterate meat-eater—the Tibetans are not given to making hypocritical excuses—but as a counterblast he was as uncompromising a teetotaller as ever came out of Wales. For my friend, the future life resolved itself simply into a matter of efficient book-keeping. Unfortunately for his naïve schemes, he left out of account the besetting sin of Ignorance, which accompanied his well-planned acts of merit. He was a very kind and pleasant man, well above average, yet he will be lucky, figuratively speaking, if he does not obtain rebirth among the *Yidags*. There are thousands more like him, who are still missing the crucial point. Like all of us, they get what they really desire and expect, not what they profess to ask for—therein lies all the difference! " Knock and it shall be opened unto you: seek and ye shall find." That is a profound truth: but much also depends upon which door one knocks at, and for which gifts one asks.

Some may be surprised that in all this lengthy discussion there has been no direct allusion to God. We have had a whole chapter on doctrine without so much as mentioning His name. Is it correct to say, as some have liked to do, that Buddhism is "atheistical," and that it precludes the belief in a Personal Deity? This is a question which loses its substance once it has been realized that Personality already implies some degree of limitation: every specification must always be clearly distinguished from the unspecifiable Infinite. So long as it is accepted that Personality occupies a lesser degree of universality than the Infinite, the Supreme Principle of All—there is no objection to admitting it as one among possible determinations. The enemy to be shunned at all costs is a permanently dualistic conception, an immutable persistence of pairs of contraries that refuse ultimately to be resolved in the unity of a Principle dwelling beyond their distinction. The Hindus, whose metaphysical language resembles that of the Lamas, have separate names for the Infinite (Brahma—neuter form), the Supreme Principle of Being (Brahmā—masculine form) and Īshwara, the Personified Creative Function. Christian theology applies the name of God now to one, now to the other, now to all three together, which is slightly confusing. The Hindu terminology could be valid for a Buddhist too, if need were, though, as far as I am aware, it has not actually been used in this way.

The just word on the Buddhist position with regard to God has been spoken by René Guénon who, more than any other European, is qualified for the office of interpreter of the traditional doctrines:—

"In reality, Buddhism is no more 'atheistical' than it is 'theistic' or 'pantheistic'; all that need be said is that it does not place itself at the point of view where these various terms have any meaning."

THE HERMIT AND THE PILGRIM

SPRING had given way to full summer when we got back to Lachhen and the wealthier of the inhabitants, who, like all Tibetans, dislike damp heat, were talking of moving to cooler levels up the valley, away from the heaviest rains. The abbot had already withdrawn to T'hangu (13,000 feet), to a hermitage dependent on his monastery. As we were anxious to spend some time in his society, we prepared to follow him there, but thought it wiser to let him know beforehand, lest he should be entering into one of his periods of seclusion. Meanwhile we camped, in order to save bungalow charges.

Caravans from Kampa Dzong kept coming through the village, laden with wool and barley flour to be exchanged lower down for rice. We stopped them from time to time and asked if they had any rugs for sale. These Tibetan rugs, coarsely knotted on a woollen warp and dyed in sound vegetable colours, fetch very low prices. The patterns are usually variants of one design, consisting of a central field containing one or three circles more or less decorated, with a key-pattern round the border; the style shows unmistakable Chinese influence. The art of making them is common knowledge in Tibet; happy is the artistic condition of a country where such rugs represent the low-water mark of material and craftsmanship, within reach even of the poorest.

The headman of Lachhen, who had all along been attentive to our comfort, kindly lent us one of his house servants, a young man from Shigatze, named T'hargya, to accompany us up to T'hangu. He was an unusually intelligent and sensitive youth, and after we had employed him for a few days, we were anxious to retain his services, so we did our best to persuade his master to release him. But he knew T'hargya's value too well and would not yield him up, though he promised to lend him for a future journey if still in his service.

The system of hiring such domestics is a kind of indenture.

The servant contracts to stay three years. No regular salary is paid; but he is clothed, fed, housed and given occasional pocket money. In many respects he is treated like one of the family; we noticed that a respectful address towards his employer did not affect T'hargya's ease of manner, free from all servility. When the term of service expires, the employee is given a present in money, or possibly in kind. We found the same system working in Ladak, in the houses of the Lhasa merchants who lived round Leh.

Going up towards T'hangu, the scenery is not specially striking. After a few miles, altitude begins to affect the denseness of the forests; yet here, where trees should be prized, denudation is going on apace, due to the habit of clearing new acres by fire in order to sow corn. We passed wide tracts where all the big trees stood leafless, mere blackened skeletons, surrounded by bare soil or low scrub of recent growth. The destruction seems to go on recklessly and it would be worth some attempt at regulation by the State Forestry department.

Close to T'hangu big trees give place to vegetation similar to that found near the snout of the Zemu glacier. The prevalent flowering plants are dwarf rhododendrons of several kinds, purple or white, and primulas, either small mauve, large dark purple, or, in boggy places, yellow ones like cowslips. Blue poppies are also common. T'hangu is not a village; there is only the pretty hermitage, a big cottage surrounded by a circle of prayer-flags, on a grassy knoll, and under it an eyesore of an ugly, ill-constructed rest-house. In June the surrounding hills are clear of snow; the weather was unceasingly damp, with a raw Scottish mist.

There was local excitement at the time because of the completion of a new *Mani* wall near the road, neatly built of masonry and cement, with the sacred inscriptions incised on flat stones embedded in the wall. The letters were left white on a ground made red with a kind of clay. The builders were two pilgrims who spent their time going from place to place erecting these walls; but the carving was done by a local man. The moment for consecrating the *Mani* wall had arrived and the headman of Lachhen and several monks and peasants assembled for the ceremony. A large tent with red flounces was pitched, housing a brazier, a table and a seat for the abbot. We introduced ourselves to the pilgrims, who were standing by, surveying their handiwork. One of them was a thick-set man of powerful build, with a merry, open face over which laughter was continually rippling. He was a childlike soul, delighted with the smallest things and radiating a transparent benevolence towards all. His home lay north-west of Lhasa, so he told us, and he had not seen it for twelve years, having spent all his time in pilgrimages to the most remote parts. With delight he recounted the wonders of the Holy Seat (Buddh Gaya in Bihar) where, at the foot of the Bodhi tree, the Teacher sat to receive His Enlightenment. The pilgrim was planning to visit it again, for the third time—but not before winter: for the plains of India are insufferably hot at other seasons. Five years ago, during his travels, he had met his present companion, a monk from the land of Kham, far away to the east on the China border. The latter was not so prepossessing as his friend. He was rough-looking and ragged. But on closer acquaintance we decided that his gruff voice and unkempt appearance did him an injustice. He was a decent, straightforward fellow.

Among the young lamas who had come up from Lachhen for the service there was one called Samdub to whom we felt attracted from the moment we set eyes on him. His features were fine and regular and his expression suggested the youthful saint, for a look of rapture never quite left his face. He greeted us like old friends; it is curious how many people one met with whom the tedious processes of introduction could be curtailed. Social intercourse is undoubtedly made much easier by the absence of servile manners in any class, and by the traditional forms of politeness which, once they have been complied with, indicate exactly where each man stands.

When the stage had been set for the consecration, we looked up towards the hermitage and seemed to see Chaucer's Canterbury Pilgrims approaching in procession. Our old friend the abbot, in full pontificals and wearing a mitre, was riding, not on a palfrey, but on a sturdy mule better fitted to bear the weight of his portly figure. A leopard-skin was thrown over the saddle and a young monk led the animal, while Samdub and others, armed with drums, sacred vessels and lighted tapers of incense, acted as acolytes. The dedication was long and complicated. Towards the end the abbot issued from his tent, scattered rice on the wall, and offered small conical cakes, after which the procession circled round the *mendong* several times, clockwise.

Mani walls are a typical feature of the Tibetan landscape.

The one at T'hangu was an insignificant affair compared to the vast erections that mark the approaches to villages or monasteries in Tibet proper and Ladak; but it differed from them only in length, and there is still time for it to grow, as offerings of additional inscribed stones by the faithful gradually extend it. The *Mani* wall or *mendong* consists of a cement base on which flat stones are laid, each with its sacred text, of which by far the commonest is the formula *Om mani padme hum.*

The origin of the *Mani* formula is attributed to the "All-Merciful Good Shepherd" Chenrezig, the personage who manifests himself in the Dalai Lama, and who revealed it for the profit of creatures, much as Our Lady revealed the Rosary to St. Dominic. In India, and in Tibet, where religious thought was moulded under Indian influence, a whole science of *Mantra* or Significant Sound is recognized which, in the same way as visual works of art, gestures and other rites of all sorts, helps to create "supports" or "props" for the reverence, attention and meditation of the worshippers. Of all *Mantras*, the *Mani* phrase is the favourite, and figures not only on the innumerable *Mani* walls leading into and out of every town, village, or monastery in Tibet, but also on many of the prayer-flags, and inside prayer-wheels great or small, operated by hand or turned by wind or water power. Thus every person travelling in Tibet is continually in touch with the idea, bathed in its influence, whether he responds consciously or not. The whole country, from end to end, is pervaded with a devotional atmosphere; only the wilfully blind can altogether avoid responding to it, while wandering across the austere landscape of the sacred tableland.

The precise meaning of the *Mani* words has given rise to much discussion: I should by rights have said meanings, for it is a characteristic of traditional ritual sentences to bear several senses simultaneously, some literal and some figurative; a whole tissue of ideas is woven into them, which can be teased out one after the other, till the most far-reaching principles become exposed.

The literal translation of the formula is "*Om*, the jewel in the lotus, *Hum!*" In a general way it may be described as an act of assent to the divine aim. *Om* (derived from the Sanskrit *aum*) stands for Brahma, "the one without second" or "the inexpressible Absolute." As one writer has put it, "*Om* is the ultimate word which can be uttered, after which there remains nothing but silence." In it, therefore, are summed up prayer and praise and worship. *Om* is also the sound of all sounds, audible to the initiated ear, which is produced by the act of Manifestation or, as we would say, of Creation, which produces and nourishes this and other Universes. It might also be compared with Pythagoras's music of the Spheres.

Mani means "jewel"; therefore a precious thing, the Doctrine. *Padme* means "in the lotus"; it may refer to the world which enshrines the doctrine of Buddha (the jewel), or to the spirit in whose depths he who knows how to take soundings, will discover Knowledge, Reality and Liberation, these three being really one and the same thing under different names. Or possibly the lotus, the usual throne of divinities and saints, is simply attached as a divine attribute to the gem of doctrine. *Hum* is an ejaculation denoting defiance. Its utterer hurls a challenge, as it were, at the enemy, at the passions, such as lust, hatred and stupidity, the poisons which drug beings into submitting to the tyranny of the Round of Existence. Or, viewed in yet another way, the adversary is no other than the cherished belief in an indissoluble "myself," and the desire for individual recompense.

But these explanations are elementary, a mere prelude to the secrets that await discovery by the initiate in the *Mani Mantra*. Even the shapes of the letters that compose it can be visualized, and made to correspond to ideas for the mind's eye to fix on. There is no end to the truths that a competent teacher can extract from this one phrase.

A seventh syllable is sometimes appended to the classical six, the word *Hri*. It is said to signify, in the sacred language, the underlying reality hidden behind phenomena, the Absolute veiled by Form. It is therefore, in a way, a quintessence of the whole preceding six syllables.

It must not be imagined that I am claiming that every Tibetan peasant who passes a *Mani* on the left, or tells the beads of his rosary, nor every lama who casually walks along the temple courtyard turning the prayer-wheels, is conscious of all these meanings, any more than every Catholic who says "Hail Mary" is always conscious of its connection with the doctrine of the Incarnation. There is every degree possible between a vaguely reverent feeling (as when taking off one's hat on entering a church) and a profound awakening of consciousness by the full and right use of the words as an instrument of association with metaphysical ideas.

I have gone into this example rather fully, in an endeavour to help readers to grasp the theory of "supports" for meditation, on which both ritual and art depend. Even the involuntary act of breathing can be turned into a contemplative discipline. The sounds of intaking and outgoing breath are then evoked as a *mantra*, and serve to symbolize the alternating rhythm of the manifestation and resorption of Universes. The end and aim of both Tibetan and Hindu teaching is to emancipate the being from the separatist illusions of individuality, and to raise it eventually to an effective and irreversible realization of the non-dual character of all things, something higher even than Unity. Anything whatsoever, a word, a stone, an image, can be the starting-point of the chain of ideas. From any single point in the Universe the whole remainder can be integrated. Tradition concerns itself with the two indispensables, wisdom and method; if it propounds a doctrine, it must also teach the art by which we can raise ourselves to its comprehension.

Our time at T'hangu alternated between visits to the abbot in his hermitage and to the pilgrims, who had found a comfortable, dry lodging in a cave under a huge boulder that stood in the midst of the valley. Once our friend came to feed with us in camp. He was a most lovable person, childlike, affectionate and unworried, and obviously engaged in carrying out literally the Gospel precept, "Take no thought for your life, what ye shall eat; neither for the body, what ye shall put on."

The conversation in his cave made the hours slip by unnoticed. One day, after describing different countries through which he had travelled, the pilgrim said: "Are there many goats in England? And sheep? And if I turn up one day at your home will you take me in?" I assured him that it would be an honour. As to animals, there were plenty of sheep but few goats: cows were used for milking. "Oh, cows, how lovely, you have lots of cows?" The thought made him chuckle with pleasure. "Then you will receive me if I come to your house?" After that, he inquired about my family and I explained that my mother was nearly eighty. "Did you say that your mother is one hundred and eight?" cried the pilgrim, in great excitement. He turned to his companion. "Our friend says his mother is one hundred and eight years old!" (This is a sacred number in Tibet: the beads of a rosary are so

138

numbered and a hundred and eight Buddhas are often found drawn on a single scroll picture. To reach that age is considered exceptionally lucky, a mark of divine favour.)

He showed us his possessions, which, besides clothes, blankets, food, teapot and cups, included a small library of books wrapped in silk and a set of drawings of Lamas and Divinities, the size of playing cards. The whole together must have added up to a weighty load for carrying across mountain passes, but his physique was equal to anything.

His friend related to us stories of border warfare with the Chinese, about 1906 and after. Many of his relations had lost their homes, and even their lives, in the disturbances. The Khambas are the most warlike as well as the handsomest of the Tibetan races and are noted for their raiding propensities, their victims being usually the caravans of wealthy merchants trading between China and Lhasa. Kham seems from all accounts to be a romantic country of seers and brigands, artists and armourers, hermits and Homeric heroes. The Chinese in these campaigns were not provided with artillery and the walled enclosures of the lamaseries were turned into fortresses which had to be invested in true medieval style. There were several epic sieges, in which the defenders performed prodigies of endurance and heroism. No quarter was given to the vanquished and both the Khamba irregulars and the Chinese forces inflicted terrible atrocities upon their unfortunate prisoners. Some of the tales are almost past belief; but there is not the slightest doubt about their accuracy, for they have been recorded by the eminent French scholar and traveller, Professor Bacot, who passed through some of the subjugated country not long after.

It is a relief to turn from these horrors to the reports of Sir Eric Teichman, a British official who mediated between the Chinese and the Tibetans and helped to conclude a peace. The Tibetan regular forces, which took part in the final phase of the struggle in 1918, were commanded by a churchman, the Kalon Lama, who rode to the wars like the old mace-bearing bishops. Sir Eric pays a tribute to the humane treatment of prisoners by order of the clerical general, and the absence of reprisals. The cruelties had been the work of irregulars, desperately defending their homes. The Lhasa regulars, obedient to the instructions of their commander, seem on that occasion to have shown an exemplary restraint.

In their departure our friends the pilgrims were true to their character. They said no good-byes, but disappeared one morning early from the cave, leaving no trace except some clay models of *tormas* (conical votive cakes) in a niche in the rock, a thank-offering to the daemon of the place. Our friendship with them was a great experience. From the moment we met, it was as if we had known each other all our lives. Should we ever meet again, it will be as if we had parted but yesterday. We never asked their names nor they ours (no one thought of it); it is, perhaps, more fitting so.

The pilgrims' simplicity cloaked no emptiness. Of such is the Kingdom of Heaven—at last we had actually met and recognized the prototype of the Gospel description.

Our time at T'hangu, apart from brief walks, was spent in the society of the pilgrim and the abbot. Nothing could have provided a greater contrast than these two men. The pilgrim stood at the pole of childlike and unsolicitous trustfulness, while the abbot occupied the opposite pole of extreme intellectuality and knowledge of the world—acquired, however, largely by withdrawing from the world and watching it from without. He had the urbanity, tempered with a dash of satire, that distinguishes the true man of culture everywhere. In the pilgrim we discerned the free spirit that never would grow up. Power meant nothing to him; he neither aspired to wield it nor stooped to worship it, he just ignored it. In this trait he and the hermit met on common ground; for the latter, though possessed of powers both temporal and psychic which brought with them a right to the service and obedience of others as a matter of course, yet set no store by such power because, by a ruthless stripping of all romance and sentimentality from life, he had learned to know it and the sensations which it brings for hollow things. Thus both the men, otherwise so different, conformed in their own ways to the Buddhist ideal of unattachment, towards which they had travelled by routes that suited their respective natures. Both of them were founded upon the rock of the same idea, the illusory character of the phenomenal world and of their own egos; but the one knew it instinctively and revealed it by his attitude towards the quite simple problems of daily life, while the prelate had the added power of being able to define his ideas for the benefit of others. He was a born teacher, a Lama in the technical sense of the word.

Once, at a later date, I made the half-joking remark that

"the Lachhen Lama is one of those who are said by the Tibetans to have passed to the stage beyond good and evil." I had inadvertently happened on the truth; for, after we returned home to England, I read in a travel book by the Marquis of Zetland, then Lord Ronaldshay, of how he had been told by the same abbot of Lachhen himself that he had reached a degree of realization where pairs of distinctions lose their meaning, even that of evil and good.

He who shall have mastered this doctrine will be freed from sin, and also from virtue.

This condition, recognized by all traditions, amounts to a reintegration in the state of Adam before he had tasted of the fruit of the dualistic tree. Certainly, I have never met anyone who so impressed me "as one having authority, and not as the Scribes." During daily interviews with him I felt my attention captured beyond any chance of straying. His room at T'hangu was similar to the one at Lachhen monastery. A softened light entered by the window. There was an altar on which glowed a single copper lamp; over it hung a truncated cone of paper, similar to a lampshade, inscribed with texts and tilted at a slight angle, so that the hot air in rising caused it to revolve gently. There were, besides, a few small tables with books, his finely chased teacup and an ancient painted scroll of some deity under his "fearsome" aspect. A rug was laid for guests to sit on; and a young monk, who was charged with the abbot's personal service, kept up continual relays of cups of tea and rusks of puffed rice.

There we conversed by the hour. The abbot's speech was slow, but not devoid of a humorous turn. A wide range of subjects was touched on and it seemed to me that he was turning over some plan in his mind which concerned me; but perhaps I only imagined this.

One day he suddenly asked: "Why did you go up to the Zemu and try to climb snow mountains? I would know your true purpose." A difficult question to deal with on the spur of the moment: to such a man the usual humbug about finding it good for one's health or character, or that one was pursuing some pseudo-scientific object, would have been an insult to his intelligence. His piercing glance was like Ithuriel's spear, compelling truthfulness. So I made a lame answer: "We love to go to wild places for their solitude, to avoid the bustle of town life." "You will never find it thus," he replied. "You have no idea how to seek it. It cannot be won by such methods. It will not be obtained nor acquired nor gained nor procured nor encompassed." (I have tried to give an impressionistic rendering of his words in Tibetan.) "The solitude to seek is the concentration of your own heart; if you have once found it, it will not matter where you are." Perhaps he was thinking of his own spiritual ancestor who said, "For him who hath realized Reality it is the same whether he dwell on an isolated hill-top in solitude or wanders hither and thither." Then placing a tiny image of the Buddha on the table, he said, "Learn to fix your thoughts on this, and then you may know solitude, but not otherwise." "But surely, my lord abbot, the great saint Mila Repa himself has sung the praises of mountain and wilderness, and recommended them to those who wish to master the art of solitude. He who aspired to Buddhahood within the span of a single life found that the undistracted atmosphere of mountains offered the best setting in which to woo the solitary spirit. Does he not introduce many of his poems with the couplet:—

Obeisance at the feet of Marpa the Translator
May he grant me strength to persevere in my mountain retreat?

I myself am weak and cannot easily learn even the elements of this art in the middle of crowds. If Mila Repa found it helpful, can we be blamed for wishing to escape from the turmoil sometimes?"

I felt I had just kept my end up—not that I am presuming to compare the love of solitude as the mountaineer knows it, with the retreats of a Mila Repa, or of the abbot himself either. Such a comparison would be blasphemy or pure romance. Yet in the mountaineer's conviction that there is a fulness of life to be found in the lonely places, which is lost in the hurry and noise of the world, he can claim to have more in common with the contemplative ideal than with the uneasy ambitions of the man about town.

It was now my turn to question. "Tell me truly, can anything be learned about solitude without a teacher?" "It cannot." "So it seems that a study of the sacred books by oneself won't reveal the way to it?" "It will not reveal it." "Is that, then, your final word? The first thing of all, for him who would enter on the Path, is to find a teacher?" "A teacher is essential; without him you will get nowhere, for you will not learn to fix your mind." He then quoted a popular proverb, in metre, the gist of which is:—

> Without milk you won't make butter
> Without barley you won't brew beer.

And so on, till it ends:—

> Without meditation you won't attain Buddhahood.

I then asked him: "Could we possibly stay on here now and study with you?" He replied: "Yes, if I were remaining here myself: but this year I have arranged to go to Tibet. This happens about once in six years. In a few days' time I start for Tashilhunpo." "And where do you advise us to go and seek our teacher?" He pondered a little and then spoke. "One of two places would suit you; either Tashilhunpo or else the monastery of the Great Accomplishment at Mindöling ('the place where Deliverance is ripened'): that's the place for you."

One day while we were in camp the young lama who, with a small kitten, was the sole attendant upon the hermit, arrived with a message. "Will Mr. Pallis please come at once to the hermitage? The Precious Master requests his presence." I hurried up the hill and found the hermit fingering a large book. "Be seated, please." To the novice: "Serve tea to the gentleman." Then again to me: "The other day you spoke of Mila Repa. Here is his Legend. I wish you to read it aloud to me." He pointed to a chapter and I began, regretting that I had left my reading glasses behind, though fortunately I was not helpless without them. After a few sentences the abbot interrupted me. "No, this is not what we want: it does not contain the important parts of Mila Repa. It is not the history, but the spiritual poems that you must read from." He turned up another volume and I began again. The language was classical and rather harder than the prose biography, and I was not proficient in the old tongue. I managed to extract a little sense as I went along, but must confess to have missed a lot. I read on and on. Whenever a stumble occurred, due to the worn printing of the wood-blocks, the hermit corrected me: he knew it all off by heart, no unusual accomplishment among Tibetans. Then he would recite or read a little himself and expound obscure words, turning them from the ancient into the modern idiom; sometimes he stopped to enlarge on the sense of a passage. It was a curious experience, alternating between moments of lucidity, half-understanding and total obscurity.

The afternoon passed and still the reading continued. As the sun began to decline outside, the twilight in the room increased and the print was no longer clearly distinguishable. I began to demur slightly. Looking at the master I perceived a strange look in his eyes, as if some change were about to come over him; but its nature was not, at the moment, plain. He remained silent for a minute or two and then said abruptly: "Now depart—go!" Closing the book of the poet, I rose and bowed. "And what of to-morrow? Shall I return in the morning?" "No, not till I send word. Perhaps the day after to-morrow." Next day, however, the novice came down to say that the hermit had entered into a trance out of which he would not emerge for several days. No one might seek speech with him or approach him. At that last interview his spirit must have been hovering on the brink, about to take flight to undreamed-of realms. I thought of the passage in St. Paul:— "I knew a man in Christ above fourteen years ago (whether in the body, I cannot tell; or whether out of the body, I cannot tell: God knoweth;) such an one caught up to the third heaven. How that he was caught up into paradise, and heard unspeakable words, which it is not lawful for a man to utter."

So ended my strange visit to the abbot. As he was about to leave for Tibet, we decided that there was no point in lingering in T'hangu in bad weather; otherwise we would have asked nothing better than to spend several months under his regular tuition. Leaving a letter to be delivered to him on his emergence from meditation, we packed up and walked down to Lachhen, overtaking Samdub and another monk on the road. They were returning to the village for the services of the Sacred Month (May–June) in which the entry of the Buddha into Nirvana is celebrated, the climax of the Tibetan year that corresponds with the Christian Easter.

OF MISSIONARIES AND MOTHS

At Lachhen at that time there were living two lady missionaries who ran a school and an industry for the making of blankets. I wished to find out what was the attitude of the lamas towards the representatives of an actively competing creed, so I tried to sound Samḍub by putting the innocent question: "What do those missionaries do in the village?" "They teach in a school, and weave rugs," he replied. Repeated inquiries entirely failed to elicit any resentful answer; the propaganda motive behind their work he seemed to ignore. I have had several subsequent opportunities of discussing the question of missions with other lamas, especially in Ladak, where the Moravians run an old-established proselytizing agency; but on no single occasion have I heard a spiteful word. Once, when I was moved to comment on this fact, I was told that "we are taught that it is a sin to speak disrespectfully of other religions or to treat their ministers in unfriendly fashion."

This precept, which goes back to the times of the Buddha, has been faithfully observed by His followers, with few exceptions, and makes Buddhist history pleasanter reading than the grim records of the more militant religions; and this open-minded spirit is shared by all other Traditions of Indian origin. The idea of the same truth presenting a different appearance when looked at from several view-points and of various paths converging upon one centre is familiar in Eastern thought. Furthermore, with so impersonal a conception of Divinity as the Orient tends to hold, it is almost impossible for anyone to fall into the state of thinking that he stands in a privileged position in regard to God. An anthropomorphic habit in referring to the Godhead, makes it easy to ascribe to It partisan sentiments of the most blasphemous kind. The believer with God on his side, does not take long to identify his own rivals with God's enemies. When he finds himself worsted he comforts himself with thoughts of martyrdom.

The Buddha and other Indian teachers, being aware of the human tendency to faction, showed foresight in formally condemning the sin of irreverence towards other religions, and thus cut the ground from under the feet of potential bigots. An edict of the great emperor Asoka, pattern for all humane rulers, who reigned in the third century B.C. says: "Do not decry other sects, do not run them down, but on the contrary pay honour to all that in them is worthy of honour." One sometimes wishes that the official teachings of Christianity had been equally explicit in respect of this practical application of Christ's law of Love. The early apostles of Buddhism managed to bear their good tidings to distant lands, without having to heap abuse on existing Traditions. They addressed themselves first and foremost to those who were capable of forming a considered judgment, the intellectually and spiritually gifted élite. Thence, the Doctrine percolated downward into the mass of the people, which it leavened more or less.

Bringers of new doctrines have never been unpopular in the East. One has only to remember the treatment accorded to the Jesuit Desideri who visited Lhasa in 1716. He was at once granted permission to preach and when he wrote a book to refute the errors, as he considered them, of the lamas, far from resenting it, they all rushed to borrow it. Desideri himself says: "My house suddenly became the scene of incessant comings and goings, by all sorts of people, chiefly learned men and professors, who came from the monasteries and universities, especially those of Sera and Drepung, the principal ones, to apply for permission to read the book." This was happening only a few years after the Huguenots had been driven from France and when in most of Europe heretical books would have been publicly burned by the common hangman.

Though in our eyes uncharitableness and pride are among the worst temptations, I think I am right in saying that a Buddhist or Hindu would always consider them secondary to that of wilful Ignorance. He would reserve his strongest blame for the habit of attacking other people's beliefs without first, like Desideri's lamas, making a genuine attempt to understand those beliefs as professed by their ablest exponents, not only by the unlettered herd. A scientist who presumed to find fault with a rival's hypothesis, without giving evidence of more than superficial acquaintance with its principles, would make himself ridiculous in the academic world. In one who tries to make himself the mouthpiece of God, this attitude, not at all uncommon, is not only intellectually censurable, it is a sin against the Holy Ghost.

When we returned to Lachhen we were informed that heavy rains had washed away paths in the Tista valley and that it would be advisable not to linger if we wished our baggage to reach Gangtok in safety. These rumours afterwards proved to have been exaggerated; but at the time, having no means of verifying them, we decided to stay no more than two days, just time enough to sort out the remaining stores and attend a service at the *Gompa* (monastery), to which we had been specially bidden by Samdub.

We were, however, first invited to tea by the headman, in his own house, where we were introduced to his wife and little son, as well as to his mother, who, as commonly happens in Tibet, ruled the home. There is no friction on that score, since family life is strong and governed by conventions that no one thinks of questioning. The interior of the house revealed an astonishing number of fine objects, considering the small size of the village. One has only to compare it with an Alpine village of similar character to see the difference in the level of taste. The living-rooms, as usual in Tibet, were on the first floor, the principal one being a combined chapel and entertaining room. On either side of the altar stood a tier of pigeon-holes, each harbouring a sacred tome; these books are probably seldom read; they are more often treated as mere objects of reverence. After taking our seats on rugs of very fair quality, we were served with tea in cups with finely-chased silver mounts. There was chopped mutton with spinach for the meat-eaters, and rice in china bowls for all. The best thing in the house was a beautifully fashioned copper brazier used for keeping the teapot warm, with a pair of silver handles ending in dragons' heads and a delicate band of ornament running round the edge. The shape is classical all over Tibet; but this example was outstanding.

The important event was, however, the visit to the *Gompa*. The service was most impressive. Perfect order and attention reigned, but free from any suggestion of drilled precision. The clergy were arranged in two choirs facing inwards and seated Buddha-fashion on low platforms covered with carpets. All had musical instruments; trumpets, eight feet long, oboes with a strong reedy tone, various percussion instruments such as drums of all sorts and sizes, and cymbals. Others held a handbell, with a very sweet note, in the left hand and a *dorjé* or thunder-bolt sceptre in the right, the pair which symbolizes the marriage of Wisdom and Method, the inseparable precursors of Enlightenment. From time to time the orchestra played a refrain; then chants followed, accompanied by drums or bells. The participants seemed absorbed in what they were doing: there was no shuffling or gazing around such as we had seen in the slack monastery at Gangtok. One sensed the influence of the abbot's teaching, imbuing his pupils with real seriousness and devotion. Samdub happened to be sitting facing me. As he wielded his bell and *dorjé* his hands described graceful ritual gestures. There is a whole language in these *mudras*, to give them their Sanskrit name, for one who knows how to read their message. A faint smile occasionally flitted across his seraphic countenance. Most of his companions knew the whole service off by heart; but he followed in a book placed on a stand in front of him, periodically turning the page over with a light flick of his finger. There was nothing to mar an atmosphere of perfect edification: the only thing that somewhat spoiled the picture was ourselves with our incongruously cut clothes which seemed aggressively out of place. I felt as if I ought to be sent away like the man in the Gospel who attended the King's feast without a marriage garment. It is extraordinary how hopeless it is to try to reconcile importations from the anti-traditional world with any traditional scene. I longed more than ever to be allowed to take part in the life of these people under conditions which would relieve me of all constraint.

In the evening Samdub and a friend of his came down to supper at the bungalow. When the meal was served, we waited for our guests to help themselves; but they paused as if embarrassed. Thinking they might be shy, I dipped a spoon in the curry, but had only just time to drop it unobserved as they started to intone a long metrical grace. When it was over they took some curry and conversation began. Samdub told us something of his life. He belonged to the village and was a special pupil of the abbot for whom he professed enthusiastic admiration. They used to rise at 5 a.m. and usually retired to bed about sunset. They apportioned the day between study, occasional services and meditation under the teacher's direction. They gave occasional instruction to the laymen of the village, and the Precious Master preached a sermon from time to time. They spent not less than three months of the year in meditation; at a later stage even more time might be given to it. During retirement they kept silence and each man attended to his own needs. Samdub was certainly a diligent pupil, with a grace and refinement all his own. It was strange to think that he came from one of the same peasant families as our rather argumentative and uncouth porters. Probably, had he not entered the Church, he would have been just like the others. His refinement seemed to be largely the result of his training, though with him the right material happened to be present also.

The monsoon is the season for seeing the Sikkim forests in all their glory. As we returned down the Tista valley, which we had only seen in the April drought, it was hard to believe that so much growth could have happened in two short months.

We lingered to pick some green raspberries, as delicious as the strawberries, but we had to keep a careful watch for the small black leeches that swarmed in the undergrowth. We found that a well-adjusted puttee was a sufficient protection; but a few leeches managed to evade our vigilance and made their way to exposed parts higher up, whence, after gorging themselves with blood, they eventually dropped off unperceived. If detected, a leech can always be made to release its hold by a pinch of salt. It is useless to pull them off as they may leave their grappling hooks in the flesh, and, in that climate, the sore is apt to fester. The bites bleed rather a long time because of a liquid which the leeches inject in order to retard coagulation.

Towards Dikchhu, in the tropical belt, the splendour of the woods attained its climax. Among the trees, broad-leaved varieties, reflecting much light from their leathery surfaces—a characteristic of warm damp regions throughout the world—contrasted with the feathery grace of acacias, tree ferns and bamboos, and the twisted sheaves of sword-blade *Pandanus*. The air was laden with heavy scents from invisible flowers overhead. Sometimes the path itself was strewn with fallen blossoms, the confetti of some sylvan wedding. Passing through this ordered confusion of forms and tints, where every step brought us face to face with a new fantasy, proof against every effort at analysis, we felt we were in the grip of a vital power, in whose presence man and his ethical preoccupations were of supreme unimportance. It is her very indifference which makes men fly to Nature for comfort when they are in trouble, for she is a mother who listens, but volunteers no interested advice.

Endless diversity of green gives the character to these woods. Flowers only play a subsidiary part in the landscape. The task of supplying brighter colours is left to butterflies, which emerge in great numbers at the approach of the rains. Among the common varieties are many yellow or white butterflies, related to the orange-tips and clouded-yellows; also swallow-tails, mostly velvety black, with patches of white or red on their elaborately scalloped hind-wings. In dry spots, especially on the path leading from Dikchhu up towards the Penlong pass, various members of the *Danaine* family, relatives of the common Monarch of U.S.A. hover round the trees. They are all large butterflies, some reddish-white with black wing-tips, some dappled grey and others (of the genus *Euploea*), dark brown velvet suffused with sapphire, one of the loveliest of all Indian butterflies. In addition there are no less brilliant day-flying moths, and innumerable bees and wasps of monstrous size encased in metallic panoplies of green, blue and purple. At night, moths, beetles, ant-lions and praying-mantises come out in immense variety; but we did not get much chance of observing them till we reached Gangtok itself, where the electric light standards drew vast numbers every evening. Whether we were looking at a hawk-moth or the huge Atlas himself with his nine-inch wing-span or an almost microscopic plume-like species, we never ceased to marvel at the intricacies of the designs which had been bestowed on them. How hopelessly inadequate and artificial those theories seemed that attempted to account for such beauties simply on utilitarian grounds, and which till recently were supposed to have said the last word on the subject.

At Singhik there occurred the first break in the monsoon. Till that time we had been almost continuously enveloped in mist, with heavy rain at times. We went to bed in Singhik bungalow without a hint of a change in the weather; but about midnight someone chanced to go on to the veranda and saw the mountains unveiled and silhouetted against a moon-lit sky. At dawn we witnessed a great wonder. In front of us lay the garden, bounded by a fence of purple bougainvillaea and datura bushes covered with white trumpet-shaped flowers. Looking beyond, we could see up into the side valley of Talung, thickly wooded, which drains the snows of Simvu. Suddenly that

mountain, scene of our defeat, and beyond it, the overwhelming mass of Kangchhendzönga, were aflame, not with the pink
glow of the Alps, but with an orange so unearthly that a painter
who faithfully reproduced it could hardly have escaped the
accusation of fancifulness. Then the curtain was lowered once
more over the peaks; but we walked down to Dikchhu in
radiant and unwonted sunlight. The same evening, taking two
stages in one, we reached Gangtok.

We were now forced to make fresh plans, if we wished to
carry on with our studies; Tibet for the present was out of the
question. After toying with several proposals, each of which
proved to contain insurmountable objections, we decided to go
to Ladak, a small kingdom of Tibetan affinities, which an incongruous accident of history has united to the Indian State of
Kashmir. Excepting Western China, which would have involved too long and costly a journey, it was the only district
outside the political frontier of Tibet where there were monasteries of sufficient size and importance for our purpose. It
meant that we had to go down to Calcutta and take the train
across to the western end of the Himalaya; but it was a case
of Hobson's choice, so, after saying good-bye to our friends
at Kalimpong, we set out for our new destination and were
soon speeding across the great plain, which the monsoon
had re-clothed with the lively green of growing crops.

LADAK

(1936)

KASHMIR AND PURIG

THE most pleasant way of approaching Kashmir is to detrain at Lahore and then to continue by car across the foothills, by the Banihal pass, a journey which occupies two days. Jammu, the old capital of the present ruling dynasty, is a possible half-way house. It possesses a number of Hindu temples, with elegant spires tipped with golden finials; but many people will be surprised to hear that one of its most interesting buildings is the dak-bungalow maintained for travellers. The ceilings are exquisite examples of Kashmir painted and gilt wood, covered with the most intricate geometrical and floral arabesques. Each room has a different pattern; how many passers-by must have seen them without paying the least heed!

Having emerged at last on the fabled plain of Kashmir, we drove along straight roads enclosed between rows of white-stemmed poplars, to Srinágar the capital. We occupied a house-boat on the river Jhelam. Europeans are not permitted to own freehold property, because the rulers of the State are apprehensive lest the excellence of the climate, which is like a dry and sunny version of our English one, should tempt retired employees of Government or Commerce to settle there in embarrassing numbers. As a result of this ordinance the foreign residents mostly inhabit house-boats.

The European end of the city, where the General Post Office, the club and the modern shops are situated, has become very trippery, and innumerable touts dog the footsteps of the tourist. The nuisance is less noticeable in the old quarters, where people are civil and where it is possible to wander unmolested.

Much of Srinágar looks like a blend of Holland and Venice, with a labyrinth of shady canals and bridges, through which the boats of hawkers of fruit and vegetables thread their way. There are little private landing-stages and spacious mansions dating from the seventeenth century, but now mostly falling into dilapidation. The material is a fine mellow brick; the walls are broken here and there by windows or balconies closed with lattices of wood forming complex geometrical interlacings. On most of the roofs grass is growing, and the effects of impoverishment are apparent on all sides.

In making preparations for a journey into the interior, the newcomer to Kashmir is faced with certain difficulties not met with in other parts of the Himalaya. Many of the agencies engaged in supplying the needs of tourists are far from reliable. The country is very cheap indeed, but the standard of honesty seems rather low and one cannot indulge in that carefreeness about prices and property that makes Garhwal and Sikkim so easy to travel in.

We did not, of course, think of leaving Kashmir before paying a visit by boat across the marshes and lakes to the famous Mughal pleasances of Nishat and Shalimar, the first built by Shah Jahan and the second by his father Jahangir. The craft used was not the swift *shikára*, which is the easiest method of communication on these waters, but a massive barge with a hut woven of rushes in the centre, in which the boatman and his family slept and cooked. These barges are punted in leisurely fashion through the reed-fringed channels that offer a passage in the tangle of pond-weeds which choke a great part of the lakes. Huge pink lotuses lift their heads high out of the water; they are much overpicked by natives, who offer them in bunches to tourists. In quiet backwaters the surface is starred with a small yellow water-lily. Villages and cottages, surrounded by fertile market gardens, occupy the solid ground, while floating islands formed of water-weeds bound together, on which tomatoes and marrows are planted, allow the peasants to push their productive holdings out on to the surface of the lake itself.

Punting up one of the water-alleys cleared in the reeds, we reached the steps of Nishat, below the principal pavilion of the garden, which is a simple building with projecting balconies closed with the usual lattices. This dream-garden is planned on the classical Mughal model, with a row of water-channels and fountains passing down the centre and out through the main pavilion itself. The water comes from a source in the hills which provide a background to the garden, and flows down a series of terraced levels, leaping each wall by an ornamental shoot. Lawns, like the softest of carpets, are edged by beds of sweet-scented carnations, heliotropes and every other sort of garden flower. It is probable that this part of the work has been

156

enhanced by the efforts of recent gardeners, for the English can always be trusted to make the best of a garden. It is the one art which they will never allow to be filched from them.

Another hour of punting brings one to the Shalimar, a name redolent of sentimental ballads. A short walk between rice-fields, some vivid green and some of a reddish brown, leads to the entrance. The plan is not unlike that of Nishat, but the slope is gentler and it is not possible to take in the whole at a glance; nevertheless it is just as lovely, and in the architecture of its two pavilions it surpasses its rival. One kiosk in particular, of black marble, is built in the characteristic square style of the time of Jahangir, with bracketed capitals and overhanging eaves that cast deep shadows, so that the sunlit garden outside has the magic of an enchanted realm. The ceilings are of the same decorated wood as in the dak-bungalow at Jammu; but curiously enough, the latter, though so recent and not built to house princes, is somewhat the better example.

The two gardens, rightly esteemed among the perfect achievements of human genius, must have been a rare solace to sovereigns weary of the cares of empire.

Among the minor campaigns undertaken by the generals of Aurangzib, harsh son of Shah Jahan (builder of Nishat) was one into Ladak; the king of that country had invoked Mughal aid to repel a Mongol-Tibetan invasion. It was accorded, but only at the price of conversion to Islam. The Ladaki prince, however, reaped but a short-lived advantage from his nominal apostasy from the ancestral faith, for though the Mughals routed the host of the invaders in a great battle, as soon as they had withdrawn the enemy reappeared and dictated terms afresh. From this time the fortunes of the principality, which at the height of its power had extended over all Western Tibet right into the valley of the Brahmaputra, fell into decline, though it preserved a precarious independence with its boundaries curtailed to the present limits. But the Mughal empire was also moving towards dissolution, largely as a consequence of Aurangzib's religious intolerance, which goaded the Hindus into revolt—by contempt and petty vexations, be it understood, for no case is on record where a single unbeliever suffered death or loss of property for his faith —and reduced most of India to anarchy, paving the way for the gradual subjugation of the peninsula by the British. During the period of disintegration in the eighteenth and early nineteenth centuries, Kashmir, after a spell of cruel oppression at the hands of Afghan upstarts, which ruined its prosperity, fell, in 1815, under the new military power of the Sikhs. A general of one of their vassals, the Dogra Rajput prince of Jammu, pushed the invasion into Ladak and, though meeting with fairly determined resistance, overran it between 1835 and 1840. From that moment its story as a separate state was ended, and this once glorious kingdom, in violation of its ethnic affinities, remained henceforth an unnatural appanage of a State mostly inhabited by Muslims and ruled over by a Hindu; for when the Sikhs in their turn fell foul of the British, Kashmir, and with it Ladak, were handed over to the Dogra chieftain, who, from having been a petty tributary to the Panjab, now emerged as the ally of British India, the Maharaja of Jammu and Kashmir, and has remained in control ever since.

Srinágar to Leh is an easy journey of fifteen days, but the time can be shortened by doing double stages. Rest-houses have been built at intervals along the route and the villages are bound, as part of their taxes, to provide transport animals if required, rates of payment being laid down in a schedule obtainable at the Residency office.

After crossing the Zoji pass, one enters a country of stony mountains and high-lying valleys, its barrenness relieved only where irrigation by means of leats has been able to harness the torrent-waters. In such favoured situations there occur oases of an intense green, kept moist by regular flooding, which takes the place of rain in this region, where the annual fall dwindles to a bare ten inches or less. Set at convenient distances apart, *baghs* or gardens, grassy enclosures shaded by willows, have been planted, kept fresh by daily watering. They offer charming camping-grounds; but when occupying them a watchful eye should be kept lest the caretakers charged with the duty of watering should open the irrigation channels without bothering to ascertain if any tents are standing in the grove. Otherwise the unsuspicious camper will suddenly notice a silvery edge of water stealing towards him across the turf. In a moment the peaceful camp is humming with activity; men snatch up blankets or stores from the path of the oncoming flood, others rush with stones to deflect it at a higher point, while yet others shout out to the villagers, not without uncomplimentary epithets, calling on them to run and block the main breach. The waters stop short in the nick of time, the hubbub subsides and calm enfolds the camp once more.

*It should be noted that only the principal mountain chains have been
indicated; most of the area shown, however, is mountainous.*

The number of visitors proceeding into Ladak in any one year is wisely limited, so as to avoid throwing an excessive strain on the scanty resources of the province. Permission to enter has therefore to be obtained from H.M. Resident in Srinágar. But for this measure, the peasants, tempted by a prospect of ready cash, might improvidently barter away too large a share of their produce, leaving themselves short in the lean season. The whole administration of the Treaty road is simple, efficient and to the advantage of all concerned.

At last the appointed day arrived (July 12th) and we set out for Wayl bridge where we crossed the Sind in order to follow its wide and verdant valley, which yields crops of rice and maize. We passed through prosperous-looking villages, shaded by huge walnut trees. The containing hills were not steep and their sides were clothed with conifers; we could have fancied ourselves in the Tyrol. Neither the valley itself nor the distant peaks suggested anything on a Himalayan scale; but the narrow side-valleys were wilder and more rugged. I followed a torrent some little way during a day's halt at Gund. The slopes were extremely abrupt and savage-looking, with long drifts of old avalanche snow lying about, through which sweet-smelling bushes with white flowers, probably viburnum, poked their branches. Delphiniums, almost as big as our garden varieties, made brilliant splashes of blue on the steep sides of the cutting. Chestnuts, with a few pines, formed the woods. The undergrowth was also chestnut, but of a different species, rather lanky and profusely flowering with bunches of huge pink blossoms. This was true Himalayan country again.

The pass across the main range, the Zoji La, the lowest in all the two thousand-odd miles of the Himalaya, is reached from Baltal rest-house, on the Kashmir side, by a path which rises some 3,000 feet by easy gradients. Pines soon gave place to birches, the trees that usually are found nearest to the snows, then the path, rounding a rocky corner where, in shaly crannies, grew huge tufts of pearly-white columbine, unexpectedly took a level sweeping curve to the right. Here we saw the last of the birches, save for a few gaunt stragglers higher up the pass, gnarled and riven under the lash of the storms. A biting wind attacked us; through mist we caught a distant glimpse of white peaks. Before us extended an even snow-bed, in the centre of which lay the half-eaten carcass of a horse, with a solitary vulture perched on it. The great bird, so gorged that he could only rise a few inches off the ground, scuttled away, aiding its legs with the beating of its magnificently spreading wings. Shivering we stopped to open rucksacks and take out warm sweaters and scarves, for the edge of the wind was keen: then on, over more snow-beds for some little distance, till we suddenly became aware that the streams had begun to flow the other way. It was the top: we were astride the Himalaya, but we could not quite agree upon the exact point of the divide. Where the snow had melted, skeletons of animals had been uncovered, calling up images of some old slave-route in the Sahara. Though such a low pass (11,300 feet) and a simple walk under summer conditions, the Zoji is one of the most murderous, accounting for a number of animal lives, and human lives too, levying its deadly toll by means of sudden avalanches, or engulfing its victims in bottomless drifts.

In the winter months, though trade is quiet, a number of Turkoman *Hadjis*, or pilgrims bound for Mecca, come from Yarkand to Leh by the Karakoram pass on their way to India. They are a happy-go-lucky lot and frequently get stranded in bad weather, at the cost of frostbitten fingers or toes, which are in due course amputated by local practitioners or, if they are lucky, by an English lady doctor who works devotedly in one of the Indus villages. Then, disdaining prudent counsels of delay, the *Hadjis* push towards the Zoji, their minds possessed by the sole thought of reaching the sacred goal and assured of a crown of glory if they should fall by the wayside. The inhabitants of the villages just north of the pass, though nominally co-religionists, exploit the pilgrims unmercifully, withholding their help in crossing the pass until the travellers have consumed all their food, and then reprovisioning them at an exorbitant charge. Finally, having bled them white, they help them down to safety on the Kashmir side.

Presently we came to the earthly paradise of Nimarg, a meeting place of several streams, where every inch of ground was hidden beneath a carpet of irises, potentillas, delphiniums, gentians, verbena, onions—both metallic purple and yellow—primulas, anemones and other species too numerous to mention. On certain slopes, creamy *Eremurus*, three feet high, stood up like lilliputian woods. A pink goosefoot formed the foundation in most of the spaces left unoccupied by other flowers; but on the floor of the valley the prevailing colour was the blue of cynoglossum; pink lousewort and edelweiss fringed the streams.

This alp owes its luxuriance to the fact that it receives the residue of all the heavily-charged rain-clouds that escape being precipitated on the Kashmir side of the divide. Though Nimarg is frequently drenched, the rainfall shrinks rapidly beyond this point, being only twenty-two inches at Dras, a few miles on, while at Leh it is no more than 3·26 inches.

A couple of miles from Nimarg, a group of mean hovels with a sordid little rest-house marked the village of Matayan. Most of the houses were too low to stand upright in, and the inhabitants seemed poor and suspicious of strangers. Though the moisture had markedly lessened, there were still many flowers. The marshy flats were rich with purple iris and on one bank, near the path, grew a specially lovely pale cream anemone. We gathered seeds of this exquisite flower on the way back and tried to induce them to germinate in a Cheshire garden, but unfortunately without any success. *Eremurus* was still found in abundance just below Matayan; but each mile brought fewer and fewer flowers. At Pandras, five miles farther on, the Alpines had almost disappeared and plants characteristic of dry climes, many of them aromatic, replaced them; thymes, chamomiles, huge umbels and a few leguminous plants armed with thorns were growing among rocks; great rose bushes made cascades of pink blossom down the face of the cliffs. The banks of the river were stony and at times it raced furiously through narrow gates of serpentine marble, like black slag. At Dras, which is a fairly large village with a few general utility shops and a camping-ground in the usual willow grove, we felt that India was already far away. This was the highly-coloured landscape, the invigorating air and the way of life of Central Asia.

There is one attractive halting-place some thirteen miles beyond Dras, where it is worth stopping a night for the mere pleasure of camping there. It is an oasis called Tasgam, set like a verdant island in the midst of a sea of shimmering radiation, with multi-coloured tangles of wild flowers along the edges of its corn-fields, and a bewitching willow-wood to camp in. The inhabitants of this and neighbouring hamlets vary greatly in the matter of physique: in Tasgam they looked healthy enough; but in villages farther on they were afflicted with all sorts of nameless diseases.

The administrative headquarters of the whole district between the Zoji and Ladak, which is known as Purig, are at Kargil, a small township which has grown up round a bazaar of Indian-owned shops which draw their subsistence from the Turkistan–India transit traffic. In addition it is the centre of a considerable tract of fertile land, beautifully tilled and planted with trees; its irrigated terraces reach far up the hillsides and into the minor valleys all around. It is the seat of an official of the Kashmir Government, who, among his other duties, is charged with the examination of travellers' passes into Ladak. The place is beautifully situated on a wide, fast-flowing river, the Suru, and has an air of prosperity which makes an agreeable change after the miserable villages round Dras. The inhabitants are largely Baltis, clad in hard-wearing brown woollens, with flat round caps to match.

The greenness of Kargil is more than usually joyful, because the last few miles before the village are tedious, with torrid stretches of sand, trying both for pedestrians and horses. After passing the head of an iron bridge, where the road to Skardu, capital of Baltistan, forks off, a bend brings one opposite a thin line of poplars, just over the river, which widens as one advances in the parallel direction, until the whole panorama is unfolded, with groves, bubbling rills of pure water, and waste ground covered with purple iris, different from the one we found below the Zoji. These irises have been put to charming use by the peasants, who train them in tufted belts to mark the divisions of their fields.

As we entered the first grassy patch on our side of the river, we caught sight of a couple of tents, pitched close to a tempting spring of icy water which welled up from under a bank. Some small dogs and children were playing there, two or three women sat gossiping, and the menfolk lay stretched on the ground fast asleep. One woman caught our attention by her clothes, which were not of the style usual either to Baltis or Ladakis, but looked rather like those that we had last seen on Tibetan women at Kalimpong. A closer look left us in no doubt: this was indeed a true Tibetan, there was no mistaking her cast of features. Her life-story was typical of that roving spirit which gains possession of so many Tibetans and sends them roaming from the frontiers of China to the edge of the Karakoram, quitting their homes without fear or care for the future. Our friend the T'hangu pilgrim was one of these wanderers, now here was another. Her father had died long since, but her mother was living when she quitted her home several years before. Though poor, she had made a pious resolve to go on pilgrimage to the Mountain of

Precious Snow, better known by its Indian name of Kailas, close to the sources of both the Satlej and the Brahmaputra. All the way behind Nepal she trekked, now alone, now with others on a similar quest, till she reached the foot of her mountain. Then she took part in its solemn circumambulation, clockwise of course, for it, like a *Mani* wall, being sacred, must be passed on the left, with the right side turned towards it. The circuit concluded, instead of going back to her people, a desire was born in her to proceed still farther afield to other shrines and monasteries of the far west. So she found herself at last in Ladak. At Leh she had met her husband-to-be. Now they had a large family, and she was trying to eke out her scanty resources by breeding Lhasa terriers. She had some twenty dogs with her and was taking them down to Kashmir to sell to the English ladies.

This unexpected encounter seemed a good omen. We lingered for some time talking to her, and then walked on towards our camp, at the far end of Kargil, where the Ladak road starts. We felt excited by the prospect of re-entering a Tibetan country the next day, where we would be free to take up those studies which so enticed us. We had been waiting for this moment to put into execution the long-cherished plan of adopting, as far as possible, the Tibetan way of living, both in regard to food, dress and personal habits. We wanted to absorb the spirit of the Tradition by direct experience, subjecting ourselves to its laws to the greatest possible extent; for there comes a time when it is difficult to rest satisfied with the rôle of observer; one must participate, and if this spiritual association is to be thorough, the external trappings, which provide the background, must also be made to agree.

I regard this living of the Tibetan life as an extension of the study of language. There is speech in gesture, even in the way a cup is lifted to the lips, in a bow, in a thousand light touches which go to reinforce the spoken word and lend it additional point. Without them, language remains a foreign thing to the last. Externals, such as clothes, count for a great deal. The actor who wishes to live his part, must first convince himself. He will find it much easier to transform his personality if he can banish as many incongruities as possible from his make-up. Kingliness is enhanced by the crown, a soldierly bearing by the sword, beggary by rags. Our intention was to be as thorough as possible. It was a way of saying to our hosts: "We wish to be as one of you. Please make no unusual arrangements on our behalf. We love your Tradition and hope it will not be rashly changed. We have found means of attuning ourselves to its ways."

I have studiously avoided turning any part of this book into an apologia; the recorded results must prove the soundness or folly of my methods. But I must make one slight exception, because I know that I have laid myself open to a charge of inconsistency. Someone is sure to offer the criticism, on the face of it a reasonable one, that here is a man who has all along gone out of his way to blame Indians and other Asiatics for copying Western dress and customs, yet he himself is doing just the same in regard to Tibet. I was never blind to this possible objection; nevertheless, I believe that I did not violate any of my principles; but I do not expect to convince everyone. I shall be satisfied if they admit that there was a *prima facie* case for my having adopted unusual methods.

My basic thesis is that between any traditional code of behaviour and the customs of an anti-traditional civilization like ours—the only one of its kind that history now remembers—there is no real equivalence. Modern Occidentalism is threatening to flatten out the whole world and mould it to a single, rather dull, pattern, throwing away all that diversity whereby man has expressed himself through the centuries. Not only are all the Oriental civilizations in acute danger as a result of the Western encroachment but also the West itself seems prepared to let go whatever was great or worthwhile in its own heritage. At home one can but try to make the best of its rather narrow limitations; but on stepping into a society which is still based on regular traditional principles, one cannot help feeling that in introducing *our* manners and customs we may be helping to spread a taste for things which will ultimately corrode the armour of Tradition, thus paving the way for totalitarian materialism, which seems to be the logical outcome of the non-traditional outlook. Furthermore, in the West no man can be said to follow the path of Tradition without let or hindrance, even should he be so minded, for conditions are against him, if not worse: one in whose heart the traditional fire has somehow been rekindled finds himself like a homeless exile and instinctively yearns to taste the experience of a normal human life, free from profane compromises. There was a day when all civilizations were roughly equivalent and travellers from one to the other could feel at home wherever they went. Now the odds

165

are unequally weighted, and the world pressure is all from the anti-traditional direction. Anomalous circumstances create their own problems which demand peculiar solutions.

In practice, I believe that I possess the requisite qualifications for making a free choice and that I could never have accomplished as much as I did, had that choice been made differently. From the first moment, I felt as if I had escaped from an invisible barrier, within which, like a hen in the middle of a chalked circle, I had been penned. I have felt at ease among Tibetans of all ranks as I have not often done elsewhere. I never felt that I was among strangers; rather was it a return to a long-lost home. A lama, with whom I was intimate, explained this quite simply by saying that it was no accident, but that I showed unmistakable signs of having been a Tibetan myself in a previous existence, whence I had inherited a natural sympathy with my former compatriots and a tendency to return to them, like a homing pigeon. Whatever truth may underly this utterance, which should not be taken too literally, I can at least say this about the next life: had I the choice I should be well content to be reborn as a Tibetan—always provided that Tibet is still Tibet, and has not been turned meanwhile into one of many feeble copies of America. From my limited experience I can endorse the words of that able French observer, Professor Jacques Bacot when he writes:—

The Tibetans impress one at once by the dignity of their persons. One sees them on horseback and nobly clad, scattered about the open spaces of their deserts . . . In all Tibet one would be hard put to it to discover one fool . . . The Tibetans are not barbarous or uncultivated; nor for that matter is their country. Under their rough hide they conceal refinements that we lack, much courtesy and philosophy, and the need for beautifying common things, whatever happens to be useful to them, be it a tent, a knife or a stirrup . . . Moreover they are gay, these Tibetans, and happy as is not the case elsewhere to-day, more so than our wretched workers in their wretched factories, armed with the whole arsenal of their rights . . . The more densely the country is populated, the tamer is the wild game. The Tibetans are not much addicted to hunting. They have long since lost the taste for killing which we still retain . . . I love their companionship during the long rides, for they are taciturn, or else they only speak with good sense, originality and a taste for speculative things.

KARGIL TO YURU :
SYMBOLISM OF THE " TANTRA "

TWENTY-THREE hot miles separated Kargil from the next halting-place. At first the way crossed an arid plateau, its monotony relieved only by a momentary glimpse of an impressive snow-mountain lying to the south-west. The lifeless tableland seemed as if it would extend for ever, when suddenly, without warning, we found ourselves looking over the edge of a huge sunken valley watered by a river from which numerous artificial rivulets conducted the life-giving water to smiling corn-fields and shady groves. The place seemed so secluded and out of keeping with the dead wastes immediately surrounding it, that it might well have been taken for a mirage. These unexpected encounters with life in the midst of desert are always dramatic, and man never fails in his emotional response to the first sight of green. It is one of the peculiar charms which belong only to barren countries and cannot be shared by luxuriant ones.

The track led down into the hollow and then hugged the margin of the fields so as not to waste a foot of arable ground. As at Kargil, here also, the wild iris was planted to mark the boundaries between properties. Gradually the gorge closed in: it was thirsty work riding through it in the heat of the early afternoon, especially as most of the ponies offered for hire along this road are not of very high quality.

As it was our first day on horseback and a specially hot one, we were beginning to feel rather sore and weary, when we emerged unexpectedly into a wider part of the valley with open views in several directions. There was a bridge to the right giving access to the small village of Shergol. From a gravel bank on the left several cold springs gushed out as if placed there specially for the convenience of thirsty travellers. But what immediately arrested our gaze and held it riveted was the sight of something like a stone bell terminating in a needle-like pinnacle —it was a *chhorten*, the symbol of Nirvana, found in all Buddhist lands. Presently, looking across the river, we discerned a cliff face some two miles away, against which nestled a white façade with a red frieze, evidently where some huge caverns provided natural chambers. Our first lamasery! We were in Ladak at last!

Yet a little farther on and Mulbek *Gompa* came into view, perched on the summit of a precipitous *aiguille*, its white and red walls outlined in the golden evening light. It looked like a small fortress, with its projecting balconies that hung airily over the gulf. Standards, like closed parasols, marked the angles of the roof.

As we approached, the little Government rest-house presented an animated scene. Our friend Khan Muhammad Din was seated in the porch, receiving petty notables and making his annual settlement of local business. A gay crowd of villagers was gathered round; their cheerful faces made a pleasant change from the dour looks of many of the Purig people. Nor were the women any less assured than the men. The Ladaki wife is anything but a doormat; more often than not, she is the real ruler in the home, and children, when asked about their parentage, will often give their mother's name before their father's. The Italian explorer, De Filippi, was not wrong in saying:—"The woman has considerable influence in family affairs—though the situation is hardly a true matriarchy—with a dignity, a social position not surpassed in any country in the world."

The male costume is not unlike that of Khunu, consisting of a long *chuba* or gown of brown or grey or sometimes purple homespun secured with a sash, in which are stuck a brass spoon and a flute. It is common to meet people playing merry tunes as they walk along the road. The shoes are quite different from the high Tibetan model and are often decorated with swastikas. The cap is peculiar to Ladak, made of cloth or of a velvety material, flattened on the crown, but with the edges turned up, something like a "cap of liberty." Often solid bracelets adorn the wrists, and the ears are pierced for rings. The men tend to be big and strong-looking: nor do their looks belie them, for they are about the toughest people I know. Even the Sherpas do not treat cold or bad weather with such complete disdain. At night they hardly bother to shelter, if that involves them in the smallest extra trouble. They wear their hair in flowing locks, and many grow beards, which is a proof that the race must contain a high percentage of non-Tibetan blood, though it has adopted the language and customs of its conquerors. We noticed

168

a wide range of types, from those who looked closer to Europeans in cast to others in whom Mongolian features predominated. Whatever else he may be doing, whether walking or sitting, the Ladaki is always assiduously spinning coarse woollen thread; his little shuttle hangs from the end of the thread and revolves merrily under dexterous twists periodically administered, while a thick skein of crude wool is hung over his elbow. The finished thread is wound on a stick. In this way a continual supply of yarn is spun for weaving into clothes during the winter months. The women's dress is dark, trimmed with sheepskin and decked out with silver ornaments of beautiful chain-work, one of which dangles from the shoulder; the chains terminate in a tiny manicure-set with silver tweezers and knives. A basket, like that of the Swiss peasants, is carried on the back; under the basket a goatskin with the hair turned outwards prevents chafing. The head-dress is extraordinary. It consists of a sort of bonnet, shading the face and curling snail-like over the back of the neck. On to this are sewn uncut turquoises, few or many, big or small, according to a person's means.

On the morrow the Khan and his train set out with the dawn, leaving us in sole possession. The first experiment with Tibetan clothes made us feel slightly self-conscious; but we were helped over the awkward stage by the fact that no one ever showed the least surprise. It occasionally happened that a person asked us what price we had given for this or that, or, after feeling the cloth, passed some comment on its quality; but *why* we chose to wear them, they never inquired. One or two Lhasa Tibetans, or Ladakis who had spent many years in Tibet proper, did go so far as to express positive pleasure. Usually, we were treated as if our use of Tibetan clothes was the most natural thing in the world. Twice I was asked if I had lived many years at Lhasa. What I soon noticed, however, was that the discriminative treatment accorded to Europeans was dropped automatically; people no longer tried to offer us chairs to sit on, and we were everywhere expected to produce our own teabowls out of our *ambags*, that is to say, out of the pouches formed by the fullness of our gowns.

The peasant houses were a never-ending joy throughout Ladak, with their combination of the qualities of amplitude, solidity, classical plan and appropriate detail. A mean or cramped or ill-constructed dwelling was never to be seen, while a fair proportion of the bigger ones made us feel positively envious.

Nowhere else have I seen houses to compare, on an average, with those of the Ladakis.

The lower story is usually allotted to animals and stores, and the family spends the summer on the upper floor in half-open chambers round the pillared court. When it is very warm, people often sleep out on the flat roof, usually naked, with clothes or a blanket thrown over them. Household furniture is confined to necessities. Besides cooking-pots and wooden bowls and cups for eating and drinking, with perhaps a china cup or two for special occasions, there is always a red glazed pottery charcoal stove for keeping tea warm, in form not unlike a Greek urn; and one or two brass or copper teapots, often decorated with good chasing, as well as with *appliqué* silver plates and dragon handles, earthenware pitchers for beer, small carpets for sitting on, and low tables for tea, painted gaily with flowers. All these objects are hand-made and of real artistic value: richer peasants sometimes possess quite fine utensils, and the woodwork of the principal rooms in their houses may also be richly decorated.

In each farm-house there is one room which claims pre-eminence in respect of furnishing and comfort; this is the family chapel, in which reside the images of the Tutelaries of the household, before whom lamas from time to time are summoned to hold services. Votive lamps are alight on the altar and painted scrolls line the walls. One family of peasants whom we knew and who, though well-to-do, cannot have possessed much ready cash, told us that they were about to invest in a new *t'hanka* by the most celebrated living artist of Ladak, Rigzin. Could one imagine many of our farmers at home who, even if they could afford it, would dream of placing an order with a painter of recognized eminence? Yet it must not be thought that I am trying to make out the average Ladaki to be a highly intellectual or consciously aesthetic person. Quite the reverse; compared to the Tibetans, for instance, they appear rather simple-minded; but under the guidance of Tradition there is a diffusion of knowledge throughout the country which cannot be paralleled in modern societies, for all their compulsory schooling.

A pass, the P'hotu La (13,400 feet), separates Bod Karbu from Yuru, where the first of the great monasteries is situated. It is usually called Lamayuru on maps and in books, an Indian corruption of the real name, which should be Yuru *Gompa*. I was seized by a sudden longing to wander off alone while we were sitting at supper at the Bod Karbu rest-house, so I asked my friends to bring up the baggage ponies next day, and I set off for Yuru on foot. The jagged rows of peaks that formed the sides of Karbu valley faded slowly from orange through dull red into inky black. By an isolated *Mani*, I saw in the half-light a figure with clasped hands and heard the faint whisperings of his prayers. I walked on and on, forgetting time and distance. Occasionally the dying gleam of a fire or the pawing of a horse's hoofs indicated an encampment. After a time the track began to rise and the shapes of mountains, huge and eerie, closed in on either side. I was hoping to make the top of the P'hotu La and then rest, waiting to descend on Yuru soon after dawn. A dog began to bark far off to the left, another joined in and then a third; all at once a whole chorus broke out and began to surge towards me in a furious crescendo. I felt very much alarmed, for it was evident that I had approached a shepherds' camp, guarded by some of those fierce mastiffs, rather like chows, which are used as watchdogs all over Tibet. It would have been most unpleasant to be attacked by several of them, for I was not even carrying a stick. Picking up a couple of stones, I hurried along the path, hoping to get out of their range. I caught a glimpse of a furious brute who refused to be shaken off till he had seen the intruder well out of the way. It was a great relief when the barking died away in the distance.[1]

I walked on, feeling rather nervous; then I heard another dog just ahead. I wondered what was the best thing to do; I turned up into the entrance of a ravine and decided to halt for the rest of the night. I lay down on the stones by a stream and slept fit-

[1] The instinct that drove me to pick up the stones would have been blamed by several lamas of my acquaintance as a sign of weakness. Still more they would have criticized the egotism, expressed as *fear of others*, root-poison of hatreds, that prompted the act. They would probably have voiced their opinion thus:—"When you heard the dogs barking, no doubt your own fear aggravated their ferocity. You underrate your own powers; for you might have proceeded on your way calmly and resolutely, fending off the phantoms of this contingent world with the buckler of profound Meditation on the all-embracing Compassion. Why put your trust in other defences?" I must record events as they actually happened; but I admit that the criticism does not lack force. Viewed from the standpoint of Enlightenment, my act of warlike preparation deserved the epithet "ill-considered." I believe that it is no exaggeration to say that persons capable of this degree of Non-attachment even in the face of danger are far from extinct in Tibet: for them, the demons of fear and worry have been exorcized, and they enjoy a serenity that even a savage mastiff might respect.

fully. At the first glimmer of dawn, I got up and unpacked some bits of wood that I had brought, to boil up a pot of tea. It was the first time that I had tried to light a fire on a hearth of three stones, such as the natives use all over Asia. It is extraordinary how clumsy an inexperienced hand can be; I wasted many matches and sticks before I got the draught properly regulated; but I derived a childish pleasure from my cup of tea, for this too was one more tiny step into the Tibetan world.

From the head of the pass the road descended a small stream-valley with gravel-strewn sides and sparse vegetation. It widened out near a point where a solitary *chhorten* had been set up, in the middle of the pebbly bed, as if to suggest that something important waited round the corner. The path turned abruptly left for a few yards up a small col with another *chhorten* standing on it. Then I stopped, in face of one of the world's wonders, overcome by the whirlpool of emotions that suddenly surged through me. A hollow, shut in between red hills, lay below, its floor filled by fields and a tiny willow copse: the brick-red background threw up the greenness of the leaves in unusually sharp relief. The road contoured round the left of the combe in a wide curve, to the foot of a huge sandstone cliff honeycombed with caves, which looked as if they had been specially designed to serve as cells for the meditations of hermits. On the crest of this cliff stood the magnificently proportioned pile of the *Gompa*, a tall central building, with a number of lower wings containing monks' quarters and on one side a warren of peasant houses.

A continuous line of huge *Mani* walls and white *chhortens* bordered the road, forming a sacred way and exerting on the eye an almost dynamic influence in guiding it in the direction it should go. Some of the larger *chhortens* had their bases moulded into bas-reliefs of dragons, horses, lions and phoenixes. The monastery itself was white, with the usual red frieze under the roof. These bands are always made in the same way, by laying bundles of sticks closely bound and painted red, so that the cut-off ends face outwards like a brush. The setting of Yuru *Gompa* is unsurpassed and its first view is an unforgettably stirring experience.

Unfortunately it seems to have suffered by its proximity to the main caravan route; being the first big monastery on this road, it is visited by every tourist who enters Ladak. Its monks give the impression of being venal, and they hold the record for the number of requests for *bakshish* which they address to the stranger. When I was going over the building, a group of nuns from the village also assembled in the courtyard and un-ashamedly shouted *"bakshish"* in chorus.

The temples of Yuru are in a poor state of repair. Cracks have appeared in walls which have been painted only recently, either because the plaster was too hastily laid on, or, more likely, because the outer wall itself is crumbling, but no one bothers about it. Much of the work is extremely fine, being, I think, by the same living painter Rigzin, whose name was mentioned earlier and whose work is in great demand throughout Western Tibet. He is a native of the Indus valley and started life as a monk, but apparently reverted to the lay state.

In Ladak there are, besides Rigzin, two or three more painters of major rank and numerous lesser ones who execute designs on furniture and woodwork. All these are kept continuously busy serving the needs of less than forty thousand people. From this, an idea can be formed of the number of artists required by a community in which art products are deemed no luxury, but something in which even common folk can share. No great halo surrounds the artist; but if his work is above average, he enjoys the solid esteem which is to be earned among a people who have real power to judge good workmanship.

The figures in the wall-paintings at Yuru divide into two strongly contrasted types. On the one hand we have Buddhas and Celestial Beings, their faces calm or lit up by faint smiles of rapture, seated on their lotus pedestals in attitudes of imper-turbable serenity. On the other hand there are frightful appari-tions, decked with crowns and necklaces of human skulls, dancing in convulsive frenzy on the prostrate forms of men or animals. It is not surprising that the casual traveller to Tibet takes these dreadful beings for demons more appalling than those who people the hells of Signorelli, Fra Angelico or Dürer; but that view is far from the truth. Many of those diabolical-looking figures are in essence identical with those who look so gentle. The Tibetan divinities all have a variety of aspects accord-ing to the functions that they are called upon to fulfil, perhaps even more according to the state of mind of the beholder. There are benign or peaceful, fascinating, fierce or terrifying aspects. Thus to the saint and to the evildoer the same divinity will show himself in widely differing guise. To the virtuous soul the Divine is necessarily glorious and comforting, but to an evil conscience the same can be a cause of horror and anguish.

173

Indeed the lamas teach that the various states of existence which men and animals attain to, such as the abode of gods or the purgatories, are entirely subjective in character, forming part, as they do, of the general body of illusions from which the mind suffers so long as it has failed to attain Enlightenment.

Another side of this doctrine of multiplicity of forms is equally important. Whoever tries to thread a way through the complications of the pantheon, not only of Tibet but equally so of India, will find that he starts by learning a bewildering number of names of apparently separate gods with their attributes. Later he will find out that each of these can be recognized under several forms, externally very different: and again, as he pursues his inquiry, he will find that these forms manifest themselves in yet other forms and that some of them merge into forms which have apparently been derived from other prototypes. This has been pithily expressed by Kipling in the line:—"Kali—who is Párvati, who is Sitala, who is worshipped against the smallpox."

His humorous remark enshrines a profound truth. Reversing the succession of forms, the goddess whom the villager invokes to guard him from smallpox becomes, as one traces her upward by a sort of involutionary process, Párvati, the spouse of Shiva. The goddess can also be worshipped as Kali under both gentle and fearful aspects. Further on we will see that Párvati is the Active Energy of Shiva Himself, wedded to Him in the same way as Wisdom is wedded to Method. Thus the mind, unable to find any single static form on which to rest, is led into recognition that all forms are really one, or to use still more accurate language, not-two, and that the whole complex is merely the total of Divine Manifestation in Form. The symbolism is here part of Method leading to a basic metaphysical concept, part of Wisdom. This, incidentally, disposes of the favourite accusation of polytheism which the wilfully-ignorant love to level at the Hindus, Tibetans and other "heathens." That the followers of these Traditions are clear in their own minds on this doctrine can be proved from innumerable quotations.

In one of the chapels at Yuru, stands a colossal image of the Bodhisat Chenrezig, the same one who is manifested through the Dalai Lama, under the form known as the All Merciful Lord. He is portrayed as a tall figure with innumerable arms forming a circle which surrounds him like an aureole; he has not one head but eleven, disposed in a pyramid. This strange symbolism was explained to me by a lama, who was almost carried away by his own eloquence. "Chenrezig is filled with boundless compassion for all creatures," he said. "You simply cannot imagine how compassionate he is. When he saw their constant sufferings and struggles in the Round of Existence, from which they vainly sought a way of escape, so overcome with pity was he that his head burst and was shivered into fragments. Then his own Lama, the Buddha of Immeasurable Light, provided him with a fresh head and this happened no less than ten times making eleven in all." Chenrezig's typical representation is, however, not the eleven-faced form, but the likeness of a young and beautiful white prince, with four arms. That is why an imprint, indicating the rudiments of the extra pair of arms, is one of the signs sought for on the body of the baby that is chosen to act as the earthly sanctuary of the Bodhisat's influence.

Chenrezig is often likened to a shepherd in terms which cannot but recall the Good Shepherd of the Gospel. The Shepherd-like Lord, in the Tibetan version, is so called because his action is that of a shepherd who, having led his flock to the entrance of the fold, lets them enter in first, and then, when all are safely inside, goes in himself last of all and closes the gate. Chenrezig, in his capacity as Bodhisat, is freed from sin and illusion, and is able at any moment to assume Buddhahood; but moved by his compassion for suffering creatures, he abstains from final Deliverance while so many are left behind in their imperfections and sorrows. "What is it to be saved oneself if others are still lost and suffering?" He therefore elects to continue in the Current of Forms so that he may aid all beings to pass in together to Nirvana. Then, and only then, he also will take the final step across the threshold. Chenrezig and his fellow Bodhisats, who again are not to be regarded as objectively distinct personalities but rather as "stages in the Path" accessible to every one of us, represent the embodied aim of the Tibetan Buddhist doctrine, the Saviour who, though sinless and all-knowing, offers himself for the Universe, in the supreme and eternal sacrifice of redemptive love.

There is another peculiarity of the Yuru paintings which should be mentioned, namely, the fact that each of the figures is really composed of two figures clasped in close embrace. This is a common feature in Tibetan iconography and serves to illustrate a doctrine which has been the subject of much uninformed and derogatory comment under the name of "Tantrism," a word simply derived from the books in which it is expounded, called the *Tantras*. According to their peculiar symbolism, each divine Being is represented as a pair, composed of a male or non-acting and a female or creative principle. The latter is spoken of as the consort or wife of the former: in Sanskrit she is called *Shakti* and an adept of this school is called a *Shakta*. The *Tantras* themselves are primarily of Hindu origin, being the latest set of sacred writings to be codified. Their inspiration is considered to be the Word of Shiva Himself; but there are also a great many Buddhist *Tantras* of similar character, though the terminology is different. St. Padma, the earliest Apostle of Tibet, introduced the Doctrine under this Tantrik form. After him came the succession of the great Translators, one of whom was Marpa of Hlobrak, of whom I have spoken so much. In the Indo-Tibetan Cosmogony, the process of manifestation of the Divine Power as Form is conceived as being subject to a rhythm comparable to breath, so that the expiration corresponds with the Manifesting Act and the intake of breath with the withdrawal of the Universe back into itself. Each of these cycles is termed a *Kalpa*, presided over by a supreme Buddha-teacher: the *Kalpa* contains fourteen *Manvantaras*, each made up of four *Yugas*, equivalent to the gold, silver, bronze and iron ages of European tradition. Each sub-period has its appropriate scripture, a *Tantra* being suited to the needs of the last phase in the cycle, the black age of decay, when the average degree of spiritual perception is insufficient to allow of the truth being encountered face to face. It must then be viewed through a glass darkly, and communicated to the dwindling group of devotees chiefly by means of symbols.

"All these things are done in parables: that seeing they may see, and not perceive; and hearing they may hear, and not understand . . . And with many such parables spake He the word unto them, as they were able to hear it. But without a parable spake He not unto them."

There are some who, by certain signs, think that the present time may be the death-throes of one such dark age, the blackest hour which precedes the dawn.

The Tantrik books are chiefly concerned with methods for assisting the mind to emancipate itself from the tyranny of phenomena. We are indeed imprisoned within a world of form, whence we cannot escape by simply wishing to be free; the Tantrik teacher starts by accepting this fact, but contrives to use the very multiplicity of form as a means to freedom. He causes the thoughts of his disciple to dwell on forms, to juggle with them, to make of them puppet actors on his mental stage where they play Passions and Moralities, till through the jungle of their multiplicity he begins to notice the narrow trail that leads out to the great underlying Unity. It is this kinetic idea which has been the womb of symbolical art in India and Tibet. At the cost of seeming to labour the fact, I repeat that according to Tibetan ideas, each celestial figure is capable of a continuous succession of transformations, being himself or herself a form of a form and so on indefinitely. To regard the numerous figures seen in the temples as separate "gods" or "devils" whose "idols" are worshipped, is an error that will rob the traveller of any chance of learning how to read the symbolical language which is unfolded for his edification.

But there is another and far more serious misunderstanding of the Tantrik symbols which demands to be refuted in the public interest. This error is spread by persons who have seen just a little more than the mere name and are vaguely aware of the worship accorded to the Divinity under the form of His own consort, the Female Energy. There is little doubt that many have persuaded themselves to suspect that under this representation there lurks some vile suggestion, pandering to man's sensual appetites, and that the figures seen clasped in ecstatic union are really pornographical emblems.

I have borrowed an example out of a *Tantra* called *Demchhog* or Highest Bliss, because the Divinity who passes under that name, and who personifies a theme propounded for contemplation, is described with great wealth of detail, while a plain explanation is given of what each of these details stands for. No better instance could be given of how the Tantrik symbolism works. I can only offer an abridged paraphrase of the passage, for to quote it all would take several pages.

The Chief Divinity, "Circle of Higher Bliss," has four faces, symbolizing fourfold sets of ideas—among them the Elements of earth, water, fire and air, which, with either, constitute the material Universe, and the Four Boundless Wishes which are Compassion, Affection, Love and Impartiality; but there are several other sets of a still more profound character. The body is blue, to symbolize that He never changes from "the Wisdom, which knows that the things which are coloured differently and the like, are really not so, but they are all of a single nature and taste." Each face has three eyes, to show that the Three Worlds—the Sensual, the World of Form but without sensual craving and the Formless Spiritual World—are under His vision, and also that He knows the Three Times, past, present and future. He has twelve arms that represent His knowledge of the Twelve Interdependent Origins of the Round of Existence.

To prove that Perfected Intelligence is both the Void (that is, the Absolutely Real, which we can only indicate through a privative word, since for us the Real cannot but be void of determination, form, relativity and all that we can possibly conceive of) and Compassion (the pure sacrificial Love which characterizes the Bodhisat, the highest goal of Buddhism), He holds in the upper hands a *dorjé* (thunderbolt sceptre) and a bell. To show that Method and Wisdom are ever in union, the first pair of hands clasps His Spouse or *Shakti*. The next two hands hold a raw elephant hide which they are tearing asunder: this is the emblem of Ignorance. The third right hand holds a drum, proclaiming the most joyous tidings. The fourth hand brandishes a battle-axe, by which He cuts off births and deaths. The fifth holds a dagger to show that the six sins of pride, disbelief, want of serious devotion, distraction, inattention and boredom are cut off. The sixth right hand grasps a trident, showing the destruction of the Root-Poisons of Anger, Desire-Attachment and Sloth (the inertia of Ignorance?).

Now to turn to the left hands:—the third holds a staff surmounted by a *dorjé*, sign of supreme bliss, and the fourth holds a blood-filled skull signifying that all ideas which regard things as either material or immaterial are done away with. From the fifth hand dangles a noose, the Knowledge that grasps the nature of sentient beings. In the sixth left hand is the head of four-faced Brahmā, showing that all the delusions of the Round have been finally shaken off.

Under His feet He tramples an emaciated figure of Time, proving that out of His boundless Compassion He voluntarily remains in the world of sentient beings as Saviour. His bent left leg spurns the form of a Black Destroyer, for Wisdom has got rid of every antithesis such as subject-object and enjoyer-enjoyment. His hair is tied in a knot on the crown of His head, because merit has been acquired in the fullest measure. Each of His heads is adorned with a chaplet of five skulls, standing for the five kinds of Wisdom. His face frowns and His teeth are set, for by Him all heresies are overcome. His ear-rings are Fortitude, His necklace Charity, His bracelets Chastity, His girdle Energy, the wheel of bone over His Head is Meditation.

Round His waist is draped a tiger-skin, not tightly fastened, because He is released from all belief in the real distinction of Body and Spirit. His limbs have symmetry and grace, His visage is heroic, stern and severe, He is full of energy, He is awe-inspiring, and yet He is compassionate and His features are of a peaceful cast. (This form belongs to a type called semi-wrathful, not one of the "terrible" forms, nor yet wholly "peaceful.")

We now come to His Consort-Energy, who clings to Him in inextricable embrace. She is red in colour, because She is devoted to the service of all beings. She has only one face, because all things have but one taste—they are basically one. She possesses two hands, for She comprehends both aspects of Truth, the apparent and the real. Her right hand holds a curved knife which is Wisdom-Consciousness, that cuts away qualifying thoughts and all passions. This weapon She thrusts in all directions. With Her left hand She clasps Her partner. To show that She has untied the knot which holds all things to be what they appear, Her hair is loose and flowing. She is naked, for She is free from the obscuring veil of Passion. She, like Her male partner, is three-eyed and crowned with the Five Wisdoms, shown by skulls. He should be regarded as Appearance (that is, the Phenomenal Universe), as Method and as Boundless Compassion; while She is the Void (the symbol of the Absolute, the Empty of all relativities), Wisdom, Tranquillity and Bliss. The pair are inseparable, so they are shown interlocked in sexual union, touching at all possible points of contact. The marriage is consummated in the midst of a halo of flames, the fire of Supreme Wisdom which burns up all obstacles.

"IF I FORGET THEE O JERUSALEM"

BELOW Yuru, a rocky defile, straightly hemmed in by sheer cliffs, falls away in a succession of huge steps down towards the Indus. The sky, far overhead, shows as a narrow strip of blue. A rivulet, born of an insignificant trickle, is crossed and recrossed. Gathering volume, it swells into a quite sizable river which after an all too brief independent life goes to merge its identity, with breath-taking suddenness, in the coffee-like waters of the greater stream, which here races along between forbidding banks of scorching rocks and sand.

A mile or two eastwards from the confluence, a suspension bridge leads over to the right bank, defended by a fort of sun-baked mud, built by the Dogra invaders of Ladak to command the passage. In this part of the Indus valley the road goes through three villages, Kalatze, Nyungla and Saspul, a few hours' ride apart. They are some of the most prosperous settlements in the land. Each of them has sprung up close to the entrance of a tributary valley, whence issues the torrent which, through its leats, allows wide terraces to be irrigated. Every large village thus owns its own hinterland, with a chain of lesser hamlets extending inland from the river. Usually in each of these districts there is one important monastery, which fills the part of feudal overlord for the valley, and receives a contribution of novices from all the leading families around. Most of these youths, before being admitted to the rank of full choir-monks, must first visit Lhasa for a long term of study, so that the holy city continues to be a nerve-centre for all Buddhist Central Asia. Young scholars from outlying provinces as far apart as Ladak and Mongolia gather there and meet their fellows from the Chinese border, Sikkim and every part of politically independent Tibet.

To the rider in the desert, the sight of long *Mani* walls dividing the road into two always heralds the approaches to a village. Some of these *mendongs* are colossal, especially those built beside the trails that converge on Leh. Huge *chhortens* are set up at intervals along the walls, which suggest a breakwater with lighthouses, except that here the ocean is of sand instead of water.

At the beginning of the fields, the roadway passes under several *chhorten*-crowned gateways which, though modelled to one pattern, yet somehow always contrive to reveal the play of individual fancy. So also the houses, though conforming roughly to the plan described in the preceding chapter, remain a never-ending source of curiosity and delight.

The valley of the Indus, comparatively sheltered from the most biting winds, offers ideal conditions for the cultivation of the apricot. Fruit ripens almost as high as Leh, but there the climate is too rigorous. The city lies near enough to the orchards, however, for a daily supply to be brought in baskets during the months of July and August. A certain proportion of the crop is dried and stored for winter use. In this form apricots are an excellent food for travelling. They are delicious when stewed, and have a very sweet, slightly toffee-like flavour.

The inhabitants of these villages must surely be some of the happiest on the face of the earth. One can only pray that no zealous enthusiast will feel impelled to "raise their standard of living," in the name of some sociological theory worked out under totally dissimilar circumstances. Certain writers have alluded to the poverty of the people, doubtless referring to their lack of ready money and their rather Spartan simplicity of life. There is no luxury, nor a big margin of surplus food, but if the enjoyment of a sufficient, if rather unvaried, diet—composed of tasty, unadulterated materials—and the leading of a healthy, outdoor life in majestic surroundings, with work which has its leisured as well as its strenuous phases, the wearing of durable and comely homespun clothing, the dwelling in spacious, well-built homes, and the possession of a restricted number of well-designed objects—if all this be poverty, then let us deplore our wealth! To the above catalogue two more intangible amenities can be added: time to think without the sense of being driven, and the absence of organized persuasion and regimentation at the hands of the State or of a commerce that does not fall far short of it in power.

Some twelve miles above Saspul, in the upland valley of Likhir ("Circle of the Water-Serpent-Spirits"), stands the great abbey of the same name, belonging to the Gelugpa or

"Virtuous Custom" Order of monks, commonly known as "Yellow-Hats" in order to distinguish |them from the red-hatted adherents of earlier conventual organizations; all, however, without exception wear red clothes. The Yellow-Hats were founded in the fourteenth century by St. Tsong Khapa, "the man from Onion land," born near the western marches of the Chinese province of Kansu: eventually they became the most powerful association in Tibet and Mongolia, including among their members the sovereign of the country, the Dalai Lama, as well as his spiritual compeer the Panchhen Lama of Tashilhunpo. Some of their colleges number their students by the thousand, the biggest of all, Drepung ("mound of rice"), outside Lhasa, exceeding in membership both Oxford and Cambridge taken together.

The Gelugpa differ from earlier foundations mainly in allotting relatively more time to public services, to the slight attenuating perhaps—or so their critics allege—of those exercises in pure meditation which the others continue to place before all else. The Yellow monk regulates his conduct by a statute of 253 clauses, which include abstinence from alcohol, meat and marriage. The second rule is often disregarded in practice, by reason of the difficulty of obtaining enough vegetable food on the plateau of Tibet, even more so in Mongolia, where the people remain exclusively pastoral, refusing to take to agriculture. But even so, no one presumes to defend the lapse into a carnivorous diet, and all those—and they are not a few—who do remain faithful to the law against flesh-eating, are generally honoured in the land. In contrast to the Gelugpa, several of the old Red-hatted schools—to speak of Red-Hats as one Order, balancing them as one whole against the Yellow-Hats is a common inaccuracy in books—admit both fermented liquor and marriage.

Though the adherents of the various Orders usually live in harmony, they would not be human if a little rivalry did not sometimes creep in; one has only to think of the petty bickerings of Franciscans and Dominicans in our own Middle Ages. The Yellow-Hats are given to reproaching the others with slackness, especially over the question of drink, and to congratulating themselves because of their zeal for book-learning; whereas the Red-Hats, who, though they have their books too, lay rather more preponderant emphasis on the oral transmission of doctrine, turn that very same fact into a counter-accusation. Referring to the frequent daily assemblies in the temple for the choral repetition of the office which the rule of the Yellow-Hats prescribes, one Red-hatted monk voiced his criticism to me by saying: "They go in for too much chatter." It is said that these rivalries occasionally have reached the point of acrimony where brawls with iron pen-cases (the students' weapon in Tibet) have broken out, and have resulted even in the spilling of blood and the cracking of tonsured skulls.

In Ladak, though both Red and Yellow Orders are found, with a certain advantage of number in favour of the former, relations between them seem perfectly amicable. Likhir of the Gelugpa is one of the older and larger houses; it is so flourishing that a new wing containing monks' quarters has been planned. It enjoys a high reputation for strict observance, being surpassed in this only by the neighbouring convent of Rigzon, many lamas of which—so it was said—refuse to ride, lest the horses should take it amiss.

On a day of July, 1936, a band of pilgrims from a distant country arrived at Saspul bound for Likhir. By their apparel one would have taken them for Tibetans from the Central Provinces, or perhaps from Sikkim, where that fashion is copied. Instead of the Làdaki self-coloured woollen tunics, they wore kimono-like cloaks of a dark maroon, girt at the waist with silk sashes, bright red, blue or green; not yellow, for this is the privilege of the clergy, and it is a criminal offence in Tibet for an unauthorized person to be seen in it. Their caps were of black felt, with a band of gold Chinese brocade and fur-edged ear-flaps, worn turned up. Their boots were of the usual high shape, bound with coloured garters; the soles were of rope, while the uppers were black felt, gaily decorated with bits of green, blue and red cloth. There were three principal persons in the party, besides a few grooms, one of whom, a tall and ugly man called Norbu, acted as servant. Norbu had a plain face, but a heart of gold. He came from Timosgam above Nyungla, which is the home of the best porters in Ladak. The baggage of the party was on a modest scale.

The little cavalcade rode into Saspul in the afternoon and alighted at a caravanserai, where they made a meal of milk, eggs, big radishes resembling turnips and ripe apricots of prime quality, thin-skinned and succulent: the newcomers must have been thirsty from having trudged through the torrid stretch which lies between Nyungla and Saspul, for each consumed a double portion of fruit, and still was eager for more. After lunch they asked for a messenger to carry a note to Likhir, since it would have seemed discourteous to have arrived there without due warning; in no land is the virtue of politeness cultivated more than in Tibet. A peasant boy volunteered for the job, and a letter, couched in suitably honorific terms and wrapped in the white silk scarf which betokens sincere respect, was entrusted to him. He set off at great speed, not by the usual tracks, but by a short cut across the hills, promising to be back with an answer soon after sundown.

While waiting for their envoy to execute his errand, the three strangers idled away their time strolling through the fields, where the tawny crops, ripe for the sickle, were being cut down and carried to the threshing-floors. When they felt tired they sat awhile in the dense shadow of the apricot trees; the deep, intense green of the foliage was gold-spangled with fruit, which kept dropping to the ground with every puff of the clover-honeyed breezes. The air had an aromatic tang that mingled with its sweetness, a fragrance as of incense that came from the catmint which covered the walls. The three friends sat and rested on the brink of one of the leats, screened from the sun by willow trees; the water at their feet ran icy cold, though only two yards away the stones were too hot to touch.

Returning to the fields, the newcomers stood watching some peasants winnowing, to the accompaniment of shrill women's voices raised in a tune which gave its rhythm to the teams engaged in treading out the grain. Apple-cheeked girls drove their yokes of four or five yak calves round and round in circles, while others, armed with long wooden forks, threw fresh sheaves upon the pile. The women took turns at keeping up the refrain continuously; at that season the whole country resounds with song from daybreak till evening. Not only harvesting, but every kind of work has its appropriate tune. One of the most expressive is that of the log-carriers. Heavy poplar logs, to be split in half for roofing, are borne on men's shoulders. As they march along, a single voice sings a verse, which is then answered in chorus by the remainder of the gang. Similarly, when a big reservoir had to be dug at Leh, an oboe-player and drummer were engaged all day to give the rhythm to the labourers: surely the requisitioning of serious music for such a use betokens a high degree of civilization!

At nightfall the messenger returned from the monastery with a message bidding the pilgrims welcome. He also reported that

184

SHEPHERD ON THE ZOJI LA

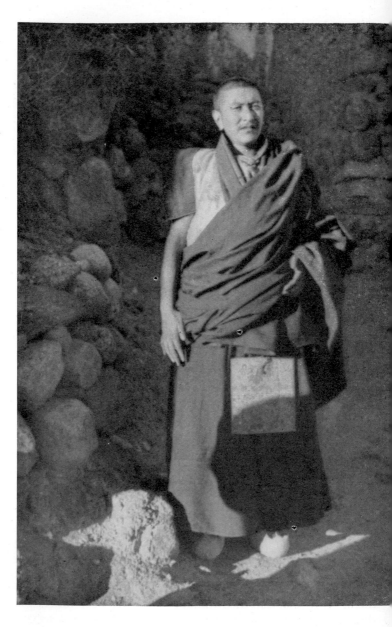

THE LAMA GYALTSAN

the abbot of Likhir was absent in Lhasa, and that the prior had been left in charge and would do the honours.

Next morning, the party rose at dawn and followed a sandy track that led away from the river into a small valley between gravel-strewn downs. Norbu acted as guide with great willingness, for that day's goal was his family *Gompa*; two of his brothers were at that time in residence, the one just ordained *Gelong* or full monk, the other a novice still in his early teens. After a few miles, the path mounted more steeply till it emerged in the Vale of Likhir, one of the most attractive in all Ladak. It was a rich expanse of cornland, dotted about with charming homesteads, each standing in its clump of willows or poplars. Since every inch of irrigated ground was precious, here, as always, the road ran in the desert, though close to the margin of cultivation. It was marked by rows of *chhortens* and *mendongs*, on which pious hands had laid innumerable flat stones bearing the *Mani* formula: the long chain of *Mani* walls constituted the Sacred Way leading towards the Water-Serpent-Spirits' abode.

Likhir *Gompa* stands on a bold eminence commanding a view of the whole valley: as one approaches it from the direction of the Indus there is a break in the curtain of hills to the right, through which a shimmering panorama of snowy peaks appears, like an immense diamond tiara. These are the higher portions of the Ladak range, mostly attaining about 19,000 or 20,000 feet.

The abbey forms a magnificent architectural pile, terrace upon terrace, which looks as if it is growing out of the very rock, an effect due to the fact that every wall, window and door is given a slight inward slope. It is this habit which makes the Tibetan style fit ideally into a mountain landscape, so that the handiworks of man, far from detracting from Nature's perfections, seem merely to heighten and extend her rhythms.

About a mile and a half from the *Gompa*, the party was greeted by a young and handsome lama, who had been sent out to meet them. The distance to which a person walks to receive a guest is proportional to the latter's rank. For a prince they might ride out a whole week's journey. A ravine had to be crossed to reach the end of a spiral path which led round the hillock forming the emplacement of the abbey. As soon as the riders came within sight of the lowest bastions, the deep purr of a bass drum greeted them. Next, added to the rumbling of the drum, sounded forth the majestic voices of the twelve-foot trumpets which serve to hold a pedal in every Tibetan temple orchestra, the foundation-

G

tone above which the higher-pitched instruments weave their symphonies. The players take turns in breathing, so that the note is maintained unbroken, heaving like the swell of some ocean of molten brass. The descant is rendered by oboes, not unlike bagpipe chanters, while complexities of rhythm are contributed by smaller drums, handbells and cymbals. The clashing sonority produced by a good orchestra is strangely thrilling when heard in the open. Raising their heads, the wayfarers caught sight of the group of red-robed musicians high up on the walls.

As the riders rounded the last bend, a throng of lamas and peasants ran out towards them. They dismounted from their ponies and, casting the bridles into willing hands, advanced to an alleyway, where a tall and venerable figure stood a little apart. He was the prior, before whom knees were bent and foreheads touched the ground. Signing to the party to follow, he turned and led the way at a rapid pace, threading a labyrinth of courts and stairs and passages to the topmost terrace of all, marked at the angles by banners, rather like furled umbrellas. Then he passed through the doorway of the abbot's private apartment, which, as was customary, was situated at the top of the building. They removed their shoes, and stepped inside a chamber of surpassing magnificence.

It was supported on wooden posts, the bracketed capitals of which, as well as all the beams, window-frames and other woodwork, were picked out in delicate patterns of flowers and dragons of brilliant hue. The windows, which were flung wide open affording a grand view over the mountains, were of Chinese design, with a kind of translucent paper to take the place of glass. The walls of the room were hung with scroll paintings representing saints or angelic beings, each picture being mounted on Chinese brocade of richest design. The ceiling was like a tent, with an awning of peach-coloured Chinese embroidery of ancient date. Along one wall, facing the window, stood the altar, behind which presided a row of gilt, lotus-throned figures shaded by elaborate carved canopies. The floor was spread with fine rugs of Turkistan and Tibet, on which the guests were bidden to take their seats; a charming little carved and painted table was placed before each man to hold his teacup and food-bowl. Each article was a work of art of real worth, and had been kept in spotless condition, though put to reasonable use.

186

No sooner was everybody seated, than tea—that inevitable preliminary to all business in Tibet—was served out of a fine teapot, which after use was kept warm on an earthenware stove, which might have been Etruscan. The tea was equal to everything else at Likhir, prepared from the best brand, with the usual butter and salt and a pinch of soda added. The Tibetans daily consume a prodigious quantity of this tea, which to our taste seems rather more like soup. At every sip, the cup is promptly refilled to the brim, and this goes on till the guest, after repeatedly making a polite show of refusal, finally decides to make a stand and covers his bowl with his hand, turns it upside down, or hides it under the table.

After the guests had drunk a good many cups of tea, food was also served; apricots both fresh and dried, a hard crystalline candy and a kind of rice pudding containing currants, lightly fried and dusted with sugar. During the meal the old prior and one or two senior monks sat on the floor and carried on an elegant conversation covering a varied range of topics, while the young novices crowded in the doorway to watch and listen.

Our three pilgrims gained some prestige from the fact that their dialect, clothes and customs derived from the Central Provinces. Their own home, however was in New Babylon on the farthest confines of the Lands of the Setting Sun, a region which was in process of being enslaved by three malignant demon-kings named Progress, Hurry-Hasty, and Propaganda —like many felons, the last-named has several aliases, the commonest of which is simple Mr. Education: these tyrants forced their subjects to work at a rate so intense that they might well have envied the pyramid-builders. From time to time the three fiends would set their subjects to battle, inflaming one against another like fighting-cocks, so that they were roused to the pitch of blind and furious hatred. Possibly the motive behind all this strife originated from a desire to distract men from calm thinking, lest having leisure to view things, and themselves, as they really are, they might discover, in non-attachment to self, a way of escape out of the sufferings of the Round of Existence in which they were imprisoned.

The majority of the servants of the demons lived in want, but some of them had persuaded themselves that their lot was enviable and should be shared by other races that had so far managed to avoid adopting their customs. Numerous busybodies were recruited, under all sorts of specious pleas, and despatched to remote corners of the globe in order to disseminate the demons' influence. The company offered up an earnest prayer that Ladak and Tibet might be spared as a preserving-ground for other ideas and that, by the power of the five kinds of Wisdom embodied in the Buddhas of the five directions, assisted by their active Consort-Energies under their sternest aspects, the malice of the demons might be exorcized, so that all mankind might return to peace.

After tea, the guests were led into a small adjoining chamber, the bedroom of the abbot. In it there was a fine chest painted in delicate gold arabesques; otherwise the room was bare except for five large scroll pictures so wonderful that to describe them there are no words sufficient in language.

Finally, everyone repaired to the main temple or Hall of Assemblies for the afternoon service. It was a lofty church, divided into three aisles by massive wooden piers, on which the flat ceiling rested. The walls were brilliantly painted or hung with *t'hankas,* so that every corner of the building offered to the eye some new play of colour under the intense rays of the Central Asian sun, streaming in by open windows opposite the high altar. There were two thrones, a higher one for the abbot and one slightly lower, on which the prior sat cross-legged. A double row of wooden platforms, raised a few inches off the floor and covered with thick rugs, formed a choir on either side, facing in towards the central space. On these the monks sat cross-legged, those of the inner row holding musical instruments. Each man, before taking his seat, drew over his shoulders a yellow cape.

All through the service a little black kitten, the pet of one of the lamas, kept playing in and out under the platforms on which the officiants were sitting. No one paid attention to it, and it was allowed to gambol to its heart's content up to the very feet of Him who did not try to distinguish between man and beast, nor even between god and devil, in pointing out the road of escape from suffering.

A brief meditation preceded the rite, the offering of the Universe to the Buddha. This idea runs through all the public worship like a central theme. St. Tsong Khapa, who fixed the order of service for his own Yellow monks, tells them to start by imagining themselves each to be endowed with a hundred heads, and each head with a thousand mouths, and each mouth with unnumbered tongues, all eloquent in praise. In making votive

188

offerings, at first separate gifts must be presented, such as flowers, incense and music. What cannot be given in kind, may be offered up in imagination, and gradually added to, until the whole Universe is ready to be laid at the divine feet "as a gift tendered by the mightiest of kings, its possessor."

The hands of the worshipper are joined in a gesture called *mandala* (globe) which is the regular symbol of the Universe. The hands are turned palms upwards, with the little fingers crossed. The tip of the right thumb touches the left little finger, the right index finger touches the left middle finger, and *vice versa*. These four pairs make the four points of the compass, or quarters. The fifth pair, the fourth fingers, sticks up in the middle and represents Mount Meru, the central axis, which is itself the path of Exaltation, of ascent from the partial and limited to the integral and infinite.

The office consisted of psalms, some sung to a marked chant, others merely droned in a low voice, diversified with symphonies rendered by the orchestra. The oboe-players held the main tune. Some of the chants were metrical and supported by drum alone; with others, handbells were rung. A precentor with a deep bass voice led the service, giving the signal with his cymbals to start or end each section. He had a peculiar way of indicating the final cadences, letting his voice sink in a long chromatic *glissando* into the depths of the bass, not unlike bagpipes from which the air is being emptied. Every ten minutes or so there was an interval, when everyone could relax and look about him; during actual prayers in the strictest Tibetan monasteries, inattention is apt to be summarily dealt with by a censor, who surveys the congregation from a point of vantage, his leather scourge kept handy for administering instant correction. Woe to the man who stares about or shuffles his knees or makes a whispered remark and thinks he can elude the watchful eye. He is seized by the scruff of the neck and led out into the middle, where he can only bow down humbly and take his punishment like a man. When officiating, the monks are expected to sit motionless, though without stiffness; their hands only move in the ritual gestures. In the pauses for relaxation, the novices get up and fill the wooden bowl set before each monk, with tea out of a monster pot; they drink, and sometimes also add to the tea a little of the parched barley-meal which takes the place of bread; this is kneaded into a lump and then eaten.

When the service was over it was time to think, reluctantly, of departure. Many were the requests on the part of the good monks that the three friends would return later and make a stay of several days or even longer. The ponies were led round by a groom; before mounting, the visitors saluted the kind old prior who, bending, imprinted on each of them a light tap with his forehead, bestowing a blessing. Then they turned and disappeared down the hill. How often since that time have they dreamed of Likhir and of the day when, like the foretaste of a beatific vision, they were admitted to the threefold joys of Nature, the Arts, and Human Intercourse combined in one single all-embracing synthesis. Now they are back in Babylon: how shall they sing the Lord's song in a strange land?

THE BURSAR OF SPITUK

THE ride from Saspul to Spituk, where the road enters the wider portion of the Indus valley, is on the whole monotonous, with sandy stretches strewn with round pebbles—an unpleasant surface, whether for riding or walking. At first, abandoning the Indus, which is only rejoined close to Spituk, the Likhir path is followed for a couple of miles to a fork; there the Leh road turns off to the right up an extremely hot and sandy pass, and leads on to a wide plateau, which it crosses before descending into the next cultivated strip near the village of Basgo. This village is surrounded by apple orchards, and dominated by an ancient ruined castle built to command the entrance to a long side valley through which it is possible to approach the river Shyok. Possibly in olden times Turkoman raiders may have come down this way.

After so many days in stony gorges the open scenery round Spituk came as a refreshing surprise. The banks of the river were marshy in many places, with reeds and low bushes, and strips of damp meadow where cattle were grazing. Spituk itself is dominated by a famous monastery of the Yellow-hatted Order; its silhouette stood out sharp in the evening light as we approached from the west. The main road to Leh passes, not on the river side, but between the hill on which the *Gompa* stands and a low line of fantastic limestone cliffs, where, so we were told, the lime is collected which is used for the foundation coating of sacred paintings. On passing through the opening, one enters a great sandy amphitheatre, the meeting-place of several valleys. On the south side, the Indus, now broken into two or three shallower channels, is fringed on either side with a broad belt of cultivation, set here and there with clumps of poplars. At the entrance bay of each subsidiary valley there is a fan of irrigated land; the nearest of these to the north contains the city of Leh itself. Across the Indus, in the shadow of a snow mountain, stands Stok with its castle, half monastery, half palace, in

191

which resides the descendant of the great line of Ladak kings, a State pensioner, who still bears the courtesy title and owns the fief.

As we wished to visit Spituk monastery at leisure, we decided to stop the night in the rest-house and to postpone entering the capital for one more day. An abrupt staircase, up which we were taken at a breathless pace, led to the main buildings, which occupied different levels on the hillside. The main temple is a fine building containing mural paintings and festooned with scrolls. There we made our offering of five precious stones, which were taken over by a tall and lithe-looking lama with a very keen, vivacious face, who discharged the office of bursar. He asked if we preferred to have the stones set in a decorated *chhorten* at the end of the aisle or in the gilt diadem of Tsepagmed, whose beautiful image stood on the right of the Buddha, behind the altar. We chose the latter as the most suitable setting for the jewels.

From the first moment we felt powerfully drawn towards the personality of our new acquaintance, whose name was Dawa (Moon); he seemed to reciprocate the feeling, for he spoke to us as if he had all along been expecting our arrival and knew that our fates, already connected by an unseen link, were pre-destined to move along parallel lines in the future. Looking back, I think that the bursar of Spituk is one of the most remarkable people I have ever met, though the abbot of Lachhen must probably be accorded the first place. The lama Dawa was a man, who, both in theory and practice, exemplified a dedi-cated life of high quality. He was not only a well-informed ex-ponent of the Doctrine, but he was the thing itself. It showed up in his smallest action and in his lightest word; above all it revealed itself in the extreme detachment of his judgment. It had even affected his bodily movements, which had a peculiar flexibility that seemed more than just physical, a reflection of the suppleness of his mind. To this list of qualities there must be added a trenchant wit and a sweet and lovable disposition. He told us that he had three pupils, whom he was coaching before they went off to Tibet for their final studies. He con-sidered that a teacher could not adequately deal with more than that number at one time; certainly they were greatly to be envied in their master.

From the temple we were led to an upper chamber containing fine *t'hankas*; carpets were spread, and tea and rice pudding were served. The room belonged to the Incarnate Abbot of Spituk, the Lord Bakula. We remembered the tributes paid to the good taste, wisdom and urbanity of that prelate in various writings of the eminent Italian anthropologist, Professor Giotto Dainelli. But his Bakula was no more to be found among the living and the monastery was being run by a prior, in expectation of the day when the newly-chosen Bakula, now about eighteen years old, should return and take his seat on the abbatial throne. He had been found by the process of divination used for discovering the child on whom the influence of the preceding line of abbots had again descended, and on reaching the age of about sixteen he had been duly sent to Lhasa to the vast college of Drepung, where the men of Spituk, as also those of Likhir, usually take their course in divinity. The young Bakula was due to return only after obtaining his degree of *Geshé* or Doctor, which demanded many years of work.

We invited the bursar to supper: towards sunset he arrived, but would touch nothing but a cup of tea, since, as he told us, he never took anything after the midday meal. He was very strict in abstaining from alcohol and meat, and pronounced severe censure against those who were self-indulgent in these respects. According to him, many of the monastic houses in Ladak had deteriorated markedly of recent years: even Rigzon, reputed to be of the purest observance, had somewhat lowered its standard, while certain of the other *Gompas* were falling into deplorable laxity and were simply vegetating, with hardly a thought to spare for the Doctrine. In Tibet he declared things to be, on the whole, much better, though even at his own university of Drepung he considered that devotion needed rekindling. "There are nine thousand monks and students there," he said, "but go any day into the temple and you will find it far from sufficiently attended." On the other hand the University of Sera, also near Lhasa, was still a model, he thought, while at Ganden, the third of the great trio of Yellow-Hat Houses at Lhasa, the standard was about average. There were, however, scores of excellent teachers to be found scattered over Tibet, but oftener in the smaller monasteries, both Yellow and Red, than in the ones with the biggest membership.

Our newly-found friend then proceeded to inquire about our own doctrinal standpoint and this led to a discussion as to what constitutes a Buddhist and what test, if any, can be employed for his recognition. Any form of inquisition into a man's private views is considered impertinent. Buddhism, like Hinduism, has on the whole, avoided the error of trying to stamp out doubt by organised pressure. Indeed the duty of subjecting the doctrines one professes to the final test of realization, is the advice given by every teacher, good and bad alike. There is no real knowledge other than the realization of truths already immanent and waiting to be unveiled as soon as the obscuring passions and self-delusions have been cleared away. Moreover, though reverence for the person of the teacher runs through the whole tradition like a central thread, it is not expected of the pupil that he shall blind himself to the fact of human deficiencies in his master's life. His private faults in no wise impair the authority of his teaching for the disciple, or to diminish the latter's obedience and devotion to the master. It is, however, bad form for the latter ever to speak disparagingly of his master to others. Whatever he may notice, he must continue to treat him with the respect due to his function as mouthpiece of the doctrine. In this matter the wording of the books is emphatic and allows no loophole for evasion. The Master-pupil relationship, in a regular Tradition, is something far transcending any actual individualities concerned. The chain is more important than any single link. If some of the links are made of baser metal, it matters little, provided that they hold. Conversely, there may be flaws in the lessons imparted by men of the highest private virtue; care must at all times be exercised against letting the scales be weighed down by irrelevant personal and moral considerations.

The bursar's view on the touchstone for recognizing a Buddhist, was summed up as follows: "Where the Refuge is present there is Buddhism: if the Refuge is wanting there is no Buddhism. The Refuge is a question of understanding and of action based thereon. This truth must be grasped and experienced and all actions must conform to its spirit. Except in the Refuge seek no other way of Deliverance."

The Refuge is a triple formula which has sometimes, inappropriately, been described as the "Creed" of Buddhism. It runs thus:—

I take Refuge in the Buddha
I take Refuge in the Doctrine
I take Refuge in the Congregation.

To these three Refuges there has been given the name of the Trinity of Most Precious Things. The line one must follow in order to realize them is suggested by the following passage, copied for me by my next teacher, the lama Gyaltsan of P'hiyang, whom I shall introduce in a succeeding chapter. It is taken from the works of Dagpo Hlardjé, surnamed Gampopa, who was a pupil of Rechhung, the disciple of Mila Repa:—

This is the lesson to be learned of how to go for refuge to the Three Most Precious Things . . .

In the integral lesson are contained six special lessons and five general ones. First of all, the special lessons contain three renunciations and three attainments.

To start with, behold the three things to be renounced:—

1. Having gone to the Buddha for refuge, do not worship the gods who err in the Round.
2. Having gone to the Doctrine for refuge, do no injury to living creatures.
3. Having gone to the Congregation for refuge, do not form associations with heretics.

Here are the three things to be attained. For as much as you attain them in conformity with the word of Buddha, do so without forgetfulness and with reverence:—

4. Respectfully raise on high even a mere fragment of a sacred effigy.
5. Having gone for refuge to the Doctrine, strive to hear, ponder and meditate the imperative Doctrine. The writing, which enshrines the Doctrine, even were it a tiny shred, raise reverently on high.
6. Having gone for refuge to the Congregation, to it—the Congregation—that is to the followers of Buddha, also show reverence.
   Associate with the friends of virtue; lastly also show respect to the yellow robe.

Here follow the five ordinary precepts:—

1. Even at the sacrifice of your life, do not abandon the Three Precious Things.
2. Even for a very important reason, do not seek any other method.
3. Do not cut off periodic offerings.
4. Do not invent another Refuge.
5. In whatever direction you may be proceeding, worship its presiding Buddha.

A few comments on this passage may help to make it clearer.

Some of the phrases explain themselves and ask for no comment, but a few might give rise to doubt as to their exact significance:—

The gods who err in the Round. They are one of the six classes of beings who share the Round of Existence (See Chapter XI, page 112). Though temporarily possessed of superior powers, they are our fellow-creatures, subject to the same vicissitudes of birth and death as ourselves. To worship them is senseless and therefore idolatrous. Real worship can only be paid to what is permanent and truly divine: that is, to the Buddha, apart from whose essence nothing is, though we know it not, because of the illusion of individual existence and the dualistic notions to which it gives birth. Reality and permanence can only belong to That which contains within Itself Its own sufficient Cause and That can only be One. To offer real worship to anything else is idolatry, though reverence of a qualified kind (what in Christian theological language was termed *dulia* as distinct from *latreia* or true worship due to God alone) is offered to Saints and Heavenly Personalities of inferior grades, who play the part of Teachers, Protectors and Intercessors. This statement of doctrine is practically the same as that which has obtained in the Catholic Church·since the Council of Constantinople, which settled the controversy over the revering of images and the invocation of Saints. It is furthermore interesting to note that all these heavenly Lamas and Divinities, including the Bodhisats like Chenrezig, who fulfil the redemptive function on behalf of all suffering creatures, are comprised in the Third Most Precious Thing—the Church. They correspond in idea to the Church Triumphant, while the lamas on earth, members of the Order set up by the Buddha, the authorized transmitters of His Tradition, correspond to the Church Militant. The concordance with Christian doctrine here revealed, is a striking illustration of the common thread which, under many external differences of form and expression, runs through all traditional teachings.

The second renunciation, which discourages us from inflicting harm on other sentient beings, is interpreted very strictly, and a man is considered to have fulfilled his duty in this matter in proportion as he finds it possible to avoid occasions for injuring even the lowliest creatures. Like many of the Jains in India to-day, the ancient Buddhist monks swept their path as they walked, lest they might tread inadvertently on an insect, and they carried a filter so that the water they drank might be cleared of animalcules that would otherwise have been swallowed. One of the first things that a Gelugpa, or Yellow monk, must do on getting up in the morning, is to anoint the soles of his feet with spittle as a sign that he prays that any animals which he may trample on by mistake may be reborn in the happy sphere of the Western Paradise.

The third renunciation is open to slight misconstruction. The word which, for lack of a better, I have translated as "heretics," is given in the original Tibetan as *Mutegpa*, which literally denotes a Brahmin devotee. It comes down from the early centuries when regular debates used to take place between rival sectaries in India. There are many tales of the discomfiture of the spokesmen of one or other party—which party, depended on the sympathies of the teller; but there is also little evidence that religious emulation ever led to bigotry: in this respect the historical record of all the Indian schools of thought is singularly blameless. I discussed the point about *Mutegpa* several times with a lama, and as far as I can tell, the passage means no more than that one should avoid associating constantly with people who are likely to try to distract one by their bad example; it must never be read in the sense of authorizing an unfriendly, stand-offish attitude even towards aggressive opponents of the Doctrine.

Turning to the three things to be Attained, one notices that the first proposition, the latter half of the second, and the third, are all concerned with treating sacred objects with reverence—images, books and persons who have the right to wear the sacred colour. The most positive of the Attainments is the first half of the second precept, which describes the process by which Knowledge is to be acquired. First one must listen to the Doctrine, then one must consider it in a theoretical sense, and finally it will be realized in Meditation. Then only can it be spoken of as Known.

"The Writing which enshrines the Doctrine"—that is, books or portions of books—is reverenced almost more than anything else by the Tibetans. They will not pack up their belongings for a journey without making sure that the books have the place of honour on top and will not be crushed under everyday objects. If a Tibetan is handed a book he will lay it on his head, murmuring a prayer that he may be helped to profit by its wisdom.

The five general injunctions call for little comment: the only one which is not quite clear is that which refers to periodic offerings. I fancy that it means that those who devote themselves to the religious calling, deserve the alms of the faithful for their support, but I am not quite sure if I have read this sentence aright.

One final remark must be added to this commentary on the Refuge. When a Tibetan is about to invoke the Three Precious Things, he usually precedes them with another Refuge phrase:—

"I go for Refuge to the Lama."

The Lama here referred to is not synonymous with the third Precious Thing, the Congregation: it denotes the disciple's private spiritual director—"his own Lama," or *Guru*, as a Hindu would call him—through whom the Doctrine is transmitted and in virtue of whose teaching the pupil is made an effective participant in the Tradition from the beginning of time. In the Lama is seen personified the Teacher function, the highest that can be conceived in the Universe. To him boundless reverence, obedience and devotion are enjoined and no important step must be taken unless preceded by his formal authorization. He is the symbol of Tradition, through which the Three Precious Things are revealed.

These explanations about the Refuge are the fruits of several discussions. On that first occasion at Spituk we naturally could only begin to approach the subject. After talking for some time of the traits which denote the Buddhist, the lama Dawa, in his turn, addressed a few inquiries to us about the teachings of Christianity. "I have noticed that Christians, as a rule, seem indifferent to the sufferings of animals. Not only do they all eat meat freely, but they do not seem to mind killing animals on the slightest provocation. Tell me, have they the authority of their Founder for this? Did He really teach that sentient creatures can be exploited in the service of man and injured at his mere convenience? It is the one thing which appears to me evil in what I know of Christianity."

There is an instinct of loyalty in man which makes it repugnant to him to run down his own countrymen before a foreigner; one feels a strong impulse to present the least unfavourable case. I believe that Christianity has been one of the great

198

traditional avenues for the revelation of true Doctrine, and I also think that the general idea of Charity as taught in the Gospel is utterly incompatible with the heartless exploitation of animals for supplying man's material wants. I deny that it is reasonable or indeed possible to practise Charity towards one's fellow-men, and callousness towards one's fellow-creatures of the animal world, acting tenderly towards the former and cruelly towards the latter; though it must be confessed that some otherwise virtuous people have attempted to justify such a policy. The theory that creatures endowed with any degree of sensibility were created to be used at the unrestricted will and pleasure of one species, singled out of the whole of creation, seems to make of the Creator not a God, but a fiend of unexampled malignancy. I can still remember at school, asking a master how the story of the drowning of the Gadarene swine could be squared with the rest of the life of Our Lord; the lame explanation that I received shocked even my boyish intelligence. That day at Spituk I would gladly have given the lama Dawa a simple statement that Christ's teaching on animals was as precise as he expected it to be and that the deplorable practice of Christians in this matter was simply a falling away from their professed ideal.

But to a man of the highest intellectual honesty like Dawa, one felt it impossible to give any answer that suffered from bias; he and his fellow lamas showed such a freedom from all tendencies towards special-pleading when discussing the condition of their own Church, that anything short of an equal frankness towards them would have been rank dishonesty.

The answer that I gave to the lama's question was roughly as follows:—"In the recorded life of the Founder of Christianity, contained in the four Gospels, it must be admitted that there are hardly any explicit allusions to animals. One can find two or three passages which could be read in a favourable sense, for example, the sparrows, not one of which can 'fall on the ground without your Father . . .' and 'the lilies of the field'; but there is nothing that could not be explained away as a figure of speech." It is therefore just to admit that in the Gospels the question of animals is practically not touched on and appears to be treated as a matter of no great urgency. It is my own personal opinion that the teaching of Christ, in regard to the cultivation of a generally merciful and loving outlook, is impossible to realize if it excludes animals. The Sermon on the Mount, and the sermon of the Buddha in the Park of Gazelles are, in spirit, singularly concordant. I readily grant that the absence from the Gospel of any specific mention of our duty towards animals seems rather regrettable in the light of subsequent experience.

Much cruelty to animals still exists, and though few English people would now tolerate intentional cruelty, many still refuse to forego activities which indirectly result in cruelty. If any extension of European influence in the Tibetan countries were to take place, it is to be feared that the thousands of wild animals that now live unmolested in the neighbourhood of the monasteries, would become an immediate target for the fur-hunter, the collector and the so-called sportsman. More dis-astrous still, their example would arouse the acquisitive instincts of the local inhabitants. To give one example, the tragedy of the Giant Panda is a recent object-lesson. This adorable creature had been left in peace for centuries until the exhaustive search for it, organized by a few thoughtless travellers, suggested to the natives that there was money to be made in attacking the Panda; with the result that in several localities it is already threatened with extinction, a disaster which the original col-lectors might well have thought of.

One other question was touched upon that evening, the ques-tion of Peace. The fear of war has held such a large place in men's thoughts during recent years, and there has been such perplexity of mind as to the duty both of Christians and non-Christians in respect of bearing arms, that the chance of obtaining an opinion from a Buddhist teacher of the highest authority was one not to be missed. The trend of Buddhism has, in practice, been markedly more pacific than that of Chris-tianity; but there have been schools of thought, notably that of Zen in Japan, in which a warlike attitude has been accepted under certain circumstances. Even among the lamas there are differences of opinion; we know that several of the monasteries of Kham played a big part in resisting the Chinese early in this century and that the Lhasa Government's forces were actually placed under the command of a churchman, the Kalon Lama. Nevertheless, the views of the Spituk bursar are probably fairly representative of a large section of opinion. He expressed him-self as an out and out supporter of non-violence. "Whoever wishes to act in conformity with the Refuge, the same is bound to abstain from every sort of injury towards sentient fellow-creatures whether by thought, word or deed. You cannot pretend to go to war without trying to inflict injury. If you take up arms there is no Refuge; if there is no Refuge, you are not a true Buddhist."

Those who, with our lama, share these conclusions, recall the story of the Sakyas, the clan from which the Buddha Himself sprang, and who inhabited a territory in the foothills of the Himalaya. News was brought to them of an impending attack by a hostile tribe and it was debated anxiously whether resistance should be offered or not. Eventually they decided that, as followers of the Doctrine, they were debarred from offering armed resistance, but must welcome the invaders as friends, so they threw down their arms. Pacifists among us are sometimes apt to say that Peace is not only right, but will pay automatically. The heart of the enemy will be changed and victory will rest with the non-resister. While not denying that in many cases the example of returning good for evil may produce incalculable results, such as a revulsion of feeling in the aggressor, one cannot encourage the belief that such would be the result as a matter of course, nor yet, as the lamas would add, allow a faint appeal to potential self-interest to fog the issue and taint the motive.

However, the Tibetans, not being sentimentalists, admit that the story of the Sakyas ends as it might very well end in any similar case—every convinced pacifist must face this possibility: the enemy arrived and the Sakyas were massacred to a man, the gutters of their streets ran with blood and their race was blotted out from mankind. Some people may argue that the sacrifice of the Sakyas was in vain; but, viewed in relation to the law of Cause and Effect, the chain of consequences derived from their brave refusal to compromise, even if all memory of the deed should fail, would add itself to the general store of merit on the Cosmic plane, the *Karman* of the Universe as a whole: and in the second place, as a recorded historical event, the slaughter of the Sakyas might, by force of example, affect many individual *Karmans*. To the Sakyas themselves there was no obvious profit; that is as it should be. Also we must ever remember that their own personalities were to be regarded as dissoluble; it was idle for them to trouble their heads with hopes of reward, or regrets. The fruit of the Sakyas' sacrifice was nothing less than the Enlightenment and ultimate Liberation of all creatures.

Before we quitted Spituk the lama Dawa made us promise to return to him. He was most anxious not to lose touch with us. "If you have a doctrinal difficulty, please put it in writing, so that I may have leisure to think it over. And do come back after you have been to Himi." (We had told him that we proposed to visit that celebrated monastery.) "And be sure to tell me your impressions." So he spoke, before we rode off across the last five sandy miles towards Leh.

LEH

A BELT of willows standing in rather dry ground marks the outskirts of the city. As we came to the houses, our baggage animals turned off the road abruptly. The ponies stepped over a wooden bar at the base of a gateway, and we followed, thinking it must be some short cut, and found ourselves all at once in the main bazaar, a broad and stately street flanked by rows of immense pollarded poplars. The vista is closed by the prodigious castle of the Ladak kings, its lower stories of Egyptian severity, while the upper ones are pierced with larger windows leading out on to wooden balconies. The scale of the building is colossal, dwarfing the rest of the town; though most of it is unoccupied, it is in a fair state of preservation. It is built at the end of a rocky spur, at the foot of which nestles Leh.

Immediately below the castle is the mosque—for there is a large Mussulman community—built in the usual Ladak style of architecture. Later on, it became one of our regular pleasures to walk down to it at night and wait for the muezzin's call. The first time that we happened to be there, standing in the darkness of the unlighted street, we heard from the balcony of a house a tenor voice of rare sweetness singing a melancholy rhapsody. The man now and then paused in his song and then began again. His mellow notes floated out into the surrounding stillness; he seemed to be expressing some deep joy that lay close to tears. In style his songs reminded me of those of Greece, so that I at first suspected Turkish influence, for many Turkish traders come down from the north to Leh; but on inquiry the house proved to belong to a Panjabi.

Eventually he ceased; spellbound we lingered in the hope of hearing him sing again. A bell clanged somewhere above our heads, and then the *Azan*, or Call to Prayer, resounded in ringing tones through the night, making known that: "There is no God but God and Muhammad is the Envoy of God!" It was the first time that we had listened to these words; we fell, for the moment, under the spell of the directness and simplicity of the Islamic faith, which proclaimed, in terms that clove like a sword, the unity of the Principle of all Being and the dependence of all created beings upon It, its Prime Cause.

But this is anticipating—on that first day, as we rode into the bazaar in the noon sunlight, we could overhear the remarks of the people. "They must come from Lhasa." "I hear them speaking the dialect of Tsang." We passed through the crowd to the far side of the town, where we sought out a secluded lodging in a garden to which we had been directed; it belonged to a native Muslim called Ghulam. We pitched the tents, while our host, who proved to be the kindest and most attentive imaginable, regaled us with bread, a long untasted luxury, and tea prepared in the Turkish way, with plenty of sugar forming a thick syrup, and scented with roses.

We had been in our garden only a few moments when Khan Muhammad Din came to call and invited us to a tea-party at his office, where we were to meet the principal merchants of the town. There were two of these; one was an old Muslim of seventy-five called Hadji Muhammad Siddiq, who traded with Lhasa and Gartok and knew the former city well, a humorous and hearty old man with a large family—the second one was also a Lhasa merchant, a Ladaki Buddhist, Nono Tönyod Sha, quiet and courtly; we used to see him almost every day and we owe much to his kindness. They both asked us to their houses at once, so the next day was occupied entirely with visits.

The interior of the better Ladaki house is usually extremely elegant, with spacious chambers bordering on a courtyard, windows with translucent paper in fretwork frames after the Chinese fashion and attractive painted woodwork, on which floral and dragon motives are applied with an almost endless power of invention. The ceilings are of unsquared poplar logs laid across the main beams. The furniture does not differ in principle from that used by the peasants, except in its greater richness and finer workmanship. There are carpets, Yarkandi, Tibetan and best of all, Chinese, divans round the walls, and painted chests and cupboards; in the old Hadji's house there were also Turkish pipes. He and his family wore the usual costume of Tibet except for the head-dress which, in their case, was a turban or red fez. We have since heard news of the Hadji's death: it is difficult to imagine Leh without his merry presence.

Nono Tönyod, the other merchant, possessed a magnificent house, but his taste appeared to have been affected by his journeys to Kashmir; in the midst of many beautiful things we saw much worthless junk. A cabinet contained, for instance, some lovely chased silver vessels from Lhasa, side by side with cheap English earthenware adorned in the style favoured by third-rate landladies at the seaside. A painted tea-table, a perfect specimen, stood next to a packing-case aggressively stencilled with the name of a firm in Bombay. Appalling modernized Yarkand carpets swore loudly against the soft texture, the warm browns and blues of the corresponding Tibetan products.

He showed us his treasures, not forgetting to serve delicious Tibetan tea and trays of dried kernels and sugar-candy. He had a prodigious collection of teapots, magnificent examples of the silversmith's art, also teacup-stands, one of which, made at Lhasa, was a real marvel. Later on we asked him if he would part with it—it is quite in order to offer to buy things seen in a private house—but he said we could only have it if he first sent it back to Lhasa to be copied. He had also some fine jewellery of gold filigree set with choice turquoises. Strangely enough, the central jewel of a magnificent pendant was only a cheap piece of red glass that might have come out of a Christmas cracker; but though this was intrinsically unworthy of its setting, the effect was not inartistic.

The merchant had a manager called Ishé Gyaltsan, a young man of energetic appearance, much more like a Tibetan than his master, who was a typical Ladaki of mixed blood. The manager looked after the Tibetan part of their business, while Tönyod himself dealt with the Indian side. Ishé Gyaltsan usually wore yellow shirts which matched his face, so that we called him the "Yellow Man." We were surprised that he should wear yellow, for he spent some months each year in Tibet and had, so he said, lived there without a break for fifteen years, and it is forbidden for any but members of the clerical Order to be clothed in that colour. "But I am of the clerical Order," he protested, "I was brought up as a novice at Tashilhunpo and I still can stay there whenever I like, though I have taken to trading." There are many similar cases in Tibet. He also wore his four-eared cap in a queer way, with three of the flaps tucked in, out of sight, and only the left ear sticking up asymmetrically. It gave his face a peculiarly comic air: again we asked the reason for this and were told: "It is the privilege of anyone who has served tea before either of the two great Lamas. As a boy I served the Panchhen Lama and now I always wear it thus, for if I did not, people in the road might say to themselves 'What sort of a man is this?' —now they know."

He was a curious, self-sufficient character, extremely concrete in outlook and of untiring industry in his work, for which he had a passion that had little to do with the mere making of money. He used to spend a large part of his life in solitary expeditions with only his own picked servants, all pure Tibetans, for company, going first to Gartok to the great fair which takes place there every autumn, and then eastward to Shigatze, Gyantse and Lhasa, a three months' journey on horseback.

He was just then organizing a caravan of forty ponies with Yarkandi merchandise such as carpets, green jade cups and felt rugs, also Indian cotton, to take to Lhasa, whence he would return with the precious brick tea, grown in West China, which the Tibetans in the remotest places love to drink in preference to more easily obtainable Indian-grown varieties. Ceaseless tying up of bales continued all day long on Tönyod's veranda, while piles of saddles were lying ready in the porch.

The Yellow Man had an amusing characteristic. Whenever he felt excited, he would repeat the last word of a phrase many times at great speed, for emphasis. He might be asked: "Do you think this is an excessive price?" "No, it is quite reasonable, not excessive at all, at all, at all, at all, at all . . ." Or he would say, "To sell the sacred books to foreign collectors is entirely unlawful, unlawful, unlawful, unlawful . . ."

He and I became fast friends; he seemed to make the overtures soon after we met. One day he explained himself, "You know, I took to you from the first moment, because it is plain to me that you really love and understand our Tibetan customs and know how to do things just as if you were one of us."

Another friend in Leh, of whose generous help we cannot speak too gratefully, was a Christian called Joseph Gergan who fortunately, in spite of his change of religion, had not attempted to become like a European, as is too often the case with converts. He was a man who truly deserved the name of Christian; for never have I come across anyone in whom the love of Christ and the imitation of His life were more manifest. There was no attempt to slur over the inconvenient portions of Christ's teaching; in him was seen the simplicity of a child, side by side with the wisdom of a cultivated, well-informed mind. We always spoke of him as "Gergan the Translator," borrowing the term from St. Marpa and the other eleventh-century importers of sacred books into Tibet, for Joseph too was a man who only tried to impart to others a doctrine which he had first practised himself. He had been occupied for years on the tremendous task of turning the Bible into colloquial Tibetan; eventually he completed the work but died before its publication, which has still to take place.

In the summer, when caravans from India and Turkistan enter or leave Leh almost daily, the scene in the bazaar is most picturesque. Here can be seen tall, thin, hawk-nosed Kashmiris in their unbecoming Euro-Indian rags. Across the way saunter some stocky Baltis in thick grey-brown homespuns and close-fitting caps. Tall Turks, fair as Englishmen, but with narrow slits of eyes and rather unintelligent faces, stalk about the market, clad in white shirts, sheepskin caps and high Cossack boots. Their women wear fine orange or rose embroidered dresses and are closely veiled, in contrast to their Ladaki sisters who move about freely. A few red-cloaked lamas are always to be seen and occasionally a true Tibetan, or an Afghan youth of great beauty, with white skin and long eyelashes and oval face, an amorous prince from the brush of Persian Bihzad come back to life.[1]

Huge yaks ruminate contentedly in the courts of the Turko-man caravanserais, over which, like a shower of wool, floats the clinging white down of the poplars. The average condition of the animals is quite good, but many ponies or mules employed on long-distance traffic show the usual sore-marks from the hard pack-saddles, suffered during the protracted journey across the Karakoram. I have heard that many animals fall from fatigue and are abandoned on the passes there, where they fall a prey to the wolves. The Turks are extremely callous and frequently inflict cruelties out of sheer stupidity. I cannot say that I have witnessed any ill-treatment in Leh itself, even from Turks, or heard an animal abused; so I am prepared to believe that insensitiveness, rather than an actively cruel instinct, is responsible for the evil. As for the Ladakis, they treat their

[1] Since writing this description I have heard that the regular caravan traffic from Turkistan has been suspended owing to political machinations in the province of Sinkiang.

animals well, on the whole; in their general attitude they do not differ from pure Tibetans.

From Nono Tönyod we managed to collect a good deal of information about the local craftsmen. The principal metal-worker of Ladak, who was the maker of many of the best examples in our friend's possession, did not live close to the capital, but in a village a couple of days' journey away, in a subsidiary valley on the south side of the Indus. The place is called Chhiling, and one large family, probably including cousins and brothers as well as children of the master, supplies most of the high-class copper and silver work for all Ladak. The master used to make periodic visits to the capital for a few weeks to take orders and carry out repairs. He luckily happened to be at Leh at the same time as ourselves and Tönyod took us round to a house on the outskirts of the town where he was at work. He had set up his furnace under a huge tree and was busy mending teapots, assisted by a pupil. Later he came over to Tönyod's house to discuss with us the price of a new brass teapot. Several examples from his own hand were shown to us, in every degree of elaboration, from one covered with silver *appliqué* to a plain copper one tinned inside, with a particularly fine dragon for a handle; according to custom its spout was inserted into the mouth of a tusked marine monster. We decided on one of the latter pattern as the proportions were the best and the price was very reasonable: this teapot reached me in 1938 and proved to be a masterpiece of the art of the hammer. The same smith was also asked whether he could make a faithful copy of Tönyod's best silver teacup-stand, to save sending it as far as Lhasa for reproduction; but, after thinking it over, he said that though he might possibly manage it, he was not sure: and it would necessitate the forging of a large number of special tools. The fact was that he was not keen on the commission; he was too honest to disguise his doubts as to whether his own skill could quite rise to the heights required for producing a replica of a work by a still greater master.

It is instructive to note the distribution of the leading artists in Ladak. The chief woodcarver and also the best jeweller lived in Leh itself. Gonbo, the silversmith with the greatest reputation, dwelt at Chhiling, but the potter whose wares were most valued belonged to the Likhir valley. Rigzin, the leading painter, came from down the Indus, while at Kalatze, on the same river four days short of Leh, lived the only man with any reputation for weaving rugs. Besides these there were many assistant craftsmen and painters, both lay and monastic.

We were given an introduction to another merchant, this time a native of Lhasa, who was married to a Ladaki lady and lived out of the town in a country house at Sabu. I rode out to pay him a call across a stretch of desert which, being free from stones and not too heavy going, gave the opportunity of an enjoyable canter. The house, which was on the usual plan with the family apartments on the first floor, was approached through a courtyard in which three chained dogs, veritable hell-hounds (but made so by man's folly), growled threateningly as I entered.

The squire—for such a title seemed to fit him better than that of trader—received me hospitably and accepted my present of a ring together with a white scarf, offered in accordance with etiquette. I had chosen for him a silver ring with a cornelian; it had been designed to slip over a finger of normal size, but he had great difficulty in discovering one thin enough to take it. He was huge and burly, and surely one of the ugliest of men; he was dressed in a dirty old shirt and greasy gown, with high velvet boots such as are affected by smart Lhasa society, all smeared with mud. On his head he wore a pointed hat of violet silk, also in the latest fashion. He was rough of speech and hearty, and he certainly might, but for the clothes, have figured as the typical squire in the days when John Bull was John Bull. He had two sons, eighteen and twelve years old respectively, both of them exceedingly beautiful and well brought up. They waited on me at table with the grace of medieval esquires, bringing a basin and pouring water over my fingers from a ewer between the courses: and when it was time to leave, they ran out to hold my stirrup. Our servant Norbu was given food in the same room; he squatted in a corner and interrupted the conversation when he thought he had a useful comment to offer. After a pleasant afternoon's small talk with the worthy squire, we returned to Leh, which we reached at sundown, just as a light breeze was rising following on the torrid heat of the afternoon. A soft tinkling, as of elfin bells, was wafted towards us; we found that it came from tiny peals attached to the pinnacles of the *chhortens*.

Next morning we had hardly finished breakfast when who should appear but the squire himself! Had we been more versed at that time in Tibetan customs, we would have known that it is conventional to return a call at the earliest possible opportunity. Luckily we managed to behave as though we had been expecting him all the time. "Please sit down," we said, "the tea is nearly ready,"—meanwhile hastily whispering to Norbu to make the tea. While our guest drank tea we had a breathing space in which to cook lunch. Actually someone had to be sent post-haste to the market to buy bread and eggs, so that omelettes, always so handy in such emergencies, could be prepared. In a few minutes lunch was served, to which, after the polite show of refusal prescribed by custom, he did full justice. When he had had enough of a dish, he passed his plate to his own servant to polish off the leavings. At the end we gave him a stiff tot of the medicinal brandy, so we felt that, though nearly caught napping, we had not fallen too far short of Tibetan standards of hospitality.

"WHERE RUST DOTH CORRUPT"

THE most celebrated as well as the largest of the Ladak monasteries is that of Himi, situated some thirty miles from Leh on the farther side of the Indus. It was founded by one Stagtsang Raspa ("Tiger's Den Cotton-clad"), whose spiritual influence continues to remanifest itself in every head Lama of that line. The present buildings date from about three and a half centuries ago, having replaced an earlier foundation that was destroyed by a landslide.

Himi is rich, owning considerable estates in various parts of the country; its subordinate houses are numerous both in the vicinity and even as far afield as Mulbek, on the border. The names of five hundred monks are inscribed on its roll. It belongs to the Order called Drugpa which, besides possessing several lamaseries in Central and Western Tibet, can claim for its own almost the entire body of clergy in Bhutan.

This monastery is considered to be one of the sights that must not be missed and most visitors to the province make an excursion there. We had come provided with a letter of introduction to the abbot, since we imagined his home to be a seat of learning, where it might be worth while staying for some time in order to study. The letter, wrapped in a silk scarf of the best quality, was despatched to him by messenger, together with our customary offering of five stones, among them an aquamarine. In a gift of this sort, coins, or whatever else is tendered, should add up to an odd number, as an even one is deemed unlucky.

The bearer of the missive completed the journey from Leh to Himi and back in an amazingly short time, having started homewards the very moment an answer was handed to him. This is typical of the Ladakis when they travel; they pause as little as possible till they have accomplished all their business and can relax properly. Their speed never fails to astonish foreigners. The abbot's reply, duly signed in English "Yours sincerely S. Raspa," conveyed an invitation to visit him as soon

211

as possible, since he was on the point of leaving for a tour of the neighbouring province of Spiti.

The ride from Leh to the great *Gompa* is sometimes taken in two stages; a halt can be made at a half-way house, the Muslim village of Shushot. After crossing the Indus, which here splits into several channels, the road follows the edge of a riverside strip of farmland for several miles, before entering the desert. A long and scorching ride lies ahead, over a tedious stretch of sandy ground. The reflection of the sun's rays from the dazzling sand is so fierce that fair-complexioned people are well-advised to use some kind of protective ointment just as if they were crossing a snowfield. If this precaution is neglected, their faces may be severely blistered. The monastery itself lies concealed inside a narrow side-valley running down to the river from the south-west. It undoubtedly merits its title of *Gompa*, which means literally "a solitary place."

At length, after going past the houses of the village, one arrives suddenly close under the monastery, which forms an impressive block of buildings nestling up against the side of the mountain. From its upper story projects a row of wooden galleries of charming design, and this gives it an unusual lightness in contrast to 'the fortress-like severity of other *Gompas*, which are almost always situated on rugged eminences, where they seem to grow out of the very rock; this magnifies the apparent size of the buildings, whereas in the case of Himi its real proportions are overshadowed by the mountain towering above.

Just under the lowest terrace there is a small guest-house with a pillared portico facing into a garden enclosed between high walls, with a strip of grass down the middle and a row of poplars along each side. As soon as we arrived we were met and conducted to this lodging by the *chyagdzöd* or bursar, a rather villainous-looking old monk dressed in grimy garments. To do him justice, however, he had arranged the little rest-house cosily, with fine brown and blue Tibetan rugs on mattresses along the platform under the porch, and a separate tea-table for each guest. He asked if we would eat meat and drink barley-beer or *chhang*—his eyes lighted up as he pronounced the magic word. We replied that we would gladly drink one cup each, and that we did not take meat. We then took our seats upon the dais, while food was cooked and served by our own men. The bursar came and sat down beside us, after directing that a big brass *chhang*-pot, like a jug with a very long lip and a lid, should be set before us. We drained our cups, and then there ensued a contest between us and our host as he did his best to refill them, while we resisted, covering the cups with our hands. Though he filled his own cup time and time again, it seemed to hurt him cruelly to think of all the good liquor being wasted, while there were still more throats down which to pour it. It is the sign of a confirmed drinker to derive inordinate satisfaction from vicarious tippling. At length we were able to pacify him with the offer of some blocks of chocolate, which was found to rank next to beer in his affections, so he went off happily, inviting the party to call on the lord abbot in the morning.

That day a small incident occurred which helps to throw light on a certain trait of the Ladaki character. We had ridden ahead of our baggage, but did not expect it to reach its destination very long after us, since experience had shown that the pony-drivers on foot could keep up with the riders extraordinarily well, in spite of the latter trotting their horses on favourable ground. We were rather annoyed, therefore, when the transport did not turn up for several hours. So unusual did this seem that we even began to feel a little anxious; but eventually the men appeared, looking fresh and unhurried, so we asked them somewhat sharply to explain the delay. They frankly admitted that they had lain down to have a good sleep; though they knew they had done wrong and were liable to a scolding, and even to some loss of pay, they did not try to make excuses. This is very typical; these people hardly know how to lie. An official subsequently related to us that when any small offence is committed it is only necessary to question the suspects in order to elicit a truthful version with full details. There is no regularly organized constabulary in Ladak, though the Wazir, in addition to his other offices, holds police rank. Apparently it is thought that among such an honest and law-abiding population, the police, having no crime to repress, could only pass their time in creating it!

Our first contact with Himi did not seem too promising, nor was a walk round the monastery reassuring. The whole area was polluted, and the air was charged with nauseating smells which, owing to the place being so shut in, never drifted away. We had been warned in Leh that the water was liable to produce a form of diarrhœa like a minor dysentery; but it is just as likely that it is not so much the water itself, as the filth-infected dust, which causes the trouble. By walking to a point well above the monastic settlement, water can be drawn where there is no reason for doubting its purity; whereas it is hardly possible to avoid consuming a certain amount of foul dust with one's food. Naturally any water drawn from below the inhabited area must be regarded as the most dangerous of all.

After a night lying on fine pile carpets—surely the most restful of all couches—we made ready for the visit to the Lama himself. Passing through a vast and stately courtyard, where several ferocious dogs struggled, howling, at their chains, we mounted a staircase to the upper story, holding our noses to keep out the stench of a leaky drain, and were ushered into a lofty chamber, magnificently painted with floral designs, carried out with the utmost delicacy and taste. The staring white dial of a huge post-office clock disfigured the farther wall, while the floor was strewn with a litter of papers, boxes, small mechanical toys and nameless junk, out of the midst of which, like a reef half-submerged by the oncoming tide, rose a platform on which the prelate was sitting, while a secretary and the old bursar stood by and assisted him with correspondence.

The man himself was a heavy, insensitive-looking person, from whose countenance any traces of learning or intelligence, if he ever possessed them, had long since faded. He signed to us to sit down before him and welcomed us with a string of inane banalities, which made us feel every moment more depressed and uncomfortable, and filled us with regret at having sent that beautiful aquamarine!

We spent the rest of the morning in a tour of the temples, which are of great size and magnificence, or rather were; for the state of the interior is enough to break the heart of any art-lover. Massive brass-studded doors, with bosses cast in the form of wreathed dragons, gave admittance to the three main halls of worship, which opened on to the central courtyard. They were crowded to the ceiling with works of art, in various stages of disintegration. Marvellous paintings, executed when the art was at its acme of creative power, had once lined the entire wall-space. Fairly large expanses still kept their rich colouring, though the colours were mellowed by time to a certain sombreness which did not detract from their beauty. But elsewhere, the plaster had cracked and flaked off badly, exposing the rubble-masonry beneath. Here the face of a Bodhisat, his finely chiselled features still composed under the impenetrable calm of Knowledge, looked out on us, though his body had all but crumbled away. There we saw a torso, there a pair of hands still making the gesture that bespeaks mercy. In a corner we discovered piles of books, volumes upon volumes, wood-block prints and manuscripts, all jumbled together, their loose leaves drifting about in hopeless confusion: who could tell what wisdom was on its way to oblivion? Passing along a side-aisle, we came upon a stack of *t'hankas*, some tied up and others half-unrolled, all cracked, torn and thick with dust. The piety of generations had turned Himi into one vast treasure-house; on every side were to be found scrolls, Chinese embroideries and statues; we also saw a throne covered with exquisite flowers that we took for Persian lacquer, but which may have been Kashmiri work, the gift of some former ruler.

In a small upper room, as if a sharp contrast were needed to point the sad lesson, we discovered a wonderful set of *t'hankas*, a riot of figures, birds and rainbow-like halos, which sent out luminous streamers that glowed like rainbows, all still in perfect preservation; also a collection of books, equally well cared for. Some of the volumes were bound between thick boards, with scenes in relief: the undersides were of gold lacquer, on which line-patterns were traced with a delicacy worthy of the Japanese. How this one corner came to escape the general dirt and untidiness was a mystery.

We wondered if any of the treasures would survive; in that climate the process of decay is slow, and a little timely energy might result in cleaning up the place and restoring some, at least, of its ancient glory; but with such a governor in charge the outlook seemed almost hopeless. "Fish stinketh from the head,' as they say in my own country of Greece. I was told that a certain sum was once sent by the Maharaja of Kashmir for repairs to Himi; but there were no signs of recent restoration to be seen. Unless a miracle happens, I fear that Himi and its treasures will soon have to be written off on the debit side of history.

In the afternoon we received another summons to the presence of the lord Raspa; reluctantly we re-ascended to his apartment, where tea was served. At the Lama's right hand was placed another low platform on which sat an aged and decrepit priest, with one wall-eye which intensified his look of dotage, yet he was evidently a man of some rank, for a silver-mounted cup stood on the little table in front of him, which attendants re-filled at intervals. No further notice was taken of him, however, but a number of European volumes were produced for our in-spection, chiefly books of travel or albums of photographs. The abbot signed to us to approach, and rapidly turning over the pages, stopped at one which showed a photograph of himself seated under some trees, together with the late "Raja" of Ladak, father of the present holder of the courtesy title. He pointed to the picture of the former Raja, and then suddenly turned with a curious gloating look towards the miserable old man on his right. "That's the same man," he said. We felt a wave of hor-rified pity sweep over us. Could that dried-up half-wit really be the lineal descendant of the talented dynasty which had reigned in the far west of Tibet for so many centuries and had endowed the country with all those marvellous monuments?

"Can you get me any stamps of this country?" broke in the voice of the abbot, while his finger pointed to the title "Czecho-Slovakia" at the top of a page in a small stamp album.

"This thing isn't working, can you mend it?" A broken bicycle bell was handed to us.

"Could you please translate this set of instructions into Tibetan and write them down?" This time it was the secretary who handed me an old dry-cell battery, with explanations for re-charging attached.

Borrowing Sir Charles Bell's dictionary, a copy of which they happened to have, I tried to make a paraphrase, ingeniously dodging unfamiliar technical terms. Finally an old catalogue of the Bombay Branch of the Army and Navy Stores was brought out and we were all kept busy trying to find descriptions and prices for various small machines. The amassing of gadgets was evidently a ruling passion with the abbot of Himi; this char-acteristic of his was even remarked on by De Filippi years before. His room was full of knick-knacks, none of them in working order. As soon as we had dealt with one problem to the best of our ability, he produced another and it was apparent that this was to go on the whole afternoon. We felt that if we stayed much longer in this lunatic atmosphere we might ourselves go crazy, so after a hurried whisper of consultation, one of us deflected the next proffered gadget by a desperate parry and we all three rose and bowed our farewells as briefly as Tibetan etiquette would allow, and filed into the outer air. But even that seemed to be pervaded with a miasma of mouldy decay. After

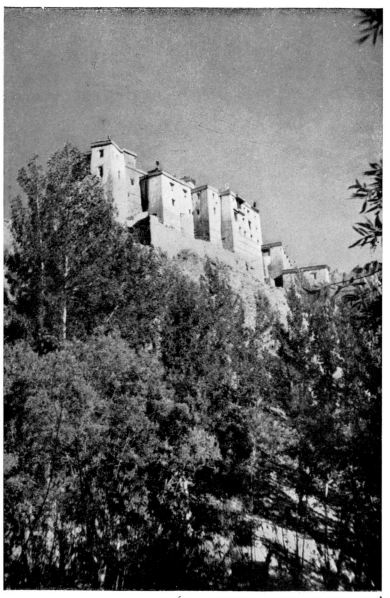

'IF I FORGET THEE O JERUSALEM'
Monastery at Likhir, Ladak

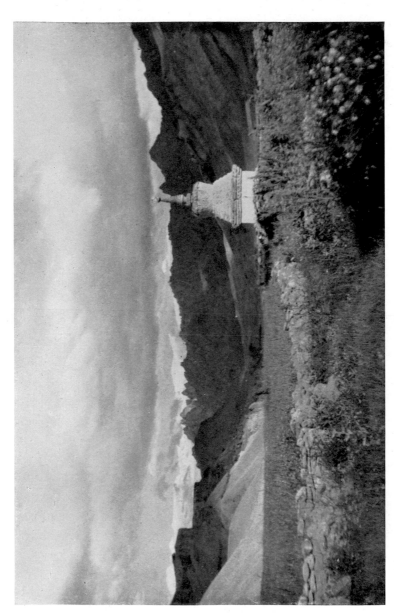

WAYSIDE CHHORTEN

leaving Himi a full day passed before the nightmare atmosphere created by the sight of the old Raja could be shaken off.

It was our intention not to return to Leh by the same track, but to penetrate beyond the Ladak range by an 18,000-foot pass, the Chang La or North Pass. Apart from the interest of seeing new country, we wished to call on another important Lama, the Abbot of Sgang-Ngon *Gompa*, which is situated not very far from Leh, at P'hiyang. Later on we spent a very happy time there. This dignitary, who ruled over Yuru and a number of minor dependencies in addition to P'hiyang, was believed to be staying at the distant *Gompa* of Satsukul two days beyond the Chang La. He enjoyed a reputation for holiness which, after seeing Himi, we might have doubted, but for the fact that Khan Muhammad Din himself had described him as a sincere, God-fearing man. There is none whose certificate of godliness could be more safely relied on than that of the Khan. If he used the term "God-fearing" it was because he himself knew what that meant.

The morning appointed for the ascent of the Chang La dawned stormily; we had hardly passed the last of the crops when showers of rain, turning to sleet and snow higher up, made us dismount, shivering, in an effort to warm ourselves by walking. Fortunately the storm did not last as long as we feared; by the time we had advanced well up the torrent valley the sun began to break through fitfully. After some time we crossed an alp, in which some specially magnificent black yaks were grazing, and then we saw the final slopes close ahead. It was gratifying to note that we might have been walking at sea level for all the effect that altitude made on us. It was evident that our acclimatization in Sikkim had been thorough.

Just short of the crest of the pass there were many flowers growing among the stones. It was a joy to see the Alpines again after so long: there were yellow Welsh poppies—rather a surprise, a pinkish mauve pyrethrum creeping close to the ground and mauve delphiniums with heavy blooms, the same kind that we had found in 1933 on Riwo Pargyul. In addition there were nettles, of a kind new to us, which, as Norbu reminded us, had been the food of St. Mila Repa.

The story is a famous one. The saint had been spending several months in a favourite cave of his, called "White Rock Horse's Tooth." His principal food consisted of nettles, which grew round the entrance to his retreat and which he boiled in

H

an earthenware pot. One day, weakened by fasting during an unusually protracted meditation, he slipped and fell on the threshold and broke the handle of his pitcher, so that it went rolling down the hill. It was smashed to bits; but the accumulated layers of residue from the nettles came out as a single greenish pot-shaped block. This episode forms the theme of one of Mila's best-known poems:—

> In the same moment I had a pot and have one no more.
> This example shows the whole law of the impermanence of
>   things.
> Chiefly it shows what is the state of man.
> If this is certain, I, the hermit Mila,
> Shall strive to meditate without distraction.
> The desirable pot that contained my wealth,
> In the very hour when it is broken, becomes my teacher.
> This lesson of the fateful impermanence of things is a great
>   wonder.

The crest of the Chang La is marked by a cairn adorned with horns of cattle and flags. It is customary in Tibet, on reaching the top of a pass, to cast a stone on the cairn and call out: "*So, so, so, so, so! Hla gyalo, De t'hamche p'ham!*" which means "Ho! ho! ho! The Gods conquer, the devils are defeated!" Travellers in the Himalaya should learn the formula and say it either when crossing a pass or a bridge. They will find it a help in gaining popularity with their porters!

The locality abounds in marmots, which are very tame. On the way back, when the weather was sunny, many of these attractive animals were to be seen lying stretched out on boulders, basking in the warmth. Some way beyond the pass was a good but cold camping-ground near a lake, the resort of many water-birds. Near by there was a hut where fuel and food were stored by Government order, for the use of caravans arriving from Turkistan. The fuel of the country is dried dung, as in most parts of Tibet. It smoulders like peat and does not smell un-pleasantly: a pair of bellows is a help when tending the fire, otherwise one must use one's own lungs.

The sparsely cultivated valleys on the farther side of the Chang La, which lie between the Ladak and Pangong ranges, are watered by streams which flow into the Shyok. Riding about eight miles along the nearest valley, we reached a place which was marked by a number of unusually large *Mani* inscriptions clearly chiselled on the rocks. There the ways branched, one

218

leading up a side valley towards our own objective, the village of Satsukul, while the other would have brought us out near the huge lake, Pangong Ts'ho, which, however, we had no time to visit. The spot where the ways divide is called T'hangtse and is famed for its cross and carved inscription in ancient Syriac, recording the journey of an old Nestorian Christian.

The Satsukul valley, which lies at an altitude of 13,300 feet, consists largely of sandy desert with a few restricted tracts where barley can be grown as well as a species of pea, quite pleasant in flavour, with flowers resembling those of a diminutive broad-bean. Along the streams there are marshy patches, which in the month of August are spangled with little flowers of bright gold, having one larger lip-like petal bearing a black mark. The peasants' houses are not the ample and artistic structures of the Indus valley, being markedly poorer: it would almost seem as if one is nearing the limit where it is profitable to try to maintain human life. The people eke out a living under severe climatic difficulties; and they show the effects of hard conditions in their less good physique, for bodily and mental deformities seem not uncommon.

The *Gompa* itself stands out in the open, not on the customary eminence. It accommodates about thirty monks; but it must be fairly prosperous since we saw an extra wing actually in course of erection. At the moment of our arrival the whole village was gathered in the courtyard; loaded ponies and riding horses stood by the gate, while there was a constant coming and going such as foreshadowed a move of some sort. On inquiry, we learned that the abbot whom we had ridden so far to visit was on the point of eluding us by departing to an even more distant spot, to which there would not be time to follow him. Before we could collect our wits we found ourselves hustled into his presence, in a room crowded with chattering peasants. The Lama, an elderly man with a kindly smile, was standing up, ready to set out. Though we attempted to explain the purpose of our journey from Leh, we really only had time for a mere exchange of formalities. A few moments later he passed from the room and, after donning a helmet-like mitre, mounted and disappeared down the valley, followed by his train, to the sound of the drum.

We were tired after our fruitless journey, so we spent the next day resting, except for a visit to the monastery. It proved to be devoid of artistic interest. The *chyagdzöd*, who exercised his financial office in all the monastic houses under that abbot, was a well-fed-looking person with small, pig-like eyes and an insolent expression. We had set aside a few rupees as a contribution for the new extension and in a weak moment we handed them over to him. He hardly even made a pretence of saying "Thank you," nor did he go in for any of the polite attentions usual on meeting strangers, and, acme of impoliteness, he failed to offer us a cup of tea! This is reckoned great negligence among the Tibetans, an unpardonable offence against the code; and it was aggravated by the fact that he was aware that we had ridden hard and far in order to visit his own superior. His bad manners were the more noticeable, in that this was the only occasion, during all our intercourse with Tibetans or Ladakis, when we were not treated with hospitality and politeness.

It was in the course of the return journey that we almost charged into the middle of a herd of *bharal*. We were traversing a mountainside and had just crossed a rib into a dip when we found ourselves among them. The wind must have been peculiarly favourable to have thus concealed our scent. The whole herd, which included a number of magnificent males, and also some charming young ones, charged away at a great pace over the slopes and in a very few minutes were no more than tiny moving dots in the distance.

While we were camping at Satsukul, we were soaked by tempests of drenching rain, which seemed incongruous in such an utterly dry country; but the storm cleared the air, so that we were able to enjoy a glorious panorama of the snowy Zanskar peaks as we passed back over the Chang La. After camping once again on the old site at Sakti, we did a forced march in order to reach Leh in one day. We followed the bank of the Indus over a terribly hot and dreary stretch and eventually entered one of the longest and richest belts of farming in all Ladak, the chief centre of which was the fine monastery of Tiksé, which, however, we had only time to admire from the outside. The water was conducted all over the area through innumerable rills shaded by huge willows. The farm-houses were more than usually spacious and prosperous-looking. In the swampy flats the ground was thickly covered with irises, but they were not in flower. It must be a most attractive district in springtime.

The last stage of the return journey crossed the sandy and stony plain that leads from the river up to Leh; these last miles were very tedious at the end of a long day. Night had fallen before we entered Leh and gained the old camping-place in the garden, where our friend Ghulam gave us a splendid welcome. Turkish scented tea was brewed, and bread, sweets and apples were hastily sent for, which kept us busy till the baggage arrived. Not many moments after the tents had been pitched, we were asleep, and the phantoms of Lamas and *Chyagdzöds* had all dissolved into nothingness.

THE PAINTER OF P'HIYANG AND SPITUK DEBATES

LEH forms a compact little world, where the various elements necessary for a complete society are blended in nicely-judged proportions, resulting in stability and contentment; while the comings and goings of Central Asian caravans have until now contributed sufficient movement for the community to escape the danger of stagnation. This little country town gives the impression of being every inch a capital, worthy to be the nerve-centre of a country, which possessing, as it does, a total population that is less than that of Scarborough but somewhat exceeds that of Margate, has produced from its deserts so wonderful a culture as to put to shame all devotees of the cult of size, wealth and number.

Apart from one or two officials, the leading citizens belong to the little group of important merchants, whose operations constitute the chief link with distant countries. Next come the shopkeepers, mostly Indian, whose influence nowadays is unfortunately tending to lower the standards of taste. In addition to these there are the skilled artisans, such as silversmiths or woodworkers, who furnish artistic requisites. Lastly come those, the majority, whose livelihood depends directly or indirectly on the caravan traffic. There are also, at all times, numbers of peasants from the surrounding district who come to the town to do their shopping or to sell fruit, vegetables and fodder: the market-place is thronged with cheerful country women carrying huge loads of fresh hay in baskets on their backs: riding through the square one must watch one's horse lest it should take a sudden nip at one of these fragrant bundles.

Higher instruction is the care of the clergy, few of whom, however, dwell inside the city, though some of them are constantly to be found there. In the days of Ladak's independence there must also have existed a powerful secular aristocracy. Nowadays the centre of fashion, in the eyes of the Ladakis, is

Lhasa: it, and not the Occidentalized Indian centres, in spite of their wealth and luxury, still holds first place in the imagination of the people. As to the delegates of the paramount British power, opportunities for contact with them occur so seldom, that the respect felt for them is not untinged with a certain naïveté. When, at intervals of a few years, the Resident in Kashmir decides to pay a visit to Leh in person, he is received with almost regal honours, to the accompaniment of holiday-making and general excitement.

We were due soon to leave Leh for the valley and monastery of P'hiyang, about three hours' ride away, where we had been invited to stay. The monastery itself stands on the usual bold eminence, in the midst of a tract of beautiful corn-land, with fascinating views up and down valley. Looking up, one is faced by a huge amphitheatre of bare hills, which take on a myriad colours in the magical light characteristic of that part of the country. In the opposite direction, beyond the Indus, darker mountains rise up steeply to their sparkling diadem of snowy ridges and small glaciers.

The project of making P'hiyang, the mother-house of Satsukul and the seat of the elusive abbot, into our headquarters, came about in this way:—A few days previous to the Himi excursion, we rode out for the day to P'hiyang to look at the architecture. We were led into one of the two big temples, the walls of which were covered with brilliant paintings. On all sides serene countenances of Buddhas, of every size and colour, greeted us, attended by smiling Bodhisats and saints in ecstasy. Terrifying Protectors writhed in flames and leaped on the bodies of victims, who personified the evil passions to be subdued within the soul; the whole showed boldness in composition and remarkable precision in the drawing. These paintings struck us as being of no great age, so we inquired of an attractive-looking monk, who was showing us round, whether they were recent. "Quite new," he answered, "it is not more than five years since they were finished." "The painter was a most talented artist," we said, "was he a Ladaki?" "I painted several myself," he replied, "but I worked in collaboration with our best painter Rigzin and several junior assistants. The work took several years."

Here was a thrilling discovery indeed! We were in the presence of a gifted craftsman, engaged in producing work of a high order, by the methods that had been handed down to him through the long dynasty of his spiritual ancestors. The man himself, though he obviously took his work most seriously, yet spoke of it with little more emotion than a plumber discussing the installation of a new pipe.

We plied him with questions; did he also paint *t'hankas*? He said he did and brought out a nearly-finished picture of Buddha with two disciples, excellently done. Our admiration so amused him that he burst out laughing. We asked to buy the *t'hanka*, but he explained that it was being done to the order of a fellow-monk; if we so wished, however, he would paint others for us and we could select the subjects. We were much excited by this, for it offered a chance of watching each step in the processes of Tibetan painting, and of going into minute particulars of the technique.

Later in the day, at tea, we learned more about our friend. His name was Konchhog Gyaltsan, which means "Banner of the Most Precious Things," and he belonged to a peasant family of P'hiyang valley. His colleagues also told us that he was a man of unusual learning, well versed in doctrine, and an admirable teacher. Our chance had come at last. If we could make a longer stay at P'hiyang we would be enabled not only to observe the painting, but also to clear up various doctrinal questions at the same time. Our satisfaction was heightened by the discovery that the Order of Lamas to which P'hiyang adhered was a branch of the Red Kargyudpa or Oral Tradition Order, which traces its descent back to St. Marpa of Hlobrak and St. Mila Repa himself. The Kargyudpa include several sub-orders: P'hiyang belonged to one of these, the mother-house of which is at Dikhung in Central Tibet, a hundred miles north-east of Lhasa. We therefore did not hesitate, but asked at once whether we might return later as his pupils, I to study the Doctrine, and the other two for painting lessons. He agreed enthusiastically, and it was arranged that we should occupy a cell next to his own, as soon as we got back from Himi.

It may well be imagined that after the disillusionment at Himi and the fiasco at Satsukul, we were looking forward with added zest to our return to P'hiyang: but that did not make us forget our other friend, the good lama Dawa, bursar of Spituk, who had been insistent in making us promise to return to him at the earliest opportunity. So we sent him word of our coming and started for P'hiyang, intending to call at Spituk on the way. We had just reached the edge of the Leh oasis when we heard a

224

tinkling of bells and caught sight of Dawa himself, riding a white horse, and followed by one of his pupils, a grave monkling of about fourteen, on a chestnut pony. The latter wore no shoes but gripped the edges of the stirrups between his toes.

The lama had been on his way to the town, but learning of our intention, he turned at once and the united party ambled back towards Spituk. The horses were left in a stable at the foot of the hill, after which we were rushed up the endless steep stairs, worse than any mountain, and deposited panting in the temple, while the abbot's apartment on the top floor was made ready. In a quarter of an hour a man came to summon us to the abbot's room, where carpets were spread and tea prepared. Besides Dawa and ourselves, the *khenpo* or prior of the monastery and another lama were present.

Dawa opened the conversation:—"So you have come from Himi? How did you find things there? Which profound doctrines did you discuss with the Lama?" We recounted our sad tale of corruption at the famous *Gompa*, but the bursar, seemingly unheeding, continued: "Surely the Lama talked with you about the significance of the Refuge?" "He mentioned nothing of the kind; we heard no doctrine at Himi." Dawa burst out laughing. "When you declared your intention of making a pilgrimage to Himi in the hope of hearing some wisdom, I said nothing; but I was shaking with suppressed laughter." He continued to tease us ironically. "But did you really not discuss the Refuge? Are they not Buddhists at Himi?" It seemed to amuse him beyond measure to picture us riding out there, full of anticipation of deep spiritual experiences to come, only to be disillusioned in that ridiculous fashion. "So there wasn't a word about the Refuge?" he chuckled. "It isn't doctrines you should have sought at Himi: beer and women are more in their line!"

Strange though it may seem to anyone not used to the Tibetan mentality, there was really no uncharitableness intended in the bursar's rather grim humour. His whole behaviour was characteristic. Such humour is born of a certain ethical outlook, which not only deters a man from trying to screen his disciple from contact with temptation, but rather makes him prone to expose him deliberately to dangerous experiences, both as a test, and to cool down romantic enthusiasms. Instances can be multiplied when a Master has gone so far as to command his follower to commit an apparently sinful act, if he judged that it would, in the long run, make for his spiritual development.

The Lama Marpa and his treatment of Mila Repa is a case in point. Innumerable similar stories could be quoted, where the means employed for testing the pupil have been carried to the verge of ruthlessness and beyond. Nor are such examples by any means confined to ancient history.

It is all a natural corollary of the attempt to strip off every illusion, however dearly treasured, which might stand in the way of the acquisition of "Awareness," the real aim of the Buddhist training. Charity itself, as they see it, is but ill-founded, unless it has its roots properly planted in the soil of the knowledge of the true nature of things. St. Mila summed up this idea in two lines of one of his last poems, which I quoted before:—

The notion of emptiness (absence of real self) engenders Compassion,
Compassion does away with the distinction between "self and other."

Loving impulses are less likely to be upset by a swing of the emotional pendulum, when they are firmly linked to sound theory—firstly to the consciousness that we and all the other creatures of the Universe are together similarly afflicted, struggling to escape from the same Round of birth and death, from the same Ignorance and Desire, and secondly to a recognition of the falseness of belief in the enduring individuality of the Ego, to which St. Mila refers, and which is the real foundation of the whole edifice of selfish ambitions and of the craving to enjoy the fruits of action. Intellectual honesty is one of the traits most noticeable in the better Tibetan clergy, who shine like highlights against the duller surface of kindly mediocrity which characterizes the multitude of ordinary lamas. This sincerity is evinced in their fearless facing of facts and in a readiness to discuss their most cherished beliefs without quarrelling.

To show how little favour sentimental appeals enjoy—a preacher is not specially admired for the power of sweeping his audience off their feet by his eloquence; rather is praise bestowed on the man who, speaking in an even, unimpassioned tone, expounds the Doctrine without having recourse to aids which might conceivably sway his listeners for irrelevant reasons. An unsound motive is enough to vitiate the merit of embracing any truth: its value is strictly proportional to the clear understanding of the issues. A true proposition, accepted for an improper reason, is equivalent to a lie: the inquisitorial person finds himself at a loss under a Tradition where the value of a mere outward conformity is thus discounted.

It is perhaps needless to harp on the fact that popular piety in Tibet, as elsewhere, does not always reach these high levels. Men in their degree of spiritual discernment show a widely varying range of capability. Yet nothing has struck me so much, in my life among the Tibetans, as the way in which the Buddhist idea, much diluted no doubt, still permeates the outlook of the common people with its gentle and humanizing influence, and to some extent with its metaphysical conceptions, even though these may have been heard as the faintest of echoes. Yet this has been accomplished without quelling the natural high spirits of the race. Some writers have alleged that real Buddhism is almost unknown in Tibet, and that superstition has entirely superseded it; I, on the contrary, was surprised to find how deeply the Doctrine had left its mark even on simple, inarticulate souls.

My criticism of the management at Himi led naturally to a general discussion on *Tulkus*, or Lamas reputed to be manifestations of the influence of known personalities, whether Heavenly Beings or Saintly predecessors. I had long sought an opportunity for eliciting the views of a really thoughtful lama concerning these much-revered figures, so numerous and popular in the Tibetan Church. I put the problem thus:—

"If a *Tulku* is the manifestation of a Saint, and yet is notorious as an evil-doer, by whom is the sin committed?" The question was meant for Dawa, but the other lama, not the prior, was the first to enter the fray.

"It is not legitimate to say of a *Tulku* that he is a great sinner," he said, "for you must not judge only by appearances. Truly the Holy One who uses the *Tulku's* body commits no sin; nor may it be taken for granted that a sin has been committed at all, even if it seems so in your eyes. It may be planned to try your faith, or from some other motive judged in reference to standards far removed from yours or mine."

I was prepared for this explanation, having heard of it before, applied to the history of the sixth Dalai Lama, who caused much scandal by indulging in carnal delights. So I pressed my question, repeating it in much the same form as before. The simple-minded lama, delighted at the chance of holding forth before an audience, proceeded to cite a tale by way of illustration:—

"A man who was on his way to visit a certain saint learned that the latter had committed the crimes of murder and adultery. Horrified, he said to himself: 'This man is no saint, but a wicked criminal: I refuse to stay with him;' so he promptly departed. Just as he was leaving, the saint picked up some dust from the road and placed it in the man's pouch, telling him to take it home. On reaching his house he emptied out the pouch and instead of dust found pure gold. He repented of his rash criticism and gave praise to the name of the saint. A thing may not glitter and yet be gold: so also are the actions of *Tulkus*."

The worthy monk, by the time he had reached the end of his parable, was beaming with satisfaction at his own eloquence. As for Dawa, he seemed rather amused by the explanation propounded by his friend, but he let him have his say before contributing his own share to the debate. To him, we put a concrete case which had come under our notice in 1933:—"A certain *Tulku* formerly known to us, secretly parted with some of the sacred vessels of the temple to a collector. He seemed to know it was a sin, for he always transacted his business under cloak of darkness." (Scandalized exclamations from the prior!) "We refuse to take this action at anything but its face value, that is, sacrilege and theft. The explanation just given by our friend here seems inadequate: find us a better." To this he replied: "If a sin is committed by a *Tulku*, or by anyone else, it is no use trying to get away from the fact. The holy being who is believed to have taken up his dwelling within the *Tulku*, being illuminate, it cannot be his act: it is surely some fiend who has taken possession."

If I had to state the case anew now, I should put it rather differently, and cite an example that did not depend on an ethical test, but rather employed a metaphysical symbolism: for, couched in this form, the problem would be easier to bring home to the Tibetan mind, and would carry greater weight. I should mention the case of the late Dalai Lama and the Panchhen Lama, who also died a few years ago in China. They had a political quarrel, and the Panchhen Lama, who by all accounts was of a gentle and benevolent nature, was driven into exile by his masterful opponent, whence he never returned. Both these high Lamas were *Tulkus*. The Dalai Lama is a manifestation of the Bodhisat Chenrezig, while the Panchhen Lama is animated by the power of Öpagmed, the Buddha of Immeasurable Light, whose disciple Chenrezig is. No deadlier sin can be conceived than revolt of the pupil against the Master, against "his own Lama." How then could the Dalai Lama representing Chenrezig make violent war against the Panchhen Lama into whom the influence of Chenrezig's own Teacher emanates? The problem, put in this way, would exercise the mind of any earnest lama, and I hope some day to hear Dawa's solution of this particular difficulty.

Lest any Western reader be misled, I must explain that no special duties attach to the condition of *Ṭulku*. Such Lamas are most often, but by no means invariably, heads of monasteries; but that office confers on them administrative powers, not authority to teach doctrine. The Dalai Lama, most famous of them all, is the sovereign ruler of Tibet, but he is no Pope, and has no greater inherent right to define dogma than any of his clergy. It may happen, and often does, that a *Lama Ṭulku* is a learned person and a teacher; but this he owes to himself and to his initiation at the hands of his Master, and not to his quality of *Ṭulku*. The service offered to mankind by *Ṭulkus* is held rather to proceed from their presence among us, which in some manner localizes the sacred influence for the benefit of mankind, than from the doing of any set work. It is as if the *Ṭulku* carried out all the purposes of a sacred image, except that it is formed of flesh and blood, not wrought in bronze. In that case he must be reckoned as a special example of a "support" for worship and meditation, like any other religious object. I am inclined to think that the doctrine of *Ṭulkus* is correctly interpreted by this theory of "supports" and that our raising of a moral issue was quite beside the point. Moreover it must be remembered that the exercise of any function of a supra-individual nature is independent of all individual contingencies, such as the private character of its ministers. It is only proper that they should provide temples worthy of the service to be offered and they can be blamed for failing to do so; nevertheless, the sacred influence itself, in principle, remains as unaffected by the individual imperfections of its supports as by their private merits.

Another question which was submitted to the judgment of the lama Dawa was whether Deliverance was attainable without first passing through the state of a human being. We were desirous to see to what lengths the belief that men and animals are, in essentials, alike, would be carried. First we referred to the fact that St. Mila Repa took what is known as the "Direct Path," which enabled him to attain Buddhahood in the course of a single life. "If that is so," we said, "is it not reasonable to suppose that a member of some other class of being, whether belonging to the animals or even a resident in one of the purgatories who experienced perfect contrition could follow a Direct Path and actually reach Buddhahood, without having to be reborn into the human family?" The lama pondered a little and answered: "Yes, I am inclined to think one must accept this. Whosoever, whether he be beast or even the most malignant of demons, finds the strength to do what Mila Repa did, overcoming the distractions of his environment, the same can become Buddha in one life as he did; but it is still more difficult for those pitiable beings, since their life does not favour nonattachment to self. Continual suffering or the daily need to slay other animals for food are great obstacles in the Path."

I kept one more question to the last—in many ways it was the most important of all:—"The various divinities are commonly portrayed and spoken of under separate names, with distinctive attributes: and so they are taken to be by many men. The countless forms fierce or calm, or the Bodhisats such as Chenrezig or Djamyan, the Giver of Wisdom, are these all separate beings, or should they be regarded as begotten only within our minds?" His answer was as follows:—"From one point of view all those divinities exist, from another they are not real"—he was here following St. Tsong Khapa, founder of the Yellow Gelugpa Order to which Spituk belonged. "So long as you are confined within the present world of forms and distinctions, so long will you personify them separately. But once a man has entered the state of 'Subduer of Foes' (Perfected Saint, who is the subduer of passions and illusions), and stands on the threshold of Enlightenment, being freed from the Round, then for him these separate things simply *are not*: for such an one, nothing at all is, except Buddhahood."

I must here add a comment to the Lama Dawa's explanation in the hope of bringing out his meaning; but it is my own interpretation and I must bear responsibility for any error. He who enters into the realization of the Absolute, has no more part in conditioned or determined existence, which ceases to have any appearance of reality whatsoever. For such a person, it can be said that our Universe, and all forms, are illusion. But so long as we still have our being within the world of form, we are forced to clothe all our ideas accordingly. The stages in the path of Enlightenment become personalities, the more distinct in proportion as we are unenlightened, the more disembodied as we progress towards the goal. What concern have we with Djamyan, Lord of Wisdom, when once we have known Wisdom herself? I used the feminine of set purpose, for She is the active energy of Method, who must also collaborate if we are to hope for the unveiling of the One Light by which alone we are able to know ourselves. And Method himself, who is Compassionate Love, the same is clothed in the form of Chenrezig, for those who can only so conceive him. And he who has trodden the path of the Bodhisats and *knows* this Compassion beyond all chance of forgetting, the same knows Chenrezig, for he *is* Chenrezig. Even the Bodhisats are "supports"; when once Buddha-hood has been attained, when there is Knowledge, Reality—things which at present mean nothing to us, and are *Void* of all that we can possibly conceive of—then all supports can be done away with; they "simply are not" as the lama said.

I cannot refrain from quoting at this point a passage that might easily have been taken from some book of the Tibetan Canon, but which is, in fact, from an English work of the four-teenth century, called *The Cloud of Unknowing*, and another passage from a commentary on it, written in the early seventeenth century, by Father Augustine Baker, a Benedictine. Nothing could better illustrate the solidarity of all traditional thought, irrespective of race and period, than these teachings of an un-known Yorkshireman, who lived five centuries ago. Both the substance of the passage and its phraseology would be more readily intelligible to the bursar of Spituk than to the writer's own countrymen of to-day.

The nought . . . is God, to whom the soul may be united when she is nowhere bodily, nor hath in her any image of creatures. And when she is nowhere bodily then she is everywhere spiritually; and being in such condition she is fit to be united with the said nothing, which also is in all places . . . And this union I have elsewhere called a union of nothing with nothing . . . What is he that calleth it nought? Surely it is our outer man and not our inner. Our inner man calleth it All; for by it he is well taught to understand all things bodily or ghostly, without any special beholding to any one thing by itself.

And when she (the soul) being in such case of nothing—that is as no imaginable or intelligible thing, but as another thing which is above all images and species, and is expressible by no species . . . doth further apply and add her foresaid nothing to the said nothing of God, then remaineth there, neither in respect of the soul nor in respect of God, anything but a certain vacuity or nothing. In which nothing is acted and passeth a union between God and the soul . . . And so in this case of union there is nothing and nothing and they make nothing . . . This is the state of perfect union which is termed by some a state of nothing, and by others, with as much reason, termed a state of totality.

These quotations are strikingly akin to the Buddhist doctrine of Nirvana, and they would surely be acclaimed by the bursar of Spituk as bearing the stamp of universal truth.

These enthralling talks we had with him were spread over two days, and made us reluctant to leave. We got him to promise, however, to ride over to P'hiyang to see us before we left for England, which he agreed to do all the more readily as he was a personal friend of the painter Gyaltsan, whom he held in high regard.

On reaching P'hiyang we found all made ready for our lodging. A certain monk named Sherab (Wisdom) had vacated his set of rooms in our favour—we later paid him a small rent for their use—and had arranged to sleep on the roof for the duration of our stay; sleeping out is customary during the summer months.

Our cell, which had a balcony with a glorious view, was approached through a small lobby where dung for the fire was stored. From the lobby a ladder led out on to the flat roof, from which tall prayer-flags floated their messages. We arranged to have our meals up there, for a small kitchen was attached.

The cell was furnished with rugs and mattresses and low tables. At the end of the room stood the altar, of white wood still undecorated, on which two large books occupied places of honour. The walls were hung round with about a dozen *t'hankas* of varying age, some of them painted by our friend himself; they depicted the patrons of the Kargyudpa Order both in their mild and terrible shapes.

In the evening, dozens of unexpected people kept peeping through the doorway or even walked right in, squatting down on the floor to gaze at us. Sometimes it was a monk, sometimes a couple of peasants; now they were silent, now in conversational mood. The young novices, in particular, left us no peace. Eventually we got used to visitors entering at awkward moments. If they were of superior rank we had to be patient and behave as if we had been expecting them. With commoner folk we let them satisfy legitimate curiosity and then turned them out good-humouredly. But unless one is engaged in meditation, which no Tibetan will willingly disturb, one must learn not to demand the strict regard for privacy that people expect to enjoy at home in England.

PAINTING LESSONS AND LEAVE-TAKINGS

Our stay at P'hiyang *Gompa* was, in a way, the climax of the expedition, for in it a hope was fulfilled, round which our plans had revolved from the outset. Time was unfortunately short: we could have done with some of those extra weeks that had been frittered away earlier on, in preparations for the abortive Holbrak project. Nevertheless the results of P'hiyang cannot be measured in time; not only does it mark a definite stage in our education, but also during that brief spell so much experience was gained, so many doubts were cleared up and such wide vistas were opened, that I look back on it as a time of accomplishment and of abundant harvesting.

Life began in earnest the day after our arrival, when we went round to Gyaltsan's room, the place where we were to spend most of our waking hours during our visit to his monastery. It was not a particularly large room. A wooden post stood up in the middle supporting the roof-beam, and at the foot of this the lama spread his rug, upon which he used to sit at his work. In the morning the sun shone full upon that side of the building and large shutters were put across the window to subdue the glare. In the afternoon they were taken down, when the sun had moved round to fall dazzlingly upon the rampart-like white walls that faced south towards the Indus valley and the Zanskar peaks beyond. Then the room was cool, with a soft breeze occasionally blowing through it, and it was filled with an even light, ideal for painting.

The furniture was more than usually well-cared-for, and it included two large painted cabinets, which Gyaltsan had decorated with floral designs. The paraphernalia of an artist was to be seen in various corners: trays of brushes, saucers of paint, stretched canvases leaning against the wall, compasses, rules and set-squares; but all was arranged with remarkable neatness and taste. Three or four *t'hankas* hung on the walls, one recently finished by Gyaltsan himself, and in a corner next to the altar there was

234

a particularly fine scroll of some age, which he treasured highly. Sometimes, as I sat upon my rug by the window and watched Gyaltsan either painting or making extracts from books in his lovely handwriting, it was the easiest thing in the world to fancy myself in the workshop of a Master Jerome or a Fra Angelico.

Gyaltsan's personal novice, a boy about twelve years old, derived much entertainment from our presence in the monastery. He was constantly running to and fro between our room and his master's, but his favourite place was on our roof helping Norbu to cook the meals. I fear our coming somewhat interfered with the even course of his education. Nevertheless, on one or two afternoons, he was put through his paces and made to recite in a high piping voice, while Gyaltsan, though he might appear half engrossed in other things, would pull him up at the mistakes without ever a reference to the text. The boy also waited on the lama when he was at work, ran errands, kept the room tidy and the floor clean and brought in the tea at frequent intervals. Gyaltsan seemed to have a very successful way with him and the boy had all the high spirits and insatiable curiosity of his age.

The boy novices have their appointed place in community life, and perform all sorts of odd jobs for which children are particularly suitable. The monasteries in Tibet are so much more comparable to our universities than to their nominal counterparts in the West, at least as these survive to-day. Each lama owns or hires his own rooms, which are often like a little self-contained flat, and keeps them up out of the money remitted to him by his own family. The lamas feed separately, and except for certain prescribed gatherings for worship in the temple each man is free to use his time as he thinks fit. This general statement must be qualified somewhat in the case of the Yellow monks whose rule is laid down in greater detail, so that their life approximates rather more nearly to that of a Christian monastic community; but even in this case the points of resemblance can easily be exaggerated. If a lama desires to wander off on the highroad or to withdraw into contemplation in some remote spot, the permission which he must first seek is not the formal authorization of the abbot, but the consent of his own personal tutor, *his* Lama; this is for everyone the final authority, from which the death of one of the parties is the only dispensation. Though children are dedicated by their parents to the spiritual life at an early age, before there could be any possibility of personal inclination, they are not bound for life in the sense that they have no means of release, if they should come to doubt their vocation. The vows are dissoluble at any age and a certain number of persons avail themselves of this right: however, they are very much in a minority, for the lama is looked up to socially, and a return "to the world," though not penalized in any way, naturally seems rather a come-down.

Every monastery owns a number of "mountain retreats," where those who desire to spend periods of contemplation can retire from the distractions of social existence. These cells consist of four walls, with a raised platform at one end, where the recluse sits. Food is pushed into the cell at stated intervals: those who bring it, must on no account address a word to the contemplative or interrupt him in any way. Among the Kargyudpa, many are found who, true to the tradition of their great saint Mila Repa, withdraw into caves in the cold regions of glaciers, where a cotton cloth is their only garment (Repa literally means "cotton-clad"). Many retreats are not so rigorous, but are simply small cottages, furnished like any other house and differing only in the absence of companionship. I remember talking to one Yellow monk from Lhasa, who had been telling me that he intended to retire for several months to a "mountain retreat." "Where is this retreat," I said, "is it in a cave?" The monk, who was a man who loved his comfort, made a gesture of horror. "Oh! no," he cried, "not a cave! My mountain retreat will be provided with every convenience!" It must also be remembered that the Buddhist conception of asceticism is quite unlike that which is familiar from the history of the Christian Church. There is no idea of mortifying the flesh by painful austerities. The Buddha formally condemned the extremes both of luxury and self-torture; He was born Himself to wealth and tried to escape into violent self-repression before He discovered its uselessness. Nothing which is calculated to damage health is to be encouraged, for impaired health may create added obstacles in the pursuit of Knowledge. The austerity of a Mila has a very different motive, the renunciation of all that might distract, the cutting off of all "purposeless" activity, the lulling of the senses into quiescence, so as to permit, rather than compel, the real Knowledge-Consciousness to arise. Neither are all contemplatives ascetics in the present-day sense of the word. St. Marpa, though he laid on Mila Repa the injunction of taking "a terrible resolution of meditating for the duration of his life for the

236

profit of creatures," himself continued to live and work in the world: he tilled his farm and was happily married.

While we were at P'hiyang, I one day suddenly ran into our old enemy the bursar of Satsukul, whose office extended to all the monastic houses of a certain group. If I was surprised, he was astounded in still greater measure—in fact, disgusted would be a better word, for it must have come as a shock to him to find the three people whom he had treated so ungraciously, making themselves at home inside his own monastery. He did not say much, but I heard that after we left he tried to vent his annoyance by making himself disagreeable to Gyaltsan.

The office of *chyagdzöd* or bursar is held on a peculiar system of tenure in many of the *Gompas*. It usually lasts for three years. On appointment, the *chyagdzöd* receives a certain sum, out of which he is expected to provide for the upkeep of those amenities which are shared by all the residents in the *Gompa*. At the end he must pay back the sum intact, but in the meantime he can use it as he wishes, for trading or lending; any profits above the original sum, after he has disbursed all that is needed for the common expenses, are his own. It can well be imagined that this post offers considerable opportunities for graft, especially in a large monastery, and is much sought after by commercially ambitious monks. The position of *chyagdzöd* in one of the vast establishments near Lhasa might be worth thousands. It must not be supposed, however, that all holders of this office are corrupt. Our friend the bursar of Spituk, who discharged his duties with zeal and integrity, told us that he longed for the day when he would lay down the seals, for he found it an uncongenial task and a distraction from things of greater importance. Nevertheless the system offers certain temptations: doubtless the presense of a strict abbot would make all the difference.

Most of our time was passed in study. Both the art-pupils and I found Gyaltsan an ideal teacher, clear in exposition, strict, patient, resourceful and infectiously enthusiastic. His methods had been well worked out, but were far from stereotyped. With myself he either enlarged upon some doctrinal point by word alone, or, more often, copied selected passages from the book of St. Gampopa, from which my quotations on the Refuge in Chapter XVII were taken, and passed them on to me to make what I could of them before turning to him for help.

After I had proceeded as far as I could, the lama expounded the passage. This method of working was slow, so that the ground covered at the time was not very extensive; but we had agreed beforehand that we should not allow ourselves to race ahead, leaving unsolved doubts to harass us afterwards. To the grounding that I received from Gyaltsan I owe the knowledge which enabled me to compile the chapter on the Doctrine in Part Two of this book, though I did not gather the full fruits of his teaching immediately; it was reserved for my other good master, the lama Wangyal, to make his predecessor's work bear fruit, when he came and visited me in my Liverpool home. In my discussions with Gyaltsan I found that when I wished to illustrate this or that knotty point, I often was able to make use of stories taken from the New Testament or from the lives of the Christian Fathers, especially St. Thomas Aquinas. The quotations were always very much appreciated; the parables of the Gospel, in particular, appealed to our lama, nor did it ever occur to him to treat them as less authoritative because they belonged to a foreign religion. He was only interested in their bearing upon the points under discussion and he seemed just as ready to find truth in the sayings of "a certain ancient Lama in our country" as in those of other Lamas whose names were familiar. The lama Wangyal went still further. Speaking of Christ he said: "I see that He was a very Buddha!"

At sunset Gyaltsan and I usually made a tour of the walls, which were formed by a single huge *mendong*, ringing the *Gompa* without a break. In hot countries this is always an enchanted hour, when the spirit seems peculiarly sensitized and ready to take wing. Gyaltsan let his mind lead him whither it would like a rider who drops the reins loose on his horse's neck and trusts to it to take him in the right direction. I well remember how on one of these circuits the lama began to describe the next Golden Age, the expected reign of Chamba, "The Loving One," who will be the Buddha of the cycle succeeding to the present one. I cannot attempt to reproduce his mood of exaltation nor how it fired me as I listened to him. He spoke like a predestined prophet, and had the heavens opened in that hour and the world stood still to make way for the Second Coming, I should have felt no surprise.

While attending to me, Gyaltsan carried on simultaneously with the drawing-class. "Well now what shall we begin with?" he asked my friends the first day. "Shall we learn how to do the Teacher's hands?" He handed out to each man a sharply-pointed wooden stylus and a small drawing-board provided

238

with a handle and shaped like a butter-pat. Then, taking one of the boards himself, he dusted it over with fine chalk and proceeded to draw with the stylus the hands of the Buddha in their classical position, one hanging down to the ground and the other supporting the begging-bowl. He made them watch carefully how he made his strokes and then try to repeat the drawing. He did one model in the corner of each pupil's board. They set to work and as they both already possessed some skill with the pencil, they made rapid progress and soon began to turn out passable copies. Whenever they made a false stroke they dusted some more chalk over the place and began again. This was the first lesson, repeated a number of times with a view to greater accuracy.

The next lessons were taken up with the Teacher's feet, which were more difficult; then came His head, and after that His body. When they had reached a fair degree of proficiency with the separate parts they tried to combine them and so produce a complete nude. This course of study was spread over several days, till finally they were considered good enough to attempt to clothe the body. Gyaltsan's criticisms confined themselves to the question of exactitude; aesthetic considerations were left alone for the time being: in fact I doubt whether they are ever mentioned as an end in themselves. When the figure appeared to have approached the model, Gyaltsan tested it with a pair of dividers in order to make sure that the measurements of the different parts had been related in correct ratio; for the main proportions of the Buddha's figure are not left to the artists' discretion, being considered to have been fixed for all time by divine revelation. Gyaltsan related the story thus:—"One of the disciples of the Victorious One was desirous of placing His portrait on record for posterity; but when he attempted to measure His holy body he found no rule long enough, nor any measure sufficient. After repeated failures, he perceived the hopelessness of his task, so he prayed to the Buddha of His grace to vouchsafe to mankind the knowledge of His earthly form. The Teacher consented and the disciple drew the first picture, which has served as a Canon ever since. For a Buddha is not like other men; He has all sorts of peculiarities; a mark between the eyes, a protuberance on the head, teeth in an unusual number, His ears are not at all the same as a man's. His eyes are shaped like a bow bent by a skilful archer—and there are many other points which must be observed if you are to portray a Buddha faithfully."

239

During the early stages the whole aim of the teaching is to train hand, eyes and memory. When the pupils have proved that they are able to copy the model several times with a considerable degree of sureness, they are made to do it from memory. At the first attempt my friends found that they had remembered only a part of what they had practised; nevertheless, after referring to the model and making one or two attempts, they began to retain the proportions in their mind's eye and Gyaltsan expressed himself as satisfied with their progress. A still more advanced stage is marked by trying to draw the same figure in a material where correction by rubbing out is not possible, that is to say, in Indian ink upon paper. From time to time, for variety's sake, flowers, clouds and animals can be introduced. Drawing from Nature does not come in at all: it is a question of learning control and of memorizing the principal classical subjects.

While the pupil is busy improving his drawing he also helps the Master in such jobs as grinding the stones and earths that make the paints, pounding them in a polished stone mortar, preparing canvases and washing brushes. Later he begins to learn how to apply the paint, and is allowed to help in the more repetitive and mechanical tasks such as borders, grass, flowers or skies. Eventually the day comes when he may try his hand at a whole composition.

There was naturally no time for us to tackle anything but elementary drawing, so, as we were anxious not to miss seeing all the processes that go to the making of a *t'hanka*, we asked Gyaltsan to let us watch him work on some that were awaiting completion. We thus saw enough for me to be able to describe the various stages without omitting any important detail.

The first task is the preparation of a canvas. The material used is ordinary white cotton cloth of Indian manufacture. An oblong is cut to the required size, and it is hemmed round barley stalks, to give the edge a slight stiffening. Then it is fixed in an embroidery frame of much larger size, with a woollen thread running in zigzags all round from the canvas to the frame, lacing the two together. If the canvas sags at any time, the lace is drawn tighter and the tension is gradually distributed all round the frame till the free end is reached, which is then reknotted. When this has been done, a dressing of lime, mixed with a little size made by boiling yak-skin, is applied, but very thinly, so as not to interfere with the flexibility of the canvas, which must be supple enough to be rolled up. The surface is wetted, polished repeatedly with a flint, and allowed to dry between each polishing. In the end, the canvas does not differ essentially from a wall, and the method of painting is akin to fresco.

When the canvas is ready, the drawing is put on with charcoal pencils, but comparatively roughly, for the artist trusts to his brush to lend due precision to the finer lines and to obliterate all trace of what lies underneath. After that, it is only a question of applying the colours: as only body colours are used, either opaque or only very slightly translucent, it is easy to blot out a mistake. The folds of draperies and the features on the faces are the last details to be put in, apart from various finer embellishments in gold. Gyaltsan's art was a typical example of pleasing but not highly inspired school-work. But for the tradition, he would have been completely at a loss; but given the help of its guiding hand, his great sincerity enabled him to go to the utmost limit of his talent.

When drawing on a *t'hanka*, the artist leans his frame against a wall; it is never laid flat on a table or on the floor. In painting, the left hand holds a transverse ruler, which follows the hand that holds the brush, providing it with a steady rest. The left hand also grasps a sea-shell which serves as a palette. Brushes are prepared by the artist from selected hairs of goat, and even cat, which he fastens on to a stick. Size is used to mix with the paints, which are first ground in the mortar. White of egg is not known as a medium; that is why it is incorrect to speak of the Tibetan mural paintings as frescoes, though they resemble them so closely in appearance.

The day before we were due to leave, some ritual dances were performed in a cloistered theatre just below our own room, in honour of the visit to P'hiyang of Colonel Lang and his party. The proper time of the year for this display is January: at that time over a hundred monks take part in the service—for it is really a sacred mystery—wearing splendid Chinese costumes, and also grotesque masks decorated with yaks' horns, antlers and tusks. The dancers wear red silk skirts, banded with yellow, which describe brilliant circles of colour as they whirl round. Summer is not really a suitable time for such violent exercise. Gyaltsan, who acted as trainer and master of the ballet, allowed his troupe of about a dozen to perform three figures that lasted half an hour, after which they retired sweating profusely. At the proper season, all Ladak gathers at P'hiyang to watch the Kargyudpa mystery which lasts two whole days.

For ourselves that last afternoon brought a gathering of friends. Khan Muhammad Din was there, in attendance on the Residency party. The lama Dawa also came from Spituk and the Yellow Man from Leh. Joseph Gergan, the Christian translator, sent a messenger bearing a kind present of cakes specially baked for us by his wife. When the dancing was over, we foregathered for the last time in Konchhog Gyaltsan's room and conversed about our future plans. "My advice to you is to go to our mother-house of Dikhung in Tibet," said Gyaltsan. "The Dikhung Lama is a true saint, and if he should receive you as a pupil you will have the happiness of studying the Doctrine, under one of the greatest teachers in the land. What do you think, Reverend Doctor?"—he turned to the bursar of Spituk inquiringly. I rather expected that the latter would prefer to recommend a member of his own Yellow-Hat Order, but to my surprise he concurred, saying: "Yes, I believe you could not do better. If you should go to Tibet, seek out the Dikhung Lama. I would gladly come with you myself, if by that time I were free of the bursar's office."

Bidding good-bye to our friends should have made us sad; but after living among Tibetans, one begins to catch a little of their philosophy, which does not favour long-drawn-out regrets. Absences of months and years are such a commonplace in this land, that people settle down quickly after the departure of a friend, knowing as they do that there is little likelihood of news being received, until the day when the absentee himself turns up unexpectedly to announce his own return. Stoicism and resignation are in the blood, and a worrying disposition is quite the exception. The lama Dawa left first for Spituk; the Yellow Man lingered a little longer, and then rode off, telling us that he too expected to be on the road within a week, for he was starting for Lhasa with a caravan and might be away a year or more. Two days later we parted from Gyaltsan, who had ridden with us as far as Kalatze, on the Indus.

We reserved for ourselves one final treat, a day to be spent in revisiting our beloved Likhir. This second occasion brought no disillusionment, but on the contrary a renewal of the rapture of our first visit. When it was at last time to go, the old prior drew me apart into his cell and said that he would feel happy to welcome us back at any time for an indefinite stay, with every facility for reading or doing whatever else we wished.

The homeward stages were all taken as speedily as possible,

Yuru, Bod Karbu and lovely Mulbek: when we crossed the frontier we shed our Tibetan personalities with regret, and became our ordinary selves once more. We hurried through Purig, where the fierceness of summer had given place to the more temperate glow of autumn. Everywhere people were stacking their last hay, or walking up and down the stubble-fields with an air of busy aimlessness as if to say "the work of the year is over; now for a long hibernation." At the alp of Nimarg, which we had left a garden in full flower, many plants had died down or been cropped short, leaving no trace; but a few late-flowering species still bloomed, gentians, a monkshood, and a delphinium new to us; they were making all haste to get through their life-cycle before the first snows condemned them once more to the enforced rest of months. We spent a day gathering seeds; there is no sound more gratifying to the ear than their metallic tinkle, as the ripe pods are bent over and emptied into the envelopes. Then at last came the Zoji, now quite cleared of snow; once across the pass and we were in India again. In the Sind valley the maize harvest was ripe and also the walnuts. Buying roasted maize-cobs in the villages made us think of Soho and chestnuts.

At last Wayl bridge appeared and "civilization," represented by a couple of cars, stood waiting for us. A Kashmiri peasant with a badly abscessed hand, stopped us and asked for medicine, so we lighted our last wayside fire to boil up water for Dr. Roaf, who operated there and then. It was the final bow before the fall of the curtain. We stepped into our car and were whirled in clouds of choking dust towards Srinágar, conscious of a mounting nervousness that could not be kept in check, in spite of our recent sojourn in the land of disillusion.

EPILOGUE

THERE *is a small book, of not more than five pages, written in verse, and called* The Powerful Good Wish, *that reveals the doctrine of One who is referred to as the "Buddha of the Beginning, the Altogether Good." He is the earliest Buddha known to mankind; but not the first in point of time, for the succession of Buddhas is eternal and cannot be assigned a temporal origin. The book opens with these words:—" Listen! All apparent Being, whether of the Round or of Deliverance, is in Principle One with two paths and two fruits. This is the jugglery of Ignorance and Knowledge. By the good wish of the Altogether Good One, may all, entering the royal abode of the Divine Essence, manifestly and completely attain to Buddhahood."*

These few sentences contain the pith of the Tibetan metaphysic, the central theme that echoes through the entire Tradition. The Principle is identical with what is styled the Void, lest by giving It any other name, one may be betrayed into limiting or qualifying It. In the Principle will be realized the ultimate Unity that belongs to all things alike, despite appearances to the contrary, a Unity so infinitely real, that one dare not even give it the name of Unity—since this too is an idea borrowed from worldly experience: one can only speak of Its non-duality, that which shall be known when all pairs of oppositions have been resolved in the Supreme Identity. Therefore it is said that under every form and seeming contradiction, the illuminate eye will recognize Voidness alone.

But the multitude of undelivered beings cannot, by merely so wishing, rid themselves of their dualistic spectacles, or of all the delusions associated with the conception of a permanently individual self, towards which the rest of the Universe stands in the relationship of "other." A self-centred consciousness forces one to polarize every idea into two contrasted notions. Therefore, where there is essential unity, men will persist in seeing two paths, one might almost have said two realities. The starting-point for any return into unity can only be found situated in the existing dualism; thus, anywhere short of the supreme realization it is quite legitimate to speak of two paths, that of Ignorance, which creatures are now following, and that of Knowledge, the path or current which they hope to enter. "Entering the current" is a usual Tibetan phrase, referring to those whose course is fairly set for Illumination. The two paths are continually diverging: the one leads con-

*tinually back into the Round of Existence, which is the fruit of Ignorance
and of its associated Desires and Activities, the other path leads away
from the Round of Deliverance, which is the fruit of Knowledge.*

*All this is compared to the by-play of a conjuror, a perplexing succession
of mirages, now delightful, now terrifying, which will only fade away, leaving
Reality unmasked, when all distinctions, even those of subject and object,
Knower and Known, the Round and Liberation themselves, shall have faded
into the Knowledge of the Foundation, the Void which alone is causeless and
uncompounded, finding within Itself Its own sufficiency.*

*The Good Wish is a prayer that all without distinction, having outgrown
distinctions, may realize this Unity, the true Beatific Vision. Liberation, in
order to be perfected, must be all-embracing—"What is it to be saved oneself,
if 'others' are still lost and suffering?" Individual salvation, with its lingering
strands of attachment to the idea of self is of no interest to the follower of
the Non-dual Doctrine. Therefore this doctrine, acclaimed by the Tibetans,
as the corner-stone of all Knowledge, is known as the GREAT WAY, in which
the Bodhisats, those embodiments of impartial Love, are the guides, and all
beings, down to the last and the least, are the pilgrims. The goal is Knowledge
and the Path is Method, which is non-attached and universal Compassion.*

*The story that has formed the subject of this book is a study in contrasts
between two paths, the path of Tradition and the path of those who have cut
themselves adrift from Tradition. Many aspects of the question have been
considered, from the Doctrine on which all else depends, down to practical
suggestions for applying traditional principles to special problems that have
arisen in certain strictly delimited fields of action. The entire world is crying
out for Reform: but that word must here be understood, not in its most usual
sense, but having regard to its derivation of Re-form—the remaking of
the Tradition wherever there has been a deviation from its path, and
the requickening of its influence in the hearts of lukewarm or bewildered
followers.*

*Viewed in this sense, the present crisis does not connote the impotence of
Tradition itself, but rather it affords an incentive to seek ways of applying
traditional principles with renewed vigour. Any evil that cries out to be
righted should be looked upon as a failure to apply Tradition's teachings
with sufficient intelligence: successful suppression of the evil will result in a
reinforcement of traditional authority, and in a change of heart in all who
accept that authority.*

This is the road of Reform; but there is the other path, the one that is already being followed by half the world, often semi-consciously and with hesitation, but which will be followed by all and to the bitter end, unless timely measures are taken; this second path is the path variously known as Progress and Revolution. To enter it, is always a sign that the Tradition, in spite of all professions to the contrary, is no longer trusted; or it shows that people prefer to renounce their principles and to drift into a life of capricious opportunism. The revolutionary path, along which the West has proceeded with increasing velocity for some centuries, leads to the dispersal of thought in the whirlpool of multiple detail and action, and to the subjection of human effort to the low impulses of sentimentality, .the deadly enemy of considered and consistent thought.

The derivation of the word "Reform" was suggestive; so is that of the word "Revolution." What picture does it evoke but of something that keeps doubling back on its own tracks? It is perhaps no accident that associates this idea with the Round of Existence, the circular eddy in which all beings flounder and find again and again their brief joys and recurrent miseries. Both Progress and Revolution imply an idealization of Change, which comes to be looked upon as something desirable in itself, in which case contentment logically becomes an evil and stability a reproach.

It is between these two paths that a choice has to be made. But choice itself implies intellectual detachment, a disinterested seeking after Knowledge. How can choice be exercised by populations weighed down by the fear of impending destruction and oppressed by the futility of any effort to avoid the approaching doom? The beings of the Round scurry hither and thither, listening to the glib persuasions of every quack, and trying to charm away their anxieties by the narcotics of speed and mechanized amusements. Yet if the right choice could be made, and if those who have strayed and have perhaps learned the beginnings of wisdom in the bitter school of disaster could be guided back into the traditional path, then there might be a hope that the pernicious dualism expressed in the phrase "East is East and West is West and never the twain shall meet" might disappear, together with other similar opportunities, in Knowledge of the One Foundation. It is surely suggestive that the most violent hatred of Europeans as men is to be found precisely among those Orientals who most admire European institutions and despise their own Tradition: it is the anti-traditional mind, that has learned its lesson well and longs to out-Westernize the West, which stoops to the baser kinds of militant nationalism as well as to irreverent vandalism directed against its own spiritual heritage: the two things go together. This might serve as a warning to the Westerners who first introduced the anti-traditional error, and even more to those Orientals, like the Tibetans, who still cling to the other path. The latter might then realize how fortunate is their present lot and how precious their intellectual independence. They would then guard their inheritance more jealously than ever and redouble their caution when tempted by the meretricious triumphs of modern invention.

Tradition is the path along which pilgrims journey towards the peaks of Wisdom: but without Method for a guide, there is ever a danger of straying from the route and being caught up in the futility of the Round, through the allurements of blind sentiments and attachment to self. The higher the doctrine, the more abysmal will be the corruption if once the doctrine is rejected. Lamas have compared the man who aspires to the Light to a serpent struggling upward inside a hollow tube of bamboo. There is little room to turn; one ill-judged movement may cause a fall to the very bottom. This is Tibet's danger; this has been the fate of those traditional civilizations which, by force or consent, have been led into accepting the standards of the modern West.

For myself, the writing of this book, and the two expeditions that led up to it, have been a single voyage of exploration into a land of uncharted glaciers and unclimbed ranges, the mountains of Tradition. From far up their slopes I glanced back, and in contrast with my surroundings, the prospect of the lands whence I had come seemed dismal indeed. At the outset of my story I tried to climb peaks in a bodily sense; but in the end I discovered the Lama, who beckoned me upwards towards immaterial heights.

A popular proverb says: "Without the Lama you cannot obtain Deliverance." Every good Tibetan—and all lovers of Tradition to-day might almost lay claim to the right of honorary citizenship of Tibet—before ever he seeks refuge in the Three Most Precious Things, the Buddha, the Doctrine and the Congregation, first pronounces the words: "I go for refuge to the Lama." In a literal sense this refers to a man's own spiritual director, "his Lama," who is the visible "support" of Tradition and its audible mouthpiece: it is this quality of support that entitles the teacher to the disciple's unbounded reverence, irrespective of personal failings, just as a brass statue of the Buddha is worthy of worship, be the casting sound or flawed. But there is also an inner and more universal meaning inherent in "the Lama"; for behind every support there is the thing supported, which the symbol both veils and reveals. Here it indicates the divine guide whose hand sustains the climber as he strives to reach the summit of Enlightenment.

Taken in this sense, the Lama, the Universal Teacher, is TRADITION ITSELF.